Brand is built from the inside out. If your business is not invested in the people experience, your brand will suffer, and so will your results. In *Built to Burn*, Karl Treacher treats culture and brand as a single system, and the result is a playbook any executive team can use to create a culture that they can be proud of.

—**Lizzy Geremia,**
Group Brand and Culture Director ANZ, Reece Group

We often claim leadership is about advancing others. Karl compels us to prove it. In this powerful, unflinching book, he exposes the unintended consequences of current-day leadership and its cultural impact. Take a deep breath and prepare to redefine how you lead and elevate your people.

—**Henry Ruiz,**
CEO Lifestyle Communities,
Former Chief Strategy Officer REA Group

Built to Burn replaces the quick fixes with solutions that actually work: better systems, better cultures and better leadership.

—Georgie Harman AO,
CEO, Beyond Blue

The neuroscience is sound, the economics are sobering, and the prescription is the most clear-eyed I have read on workplace burnout. Required reading for all leaders.

—Prof. Selena Bartlett,
Neuroscientist, QUT

Karl has a wonderful way of reminding us that success means little if it comes at the expense of the people we care about. This is a thoughtful, practical and deeply human book!

—Damian Zahra,
Chief People Officer, Bunnings Group

This isn't a wellbeing book. It's a leadership book that takes burnout seriously. *Built to Burn* shows that how we've designed our companies is what's burning people out and offers leaders willing to look honestly, a genuine path to something better. The kind of book you'll mark up and come back to.

—Sally Bruce,
Non-Executive Director, former Bank CEO &
CFO / Global Tech COO & CFO

Karl always brings humanity back to leadership and this book is another example of how being human can make you the leader that is needed today.

—Mike Baird AO,
CEO NRMA, Former Premier NSW

Burnout is the issue shaping culture and performance more than anything else right now, and the cost is mounting in every business. *Built to Burn* shows why it is happening and gives leaders the tools to act. It will reset culture and performance in any organisation that takes it seriously.

—Nat Feehan,
Director, ANZ Sales & Enablement, SEEK

The principles that produce champions also produce healthy businesses, and high performance always comes from health. Karl Treacher has written the book every business needs right now.

—Guy Leech,
Former World Ironman Champion

It now makes perfect sense. Karl connects the data dots that we have all seen, and likely lived. *Built to Burn* invites all leaders to build cultures where wellbeing and performance thrive together.

—Cindy Batchelor,
Chair, Auto & General Insurance,
Victorian Chapter Chair, Chief Executive Women

Built to Burn is the most important book a leader can read right now. Karl Treacher moves the burnout conversation from individuals to leadership and culture, where it belongs, and he writes with the authority of someone who has spent his life doing this work. He asks you to examine your own leadership and you come out a better leader for it.

—Charles R. Weiser,
Former Group Chief Executive Officer,
RAMS Home Loans Corporation

BUILT to BURN

BUILT to BURN

Why Work Burns People Out and How the Best Leaders Build Cultures That Don't

Karl Treacher

WILEY

First published 2027 by John Wiley & Sons Australia, Ltd

ISBN: 978-1-394-45651-2

NATIONAL LIBRARY OF AUSTRALIA

A catalogue record for this book is available from the National Library of Australia

Registered Office
John Wiley & Sons Australia, Ltd. Level 4, 600 Bourke Street, Melbourne, VIC 3000, Australia

For details of our global editorial offices, customer services, and more information about Wiley products visit us at www.wiley.com.

Wiley also publishes its books in a variety of electronic formats and by print-on-demand. Some content that appears in standard print versions of this book may not be available in other formats.

Cover design by Wiley
Cover images: © yuphayao phankhamkerd/Getty Images, Chattranusorn09/Getty Images

Set in 11.5/15.5 pts and Minion Pro by Straive, Chennai, India.

Printed and bound by CPI Group (UK) Ltd, Croydon, CR0 4YY

C9781394456512_040926

The manufacturer's authorized representative according to the EU General Product Safety Regulation is Wiley-VCH GmbH, Boschstr. 12, 69469 Weinheim, Germany,
e-mail: Product_Safety@wiley.com.

For anyone who has felt the flames and for those who have the courage to fight them.

Contents

Acknowledgements

This book is the product of almost three decades of experience, countless conversations, and the accumulated wisdom of teachers, colleagues and clients who shaped my understanding of culture and leadership.

The foundational researchers who made this book possible each deserve more than a mention. Christina Maslach defined burnout as a measurable phenomenon when the world had not yet found words for it. Amy Edmondson's work on psychological safety transformed how we understand what teams truly need to do their best work. Edward Deci and Richard Ryan gave us self-determination theory, which explains why autonomy and intrinsic motivation are biological necessities rather than soft preferences. Martin Seligman and Mihaly Csikszentmihalyi built the foundations of positive psychology and gave us a rigorous language for human flourishing.

To the broader intellectual community whose work runs through these pages: Bruce Perry, Edgar Schein, Daniel Coyle, Carl Jung, Eckhart Tolle, Brené Brown, Adam Grant, Daniel Pink, Michael Morris and many others whose thinking about relationships, work and motivation has shaped mine over many years, I have tried to represent your work honestly. Any errors are my own.

I am as susceptible as anyone to confirmation bias, and to the particular comfort of vehemently defending my own argument in an echo chamber. One of the disciplines I imposed on myself throughout this process was to hold my conclusions up against the work of researchers I respect, rather than gathering evidence that simply confirms what I already believe. The harder and more honest work is testing your assumptions against people who have spent their lives getting to the truth of the matter.

Professor Selena Bartlett has been one of those people for me. I have known Selena for ten years and we have worked together on other projects, so I understand the rigour she brings to everything she does. The timing of her latest book, *Thriving Minds in the Age of AI*, could not have been better. It arrived as I was finalising this manuscript, and its scientific grounding on neuroplasticity, on what sustained workplace pressure does to the brain, on why recovery requires far more than a change of scenery, confirmed and deepened arguments I had been making from a consulting and cultural perspective for 25 years. Her life's work has been an extraordinary source of truth and validation. We all need to understand the weight of this challenge. It is an epidemic, and Selena's research closes the argument.

To Lucy Raymond at Wiley, who believed in this book and championed it through to completion: thank you for your patience, your judgement, and your commitment to getting this right. And to Bernadette Schwerdt, whose coaching helped me find the shape of an argument I had been carrying for years: thank you.

To the thousands of leaders and hundreds of teams I have worked with in my professional career: you taught me far more than I taught you. Your struggles, your breakthroughs, and your honest feedback about what works and what does not are the real research behind this book.

My broader social network has provided something no database can: living examples of people navigating workplaces that sustain them and workplaces that extract from them. It is through their stories and lived experiences, alongside my own research and career, that I am in a position to write this at all. This book is built on those conversations, and I am grateful for every one of them.

To my wonderful wife Dani and my daughter Cleo: thank you for accepting the hours, the weekends, the months and years I have spent in my home office at all hours working on something you didn't know was coming. Your patience made this possible and your playfulness and love grounds me in what really matters in life.

I wrote this book alone. I am a private person and this is how I work. But I did not think alone, and there are people I have engaged with and built stories alongside over the years whose fingerprints are on how I see the world: Dani Lombard-Treacher, the late Chris Lombard, Grant Hayden, Henry Ruiz, Daniel Mathews, Samantha Moore, Denise Ellis, Lloyd Lazaro, Cam Middleton, Kurt Tutt, Jo Pollard, Mike Rawling, Guy Leech, Belinda Shakespeare, Lewis Hunt, Dean Gardiner OA, Rod Browning, James Carter, Jason Pollard, James Hewitt, Dan Umphray, Martin Betts, Matt Williams, Damien Daley, Clint McDonell, Gregg Girling, Dean Gale, Geoff Guggenheimer, Chris Morsley, Paul Newman, Damien Styring, Will Hocking, Mark Watkins, Mark Poole and Jesse Price: you are in here somewhere.

I have had the privilege of working alongside leaders whose character and contribution I consider extraordinary: former Premier Mike Baird, Henry Ruiz, Natalie Feehan, Lizzy Geremia, Danny Almagor, Berry Liberman, Cindy Batchelor, Tim Reed, Sarah White, Sally Bruce, Georgie Harman, Mary Farah: each of them has shown me what becomes possible when leadership is grounded in genuine care. They are living evidence of a different way. And to the closest thing I've had to a mentor, Mark Worman: you taught me what it meant to be a leader and a dad without ever delivering a lecture. You remain for me, the closest example of the perfect leader.

To the contemplative teachers who have guided my practice: your wisdom about suffering and the path through it provides the foundation that makes the rest make sense. For me there was no greater teacher than my late father, clinical psychotherapist Don Treacher. Dad's desire to help people had a far greater impact on society than I will ever have, and his timeless, positive and balanced nature provided the platform I needed to carry on his cause, now my cause, and I hope yours: a pro-social global community built on care and respect. Dad always said he would never write a book because it would take too much time away from helping his patients. I think he would have made an exception for this one.

And to everyone currently experiencing burnout, struggling to survive workplaces that were never built with people in mind: this book is for you. You are not weak. You are not failing. The conditions are the problem, not your capacity to endure them. I hope these pages offer both validation of your experience and a genuine path towards something better.

Author's note on the scope of this book

The research and case material in this book draws on a review and synthesis of the past 30 years of work on burnout, organisational culture and leadership, with most of the focus on the past decade, where the data is densest and the workplace shifts have been sharpest. Alongside the literature sit my own years of consulting practice across Australia, the USA and Asia. The structural causes of burnout I describe, the pressures of overwork, the failures of leadership, the cultural patterns that quietly degrade people inside organisations, have been studied for long enough that we can speak about them with confidence. The frameworks in Chapter 16 have been tested in real organisations across that period and produce measurable change when applied with intent.

What this book does not yet address in depth is the impact of two pressures that have emerged with such speed that the research is still catching up with the experience and cultural impact.

The first is AI-era anxiety. The Pew Research Center's February 2025 report, based on a survey of 5273 US workers conducted in October 2024, found that 52 per cent feel worried about the future of AI in the workplace, 33 per cent feel overwhelmed by it, and only 6 per cent believe it will lead to more job opportunities for them. The World Economic Forum's Future of Jobs Report 2025, drawing on data from over 1000 global employers representing 14 million workers across 55 economies, projects 92 million jobs displaced by 2030, with 41 per cent of employers globally intending to reduce their workforce as AI capability matures. Sitting underneath those numbers is a workforce being asked to produce more, with less certainty about whether the job they are producing in will still exist in five years.

The second is financial wellbeing. PwC's 2026 Employee Financial Wellness Survey found that 85 per cent of Gen Z workers say financial stress is affecting their mental health, with 71 per cent reporting reduced productivity as a result. Across the Atlantic, a Lancaster University Work Foundation survey of 3796 UK workers in 2025 found that 43 per cent have little or nothing left at the end of the month after paying their bills. The structural picture in the United States is no kinder. US Bureau of Labor Statistics data shows that real wages, adjusted for inflation, have grown less than half a per cent in the year to early 2026, with most measures of real pay declining in the most recent quarter.

These pressures intensify everything described in this book. A workforce that is anxious about job security is less willing to push back on unreasonable workload. A workforce that is financially stressed cannot leave a bad job for a better one. They stay, depleted, and the structural causes of their depletion go unchallenged.

The frameworks still apply. The diagnostic questions, the culture redesign work, the sustainability practices. What changes is the urgency. Leaders who address burnout in 2026 and beyond are doing so against an intensifying headwind, and the cost of getting it wrong will be measured in turnover, engagement, and the mental health of an entire generation of workers.

Read what follows knowing that the conditions I describe are the baseline against which two new pressures are stacking, and that the leaders who act on what they read here will be the ones building the workplaces that the next generation wants to join.

My Story

Before the research and the case studies, there were a handful of moments that forged the lens I see every workplace culture through.

At four years old, I apparently ran some form of courtroom in the kindergarten playground, handing out sentences for inappropriate behaviour. By all accounts the courtroom was as busy as it was out of control. I have had trouble accepting injustice for as long as I can remember.

That instinct hasn't faded. Standing up for what matters when the odds say not to bother has shaped my entire life and career. This book is just another way of calling it out. The injustices now play out in accidental workplace cultures, with a predictable human cost.

What has also shaped me is competitive sport. I was generally the worst of the best. Always making the top teams, the pro wave but never the podium. I had coaches who believed that hardness was a virtue and rest was a character flaw. That pain was gain. I carried all of that into my early consulting years without examining it and believed that the people who burned out simply hadn't wanted it enough. Overwhelming evidence eventually made that position impossible to maintain. The process of letting go of a comfortable, yet incorrect idea is part of what this book is about.

My father was a man of God and a psychologist. He saw ten patients a day, six days a week for 50 years. Service was his only gear. He was an amazing human. He charged what people could afford, which the industry found baffling and his patients found lifesaving. My mother spent her career as a maternal and infant welfare nurse, with women at their most exhausted and most vulnerable. Neither of them ever looked for recognition. They just showed up, every day, for the people in front of them. Without meaning to, I appear to have absorbed my own version of that ethos. That work, with one person at a time, has been my measure of leadership ever since.

Then there was a mountain.

In 1998 I was 22 years old, on a ski trip with my girlfriend at the time, Melissa, and my best friend, Richard, to Mount Hutt in New Zealand's Canterbury region. The access road is 14 kilometres of unpaved, snow-covered, fully exposed switchbacks, with no barriers between you and a very long drop. Before we drove up, the rangers offered one piece of advice: 'Keep your doors unlocked'. They explained that if the car leaves the road, you need to be able to get out before it goes over the edge, and they delivered this with the calm professionalism of people who say it every season. We received it with the enthusiastic nodding of people who had not yet understood what they had just been told.

We white-knuckled it up, and after I parked the car we walked to the lift ticket hut in gale force winds wearing ski boots, which is less walking, more skating and controlled falling. We arrived at the ticket window to be told the weather had turned unexpectedly and the mountain, known by locals as Mount Shut because of its exposure to the elements, was closing. We needed to get back down quickly. A siren began to sound too, which helped calm my nerves.

On the way back down, roughly a kilometre from the top, we heard a loud bang as something hit the roof of the car. I looked left. The entire side of the mountain above us was moving. My instinct was to turn right, away from it, which would have taken us off the road and over the edge. Instead I turned into the snow, edging the car sideways until the avalanche covered us.

Then it was quiet and very dark.

The three of us sat in the car under the snow with no idea whether we were three feet down or 30 metres down. No idea whether anyone knew where we were. This was 1998. There were no mobile phones, no communications of any kind. The doors wouldn't open. We weren't getting out. We were completely at the mercy of the mountain, of whatever Mother Nature decided to do next. This is, as it turns out, a particularly difficult situation if you are claustrophobic. Which I am.

What happens in those first ten or so minutes is not clean, useful philosophical insight. It's fear. Fear that transitions into something that you wouldn't call calm, but close to it; the kind of stillness that arrives when there is nothing you can do. Then comes the thinking, just stripped of its usual noise. Narrow, focused thinking. Nobody buried under a mountain asks themselves whether their career is on track or how they're tracking for their annual bonus. What arrives instead, with the bluntness of something that has been waiting for an opening, something that actually matters is: what have you done with your time alive on this planet?

I was 22. The answer was: not enough.

After around six hours the ski patrol found us. We got a lift down the mountain, shaking, and spent the rest of the evening in a small bar in Ashburton not saying very much.

What stayed with me was not gratitude, though there was that. It was something more like a decision, made in conditions that forced it. Living is not a guarantee. Living a meaningful life is a choice, a commitment that has to be made. One that most aren't forced to make. I still remember the promises I made under the snow that day, and I deliver on them at every opportunity. Thankfully, most people won't have their sense of purpose challenged by an avalanche. The question is still worth answering as early as you can. Ideally not under a pile of snow.

Olive came next. With her came the first system I ever saw clearly.

To help fund university I had spent several years personal training a handful of people. One of my favourites was a man named Geoff, who owned a chain of nursing homes. Geoff was not what you would call a committed client. One cold Melbourne afternoon when he was, as was often the case, conveniently unavailable, I wandered through one of his homes looking for where he was hiding this time.

What I found changed me and my future.

In the day room, a place where residents would spend their days, elderly people sat in silence. Some stared at a small television. Some stared at windows. People who had spent entire lives building families, raising children, contributing to communities, parked in a room designed for administration rather than living. Nobody walking with them, physically or metaphorically. Nobody listening. Nobody treating their presence as anything beyond logistics to be managed. Geoff wasn't the problem. He was part of a system that had simply never been designed with the people inside it in mind. I had just never seen it that plainly before. I see it every day now.

Within weeks I had left university, five years in, and started a business providing diagnostics and allied health therapy services to nursing homes. As its first, and for a while only, employee, I spent my days doing what the system hadn't made room for. Walking with people. Listening. In many cases, dancing. Some residents had experienced strokes and confused me with late husbands. I found this almost unbearably moving every time. Often the dancing was closer to a carry. It needed to be done regardless.

Olive was 88. She had the use of only her right side. Twice a week I would arrive mid-morning at Parkside Nursing Home and we would work on her contracted side and then dance to Fred Astaire on the lino floor. I still remember the light flickering back into her eyes, even if only for a minute or two.

I sold the business after seven years. But the drive that built it has never left me. Neither has the day room.

What I saw there shaped my mission.

Since 2003 The Culture Institute of Australia has been the main vehicle. We help leaders and organisations design cultures that perform because they look after their people.

From dancing with Olive on a nursing home lino floor to corporate workshops on level 27 of a glass tower in New York, I have stayed true to what has always mattered to me: putting people first.

I don't tolerate toxic leaders, and I can't support systems designed without the people inside them in mind. That has been true since long before I could articulate why. My hope is that *Built to Burn* leaves you standing alongside me, between our people and the systems built to extract what I consider our birthright: a meaningful life.

Introduction

Not normal

> Everyone has been made for some particular work, and the desire for that work has been put in every heart.
>
> —Rumi (1207–1273)

Work should be one of the best parts of our lives.

We spend roughly 90 000 hours at work. That's more time than we spend with our children, our friends, or on our hobbies and passions. It's more time than we spend doing almost anything else. Those hours could be extraordinary. They could be filled with personal growth, connection and meaning. For some people, in some organisations, they still are. There are teams that thrive, leaders who inspire, and cultures where Monday mornings feel like possibility rather than punishment.

We've never known more about how to build such places. The science of personal and team motivation is well established, and the research on psychological safety is overwhelming. We know, with more certainty than ever, what people need to thrive at work. And yet you've probably noticed that healthy, thriving workplaces feel increasingly rare. That somewhere between the ping pong tables and the productivity software, between the mission statements and the meditation room that became Warren's daybed, something went very wrong. The gap between what work *could be* and what work *is* has become a chasm, filled with fire.

You may sense it in the 2 am emails, and if you look closely you may see it in your team's eyes, distracted by their side hustle, which is getting a new job. You may hear it in the awkward silence of meetings where everyone, including you, just wants it to end. And you may even feel it in your own chest every Sunday evening as Monday's dread settles in like the realisation that your email about Warren replied all ... including Warren.

Let me describe a day you may recognise. After a 30- or 45-minute commute, you arrive at work, on time, and before you have formed a single original thought, there are 119 emails waiting. You start reading them. Twelve minutes in, a calendar notification pulls you into the first meeting of seven. You haven't prepared for it. Nobody has. The meeting produces no decision but it produces another meeting, scheduled for Thursday, which may also produce no decision.

Between meetings, you try to do the work you were hired to do. You get nine minutes of uninterrupted focus before a Slack notification from Sally breaks your concentration. Sally sits five feet from you.

Research shows that it takes you more than 23 minutes to get back to where you were. By then, there's another meeting. You spend the afternoon performing a version of work that looks productive from the outside and feels hollow from the inside. You respond to messages quickly because responsiveness is how commitment is measured here. You stay visible because visibility is how contribution is judged. At 6 pm you leave the office, with the uneasy knowledge that you haven't done the work that matters. At 9 pm, you check your email one more time. There are 14 new messages. You answer three and tell yourself you'll get to the real work tomorrow.

If this day feels familiar, it should. While perhaps slightly exaggerated, it's the architecture of modern knowledge work, built from practices that have never been examined against the evidence of what produces results. This book will examine that evidence, and what it reveals is both infuriating and hopeful: almost every element of the day I have just described, from the open plan office to the meeting schedule to the expectation that you'll respond to emails at 9 pm, works directly against the outcomes it claims to serve. We have built our workplaces around assumptions that the research very clearly demolished years ago.

From personal experience

My own approach to work was formed inside the cultures this book is about. In my early consulting years I admired the hard chargers, the leaders who took no prisoners and saw burnout as evidence that someone simply wasn't cut out for elite performance. I believed pushing through was how you won.

Time and evidence dismantled that view. I watched talented people break under conditions I, to some extent, had helped normalise. And then, on becoming a father and watching my daughter grow, I began asking myself what kind of workplaces we were building for the next generation.

After 25 years consulting on leadership and culture, I've watched the same pattern repeat across industries and continents. Organisations that extract performance from their people rather than investing in the conditions that sustain it produce a particular kind of damage. I've seen it in Sydney boardrooms and Tokyo headquarters, in New York City startups and Singapore multinationals. Brilliant strategies built on exhausted people. Results that looked great until they didn't.

And I've learned something most of us know: culture doesn't happen by accident. When organisations burn their people, it's because they have built systems that produce fire. If the employees break, it's because they've been placed in conditions that break them. Burnout is a cultural output, as predictable as any other metric, and just as amenable to change.

A crisis of meaning

This book draws on hard data, neuroscience and organisational psychology. It maps the cultures that produce burnout, and the cultures that produce something better, where performance and human wellbeing reinforce each other, and where genuine care creates the conditions for sustained excellence.

This book has also been shaped by over 30 years of contemplative practice rooted in Eastern philosophy. Meditation has been part of my daily life for most of my adult years. Where the research tells you what is broken, contemplative wisdom explains why it matters. I draw on both throughout these pages.

What is burnout?

When you hear that someone has burned out, what's your first thought? Be honest. Not your HR-approved, politically correct thought. Your *actual* first thought. For most of us, there's an instinctive flicker of judgement. What choices did that person make? Why didn't they set better boundaries? Couldn't they have managed their time differently? Were they just not resilient enough? We have all asked these questions, most often silently.

I understand that instinct, and I shared it for years. This response is natural. We are all wired to look for individual explanations because they are simpler and far less threatening. If burnout is about personal choices, then making better choices will protect us. The alternative is deeply uncomfortable: the system itself might be broken, we might be complicit in it, and our own exhaustion might not be our fault.

The evidence tells a different story. In most cases burnout is an organisational failure, not an individual one. The burned-out employee didn't lack resilience or make poor choices, they were placed in conditions that would burn out almost anyone. Yes, in some cases there's shared responsibility. Perhaps someone ignored every warning sign or refused support that was available but these cases are the exception, and they make a convenient excuse for ignoring the rule entirely.

I ask you to resist the instinct to blame the individual. When you see burnout, look first at the architecture, not the person trapped inside it. I've watched this fire spread from isolated incidents to a global conflagration. Burnout has become an epidemic so widespread that we've begun treating it as normal.

A 2025 community poll commissioned by Beyond Blue found that roughly half of Australian workers experienced burnout in the prior year, with those aged 18 to 29 reporting the highest rates despite being early in their careers. Professor Selena Bartlett, neuroscientist at Queensland University of Technology, writes in her 2026 research that these findings confirm burnout as a systemic signal; evidence that the way we design work and the conditions we expect people to endure require urgent redesign.

The statistics are staggering. Eighty-two per cent of employees are now at risk of burnout (Mercer, 2024). We're talking about a genuine risk of the kind of chronic exhaustion that changes brain structure, destroys health and ends careers. This represents a significant escalation from previous years, and the trajectory shows no signs of reversing.

Generation Z and Millennial workers are reaching peak burnout at age 25, a full 17 years earlier than previous generations who historically experienced peak burnout at 42 (DHR Global, 2024). Many young people are burning out before they've even begun. They're exhausted before they've built careers, families or savings. They're giving up on the very concept of meaningful work because the only work they've known has been meaningless suffering dressed in corporate language and PowerPoint presentations.

Globally, the economic cost exceeds eight trillion dollars every year. That represents 9 per cent of global GDP lost to the flames of disengagement, exhaustion and despair (Gallup, 2024). More than half a billion workdays vanish each year. Healthcare systems buckle under the weight of stress-related illness. And behind every statistic is a human being, someone's partner, parent, child or friend whose life is being consumed by work that was supposed to sustain it. As someone whose life's work is building healthy organisations, I find it impossible to sit on my hands and let this play out.

How to use this book

The book is organised into three stages. Part 1 maps the furnace: its scale, its cost, and what chronic workplace stress scientifically does to the brain and body. Part 2 traces the fuel: the systems, the assumptions, and the quiet philosophical drift that allows work to consume life rather than enhance it. Part 3 is about building something better: not another wellness initiative bolted onto a broken system, but the structural and cultural work that addresses why the system broke in the first place.

Importantly, this is not a crisis of ignorance. We know exactly what's wrong and exactly what works. The open plan office, designed for collaboration, reduces satisfaction more than it improves interaction (Kim & de Dear, 2013) and decreases face-to-face collaboration by around 70 per cent compared to private workspaces (Bernstein & Turban, 2018). The employee who works 70 hours produces no more output than the one who works 55 (Pencavel, 2014). Group brainstorming consistently generates fewer ideas than the same people working independently and then combining their output, a finding replicated across dozens of studies. The annual performance review delivers ratings that are 62 per cent a reflection of the evaluator's own biases rather than the performance of the person being assessed (Scullen, Mount & Goff, 2000).

Furthermore, the return-to-office mandate typically drives away the most experienced people first, and we work five days a week because Henry Ford said so in 1926, despite trial after trial showing that four days of focused work delivers equal or greater output.

The evidence for a better way of working is overwhelming, and it has been for some time. In August 2019, Microsoft Japan ran an experiment that challenged every assumption about the relationship between hours worked and results produced. For one month, they closed their offices every Friday, giving 2300 employees a paid day off. Productivity increased by 39.9 per cent. Electricity consumption dropped by 23 per cent. Employee satisfaction hit 92 per cent. In one of the world's most overworked cultures, reducing hours by 20 per cent produced a productivity gain of nearly 40 per cent.

And it wasn't a fluke. A 2022 trial across 61 UK companies found that implementing a four-day week reduced burnout by 71 per cent while revenue held steady. Ninety-two per cent of participating companies chose to continue the model after the trial ended (Autonomy/4 Day Week Global, 2023). The path from burnout to cultural health has been mapped many times by organisations willing to walk it.

Now, I realise these opening pages have been grim. Stay with me. The fire is real, and you need to see it clearly for the rest of the book to make sense. But Part 3 is where we build. A practical guide drawing on neuroscience, organisational psychology, and the wisdom of traditions that have helped humans navigate suffering for millennia. It's also, I hope, an honest reckoning: the way we've been working is destructive, and leaders bear the primary responsibility for changing it.

Many leaders reading this book will be operating within constraints they didn't create and can't unilaterally change. You may report to an executive or leader who measures success purely in output, or work within systems that unknowingly reward burnout. You may have limited authority over the structures that shape your team's experience. This book is for you too. Not every recommendation will be available to you, but within whatever sphere you control, however small, you have choices. Those choices matter to the people you lead, and they matter to the kind of leader you choose to be ... or become.

The role of contemplative wisdom

I said earlier that burnout is a crisis of meaning. In practice, that looks like this: we've created workplaces that treat human beings as resources to be optimised and then act surprised when those resources turn out to have feelings, families, and a finite tolerance for nonsense. We've built systems that mistake activity for productivity, presence for commitment, and sacrifice for strength. We've forgotten that work exists to serve life. Somewhere along the way, we reversed the equation, and most of us were too busy answering emails at dinner to notice.

This is where contemplative wisdom earns its place alongside the research. The Buddhist concept of *The Middle Way*, a balance between extremes, has particular relevance in workplaces that oscillate between impossible demands and empty wellness gestures. Mindfulness offers leaders something rarer than another framework: the ability to see their cultures accurately, without the comfortable distortions of wishful thinking or defensive denial. The understanding of impermanence is a useful reminder that the current crisis, however entrenched it feels, won't last forever. Things can change, and with the right leadership, they will.

Dara Simkin and Tane Hunter's *Full Stack Human* makes this argument at the individual level: we are running ancient biology on superhuman technology, and the upgrade required is fundamentally human rather than technical. They are right. A 2026 global study of over 80 000 workers across 115 countries confirms the gap they describe: in 15 of 17 countries, employees rated their team's productivity higher than their own happiness. We are producing more and flourishing less, and changing culture and conditions is the only way to close that gap.

This book draws on every relevant source of wisdom leaders need in a time of crisis, neuroscience, psychology, economics, philosophy and lived experience, because the crisis we face demands everything we have. The term 'burning platform' is usually business jargon for change dressed as crisis. Not on this occasion. The platform most of us work from is on fire. This book is about putting it out and building something better.

PART 1

The Furnace

Understanding the burnout crisis

The case this book makes rests on what Part 1 establishes. These chapters map the scale of the crisis, what burnout is, what it costs, what it does to the human brain and body, and how it came to feel normal.

The burnout crisis has been described as an epidemic, a cultural failure, and a leadership problem. All of which are true. Rarely has it been described as a system working exactly as designed.

Some of what follows will be uncomfortable. It needs to be. You can't redesign a system you haven't recognised.

CHAPTER 1

The scale of the fire

> To know what you know and what you do not know, that is true knowledge.
>
> —Confucius, Analects 2.17

The first thing to understand about the burnout epidemic is its sheer scale. It affects every sector, demographic and level of organisational hierarchy, and every continent with an internet connection and a quarterly earnings call. The numbers tell a story so stark that it should be impossible to ignore it, and yet ignore it we do.

A global contagion

In the United Kingdom, 91 per cent of workers reported high or extreme levels of stress at some point over the past year (Mental Health UK/YouGov, 2024). Think about what that means for your own workplace. The colleague who seems fine possibly isn't. The direct report who never complains may be one difficult conversation away from handing in their notice, and the cheerful faces in your Monday standup could well be masking something that nine out of ten people in that virtual room are carrying.

In 2024, more than half of all sick days taken in the UK were linked to stress, anxiety or burnout. Stress-related absence now accounts for 52 per cent of all work-related illness cases in the UK. The Health and

Safety Executive's 2025 statistics documented 964 000 workers suffering from stress, depression or anxiety caused or worsened by work. There were 22.1 million working days lost to these conditions alone, out of 40.1 million total days lost to work-related ill health (HSE, 2025). The financial toll is estimated at £22.9 billion annually in lost output, healthcare costs and wider impacts.

In the United States, the situation is equally dire. More than half of the workforce, 55 per cent, is experiencing burnout (Eagle Hill Consulting, 2025). The statistics are particularly alarming for younger workers, with 66 per cent of Generation Z reporting burnout compared to 37 per cent of Baby Boomers. That's almost twice the rate. American companies lose over $300 billion annually due to stress-related absenteeism, and reduced productivity and turnover (AIS, 2023).

Across European Union member states, 29 per cent of employees report stress, depression or anxiety caused or worsened by work, making mental strain one of the top three work-related health problems on the continent. Roughly 10 per cent of European employees meet the clinical criteria for burnout.

In Asia, where long working hours and presenteeism cultures dominate, the numbers are even more concerning. Research indicates that Asian employees report higher burnout than the global average, largely due to cultural expectations around work and hierarchical workplace structures. In Japan, around 31 per cent of employees experience measurable burnout symptoms (Matsuo et al., 2022).

Australia and New Zealand, where I've spent most of my career, rank among the worst in the developed world for workplace harassment and bullying. According to the Lloyd's Register Foundation World Risk Poll 2021, which is a comprehensive global survey of over 125 000 people across 121 countries, Australia and New Zealand report the highest rates of workplace violence and harassment worldwide. Nearly half of Australian workers, around 47 to 49 per cent, have experienced some form of it, whether physical, psychological or sexual. This far exceeds the global average of 21 per cent, with psychological harassment being the most prevalent form, often involving repeated unreasonable behaviours such as yelling, humiliation or exclusion.

I find this deeply troubling. We pride ourselves on being a 'fair go' nation, yet our workplaces tell a different story. Harassment and bullying are among the most reliable producers of burnout.

These figures reveal far more than isolated incidents. They expose a profound systemic failure in which chronic stress has become the entrenched, default condition of employment in modern workplace cultures.

The generational divide

Perhaps no finding is more troubling than the generational patterns in burnout. The average American experiences peak burnout at 42 years old, but Generation Z and Millennial workers report reaching their highest levels of stress at an average age of just 25 (DHR Global, 2024). This dramatic shift represents more than a statistical anomaly. It signals a fundamental breakdown in the relationship between work and human development.

Consider what this means. Previous generations had years to build resilience, develop skills, accumulate savings, and establish identities before encountering the kind of chronic stress that leads to burnout. They had time to learn coping mechanisms, find mentors, and develop perspective on what matters. Today's young workers are being crushed before they have had any of these opportunities.

Research consistently shows that younger workers report the highest rates of burnout symptoms. Seventy-one per cent of Generation Z and 59 per cent of Millennials report low wellbeing at work (Gallup, 2024). In the UK, younger workers report significantly higher rates of stress-related absence than their older colleagues (Mental Health

UK, 2024). When young workers burn out before age 30 and leave the workforce at increasing rates, we risk losing the diverse talent necessary for innovation and growth. This represents lost potential, unfulfilled careers and damaged lives.

There is something deeply wrong with a system that exhausts people before they have begun. And there is something even more wrong with leaders who see this happening and accept it.

The gender gap

The burnout crisis does not affect all workers equally. Women experience burnout at significantly higher rates than men, with the gap more than doubling since 2019 (McKinsey, 2022). Women in the workforce are 8 per cent more likely than men to report feeling like they're struggling or in crisis (Gallup, 2024).

Multiple factors contribute to this disparity. Women continue to bear disproportionate responsibility for caregiving and domestic labour, creating a second shift that leaves less time for recovery. They are more likely to face workplace discrimination and harassment, adding psychological burden to already demanding roles. They are also more likely to work in high burnout sectors, such as healthcare, education and social services.

The gender gap in burnout belongs to the workplace and the systems within it.

Many organisations have designed systems that assume workers have few responsibilities outside the office, reward presence over productivity, and punish those who can't conform to norms built around male patterns of work. Until we address these systemic factors, women will continue to bear the heaviest burden of our collective failure.

Industry hotspots

While burnout touches every sector, certain industries have become ground zero for the crisis. Healthcare workers, who spent the pandemic years pushing themselves to breaking point, now face endemic burnout levels. Physician burnout alone costs the US healthcare system over $4.6 billion annually (Han et al., 2019), and that figure does not count the human cost of medical errors made by exhausted practitioners.

The technology sector, despite its reputation for perks and progressive policies, shows moderate to extreme burnout among 58 per cent of workers (Spill, 2024). In retail, more than half of workers report experiencing burnout in the past year (Grant Thornton, 2024). These numbers represent the majority of workers in critical economic sectors.

A word of caution, focusing on industry patterns can obscure the deeper truth: burnout follows bad management, not specific jobs. Within any industry you will find organisations with healthy cultures and organisations that churn through human beings like disposable components. The difference lies in how work is organised, led and valued. The difference is culture.

The slow erosion

Beyond the statistics on burnout lies a newer phenomenon that researchers have begun calling 'quiet cracking'. A gradual erosion of workplace satisfaction that manifests as persistent unhappiness and slow disengagement. Unlike traditional burnout, which announces itself through overwhelm, exhaustion and cynicism, quiet cracking operates beneath the surface, slowly dissolving the connection between workers and their work.

This phenomenon now affects 54 per cent of the workforce (TalentLMS, 2025). These are workers who are quietly giving up. They are showing up but not engaging, meeting minimum standards but withholding discretionary effort, and are remaining employed when emotionally they have already departed. They sit in meetings with vacant eyes, complete tasks without investment, and answer emails while mentally composing their exit.

Quiet cracking is particularly insidious because it is often invisible to managers focused on traditional performance metrics. The quietly cracking employee may hit their targets and attend their meetings while progressively disconnecting from their work, their colleagues, and their sense of purpose. By the time the problem becomes visible, it is often too late to address. They've cracked.

Crisis management or management crisis?

If a single factor predicts burnout more than any other, it's management. Toxic workplace behaviour is the single largest predictor of burnout: employees in toxic climates are *eight times* more likely to burn out (McKinsey & Company, 2022). That number is worth repeating: *eight times the likelihood*. A workplace that tolerates toxic behaviour produces burnout with industrial efficiency. Toxic management behaviours predict more than 60 per cent of burnout variance globally.

Managers themselves are also burning out at alarming rates. Global employee engagement data shows that manager engagement fell from 30 to 27 per cent in just one year (Gallup, 2025). Three percentage points sounds abstract until you realise what it represents: the people responsible for 70 per cent of team engagement are themselves disengaging. The lifeguards are drowning but they're too busy trying to save everyone else to call for help.

Young managers and female managers experienced the largest declines. Since the pandemic, managers have been asked to balance new executive demands and employee expectations, and we're only now starting to see the toll.

Seventy per cent of team engagement is attributable to the manager (Gallup, 2024). When managers burn out, their teams burn out. When managers disengage, their teams disengage. The crisis is cascading through organisational hierarchies, spreading from exhausted managers to the teams they're too depleted to lead.

It appears that we have constructed, at considerable expense and over several decades, a system in which one person's anxiety becomes their team's anxiety, their team's anxiety becomes the organisation's anxiety, and the organisation's anxiety gets described in the job ads as 'a dynamic and challenging operating environment'.

A global study of over 80 000 workers found that the Employee Net Promoter Score (eNPS) is negative in half the countries surveyed. Meaning, more than half the global workforce would not recommend their employer to a friend. Satisfaction with the mechanics of work does not automatically translate into the emotional connection that makes someone willing to put their name behind where they work (The Happiness Index, 2026).

The legal reckoning

Workplace safety law has traditionally been reactive: something went wrong, there would be an investigation, and this was followed by a fine if the breach was serious enough. The implicit message to employers was to manage your risks, but if you miss something, respond when it surfaces.

That model is changing and in several jurisdictions it has already changed entirely. Leaders who have not updated their understanding of what they are legally required to do are carrying significant personal and organisational exposure, and simply don't know it.

In Australia, the Work Health and Safety (WHS) Regulations were amended on 1 April 2023, requiring employers to proactively identify and manage psychosocial hazards at work. Unrealistic workloads, poor leadership, chronic job strain, excessive hours, and the absence of control over one's work are now legally defined hazards that employers must eliminate or minimise, in the same way they are required to manage physical safety risks. Every Australian state and territory has adopted the changes. For many leaders, it's still sinking in that this isn't guidance or best practice, it's law.

The WHS framework operates on a proactive basis. Employers can't wait for harm to occur and then respond. They are required to identify risks and prevent harm before it happens. Ignorance is not a defence, and neither is a wellness program bolted onto a toxic culture. Regulators will ask what steps were taken, proactively and systematically, to ensure workers weren't being harmed by the conditions that were built.

In October 2023, Court Services Victoria was prosecuted, pleaded guilty and fined $379 157 for failing to identify and manage psychosocial risks and address a toxic workplace culture at the Coroners Court. The conduct covered a period spanning several years. In December 2025, the Department of Defence became the first Commonwealth employer convicted for failing to manage psychosocial risks, following the death by suicide of a Royal Australian Air Force technician who was subject to an intensive performance management process. The fine was accompanied by a court-ordered adverse publicity notice. Regulators are no longer sitting around waiting for complaints. They're looking.

Those two cases sit at the lighter end of what is now possible. The industrial manslaughter laws now in force across all Australian states and territories carry penalties of $18 to $20 million for organisations, and up to 25 years imprisonment for individuals, depending on jurisdiction. The threshold is reckless or grossly negligent conduct that substantially contributes to a worker's death. Legal commentators have noted that where workplace psychological harm contributes to a worker's suicide and gross negligence can be established, industrial manslaughter provisions may apply. That possibility has been deliberately left open by regulators and the courts.

In the UK, the duty of care under the *Health and Safety at Work Act 1974* explicitly includes psychological health. The Management of Health and Safety at Work Regulations 1999 require employers to assess psychosocial hazards and implement controls. These are not aspirational standards; failure to meet them can result in enforcement notices, prosecution and civil liability. In February 2024, a UK employer was ordered to pay £300 000 in compensation to a former manager who suffered severe depression caused by an unrealistic workload and the deliberate removal of the resources he needed to do his job. The employer had received a GP letter and an occupational health referral. They did not act, and that decision had a price.

Across the European Union, Framework Directive 89/391/EEC establishes a legal requirement to assess and manage psychosocial risks in all member states. In Belgium, Finland, Ireland and Spain, criminal proceedings are available for breach of occupational health and safety obligations. The European Commission is under active pressure to introduce a specific directive on psychosocial risks that would tighten and standardise obligations further.

The burnout crisis has crossed from moral failure into legal liability. The culture that produces burnout, the leadership that maintains it, and the systems that normalise it are now, in multiple jurisdictions, legally required to be effectively addressed. The leaders who understand this are doing the work described in this book because it's the right thing to do, it's effective, and they have grasped that the alternative now carries consequences they can't afford. Leaders who do not understand it yet, will understand when the investigation starts.

What the numbers demand

The anatomy of this epidemic reveals a crisis that is global in scope, accelerating in pace, devastating in impact, and now embedded in law. The system built it, meaning that this is a collective breakdown in how we have organised work, and a failure to build cultures that meet the needs of the people inside them.

The human cost alone should be enough to compel action. For some leaders, it will be. Others will need to see the spreadsheet. The next chapter is about money.

Most leaders reading this already know which person on their team is closest to breaking. They have known for months.

CHAPTER 2

The economics of destruction

There is no wealth but life.

—John Ruskin, *Unto This Last* (1862)

In my experience, there are two kinds of leaders when it comes to burnout. The first kind are leaders who care about their people and are motivated by the human cost: the suffering, lost potential and damaged lives. The second kind need to see a business case before they will act. This chapter is for both; the evidence serves either starting position.

The hidden tax

The economic case against burnout is so overwhelming that doing nothing about it is financially irrational. Let's have a look at what burnout is likely costing your organisation.

The global economic impact of burnout and disengagement exceeds US$8.9 trillion annually (Gallup, 2024). Nine per cent of everything the world produces, lost to exhaustion, disengagement and despair. That's more than the entire GDP of Japan and Germany combined.

Every year, we burn wealth equivalent to the third and fourth largest economies on Earth, while burning the people who could have created far more.

But these headline figures understate the problem, because they primarily capture direct costs like absenteeism, turnover and reduced output. The larger burden is invisible: presenteeism, which is the phenomenon of workers who are physically present but mentally absent, too exhausted to perform but too worried about job security to stay home.

A 2025 study published in the *American Journal of Preventive Medicine* quantified this hidden tax (Merrill et al., 2025). Employee disengagement and burnout over the course of a single year costs employers an average of approximately US$4000 for an hourly employee, around US$4300 for a salaried employee, nearly US$11 000 for a manager, and more than US$20 000 for an executive.

This means a typical organisation with 1000 employees, where most staff are hourly or salaried rather than managers or executives, faces approximately US$5 million in direct burnout costs annually. For a larger enterprise with 10 000 employees, the figure climbs to US$50 million a year, quietly draining from the bottom line.

And presenteeism accounts for up to 89 per cent of these costs (Merrill et al., 2025). The visible problem, people calling in sick, represents barely a tenth of the actual damage. The rest is invisible, which is why we have always underestimated burnout. The developer staring at code without seeing it, the sales rep going through motions without conviction, the manager in back-to-back meetings while mentally composing their resignation letter. Bodies present. Minds and motivation absent.

Declan Edwards, whose research examines the psychology of happiness and emotional wellbeing, identifies the mechanism clearly. When people suppress difficult emotions rather than process them, they don't selectively numb the uncomfortable feelings, they narrow the entire emotional range. As anxiety and exhaustion grow, the capacity for enthusiasm, creativity and connection diminishes. What remains is the performance of engagement without its substance (Edwards, 2026). Presenteeism is what emotional depletion looks like from the outside.

Most of these costs go completely unrecognised because the organisation looks like it is functioning. The walls are standing, lights are on and people are at their desks. What nobody can see is the very thing many people can feel: that the temperature has been rising for years.

The healthcare burden

US businesses lose between $125 billion and $190 billion annually in healthcare costs attributable to workplace burnout (Goh, Pfeffer & Zenios, 2016). Between 5 and 8 per cent of total national healthcare spending traces back to workplace stressors: conditions that did not originate in hospitals or clinics but in open plan offices, performance management cycles and always-on email cultures.

The picture in Australia is no less striking. Safe Work Australia estimates the cost of poor psychosocial safety at approximately $6 billion per year. The cost of depression alone, through presenteeism and absenteeism, runs to a further $6.3 billion annually. Mental health conditions now account for 12 per cent of all serious workers' compensation claims in Australia, and the median time lost is almost five times that of physical injuries (SWA, 2025). Mental health has overtaken physical illness as the dominant driver of workplace productivity loss.

Burned-out employees are 23 per cent more likely to visit an emergency room (Gallup, 2018). They are more likely to develop chronic conditions, require ongoing medication and accumulate the kind of compounding health costs that don't resolve with a wellness program and a resilience workshop. These costs are felt by organisations as higher insurance premiums, increased absenteeism, and a steady erosion of the cognitive capacity that sustained performance depends on.

The turnover cascade

Burned-out employees are nearly three times more likely to say they plan to leave their employer in the coming year. When they leave, they take institutional knowledge, client relationships and team cohesion with them. The replacement costs are staggering: typically between 50 and 200 per cent of annual salary, depending on the role.

But the real damage goes deeper. High turnover rates materially destabilise teams, disrupt projects, and force remaining employees to absorb additional workload. This increases their own burnout risk, which increases their own likelihood of leaving, which creates something of a death spiral of departures.

Seventy-three per cent of Generation Z and 70 per cent of Millennials are considering changing jobs, largely driven by burnout (Deloitte, 2025). Sixty-one per cent of Generation Z workers would strongly consider leaving their current job if offered one with significantly better mental health benefits (SHRM, 2025). Nearly half of younger workers say they would rather be unemployed than stuck in a job that drains their soul (ADP Research Institute, 2025).

It's easy to dismiss this as entitlement. I hear that response frequently, mostly from Gen X leaders like me. But that interpretation misses something important. This is a rational response to intolerable conditions. Young workers are looking at what burnout does to people. They've watched their parents, their older siblings, and their early mentors burn out. They've seen what the deal looks like from the other end. And they're declining it.

The productivity paradox

The management practices most likely to cause burnout are often implemented in the name of productivity. Leaders push harder, demand more, extend hours and compress timelines precisely because they believe this will increase output. The research tells a different story: sustained pressure degrades the cognitive functions that productive work depends on. Attention narrows, decision quality drops, and creative thinking shuts down. The brain under chronic stress is running a threat response, and threat responses are not helpful for complex knowledge work.

Workers who feel burned out are significantly less likely to go above and beyond what's expected of them: 40 per cent versus 56 per cent among engaged workers (Gallup, 2020). Burned-out employees are 63 per cent more likely to take a sick day and 13 per cent less confident in their performance (Gallup, 2018). Job-related stress contributes to 550 million workdays lost annually. The World Health Organization (WHO) estimates that one trillion dollars is lost in productivity each year as a result of depression and anxiety, which are conditions strongly linked to workplace stress.

The simple reality is that it's impossible to extract sustainable performance from exhausted people. You can extract a sprint. You can get a temporary burst of effort in a crisis.

But you can't build sustained competitive advantage by running your workforce into the ground. The body quits before the mind admits defeat.

The ROI of intervention

Now for the good news. Fixing burnout pays for itself many times over. Mental health programs generate average returns of 4.7 times the investment (Deloitte, 2022). Companies implementing interventions like four-day workweeks report 71 per cent burnout reduction while maintaining revenue (Autonomy/4 Day Week Global, 2023).

Organisations with comprehensive wellbeing benefits are 8 per cent more likely to see a positive return on investment from those benefits and 13 per cent more likely to see increased employee engagement, the strongest known predictor of organisational performance (Lyra Health, 2025). Employees who feel their mental health is supported are twice as likely to report no burnout or depression (Mind Share Partners, 2025). In workplaces that offer mental health training, employees are significantly less likely to report that their productivity has suffered: 21 per cent compared to 38 per cent in workplaces without training (NAMI, 2025).

The return on investment for burnout prevention is substantial, measurable and proven. Beyond specific interventions, perception matters. Employees who strongly agree their employer cares about their wellbeing are 71 per cent less likely to report burnout, and three times more likely to be engaged (Gallup, 2020).

What healthy cultures produce

The cost of burnout and the return on getting it right are well documented. When Microsoft Japan trialled a four-day workweek, productivity increased by 39.9 per cent. Not maintained. Increased. Employees with more recovery time brought more cognitive capacity to their work. Meetings became more focused, decision-making became more efficient.

The UK's four-day workweek trial told a similar story. Participating companies reported not just maintained revenue but revenue growth.

Employees reported dramatically improved wellbeing. It turned out that the perceived tradeoff between performance and care, which seemed so obvious to so many leaders, simply did not exist.

Healthy cultures produce outcomes that depleted cultures cannot. Innovation requires psychological safety: the willingness to take risks without fear of punishment. Collaboration requires trust: the confidence that colleagues will support rather than undercut. Customer centricity requires genuine care, which is impossible when employees have nothing left to give. These are competitive advantages that determine which organisations thrive and which do not.

The investment case for culture health becomes clear when you watch what happens over time. Organisations that invest in their people build capabilities that compound. Organisations that extract from their people deplete capabilities until little remains to extract.

The most rigorous longitudinal research confirms what these examples suggest. Kotter and Heskett's landmark Harvard study tracked 207 companies across 22 industries over 11 years. Companies that managed their cultures deliberately (shaping an 'intentional culture') saw stock prices appreciate by 901 per cent, compared to 74 per cent for those that did not. Revenue grew 682 per cent versus 166 per cent. Net income increased 756 per cent versus 1 per cent. These aren't marginal differences. They represent an order of magnitude gap between organisations that treat culture as a strategic priority and those that leave it to chance.

More recent research reinforces these findings. A 2023 global study by i4cp found that organisations with the healthiest cultures reported high market performance six times more often than those with toxic or unfit cultures. Fit (intentionally aligned) cultures were four times more likely to have improved retention and three times more likely to have strengthened their ability to attract top talent. The pattern is consistent across decades of research: deliberate investment in culture health produces returns that dwarf the investments required to create them.

For leaders, the implication is straightforward. Taking time to shape intentional culture is a value creation strategy with measurable returns. Teams and organisations that treat culture development as peripheral are surrendering ground which most struggle to recover.

The shareholder fallacy

I was sitting with an executive team some years ago when the conversation turned, as it often does in the third quarter, to the gap between actual and projected revenue. The team had committed a number to the board. The response to the shortfall was immediate and unanimous: cut costs. Within a few hours, the group had identified several hundred roles that could be eliminated. It was the only idea on the table. There was no conversation about which revenue lines could be accelerated, which markets were underleveraged, or which operational inefficiencies were costing more than the headcount being discussed. Just names and numbers, and a collective relief that something decisive had been done.

Nobody asked about the longer term commercial and cultural costs. How the remaining team would absorb the work. What it would cost to replace the institutional knowledge walking out the door. What the same output would now require with 30 per cent fewer people. The number had been decided and the meeting ended on time. What followed over the next 18 months, the resignations, the errors, the client attrition, the rehiring at premium rates, was filed as a separate problem unrelated to the decision made in that room that day.

I've heard the justification for that kind of decision countless times. Shareholder obligations require maximising short-term returns, even at the cost of employee wellbeing. This argument ignores both the evidence and the actual requirements of fiduciary duty. It also represents, to my mind, the root cause of the vast majority of burnout. And it is made, with great confidence, almost exclusively by people whose own compensation is not subject to the consequences of these decisions.

Workers in firms with higher burnout risk receive lower wages, and those jobs are less productive as measured by value added per worker. Burned-out workforces are less productive workforces. Extractive practices destroy long-term value. Workers who burn out suffer severe earnings losses that persist for years, similar to the well-documented displacement effect of layoffs. We are damaging human capital that took years to develop and will take years to replace.

The organisations that will thrive in the coming decades are those that recognise human beings as the source of value rather than a cost to be managed. Those that continue treating people as disposable will find themselves unable to attract talent, unable to retain expertise and unable to compete, not as a moral consequence but as a commercial one.

If someone in your organisation can tell you exactly how many sick days were taken last quarter, ask them what they are doing about the 57 days those same people showed up and produced nothing.

CHAPTER 3

The neuroscience of breaking

> It is easy for the one who stands outside the prison-wall of pain to exhort and teach the one who suffers.
>
> —Aeschylus (c. 525–456 BC)

When I speak with leaders about burnout, I often encounter a particular form of scepticism. While some acknowledge that burnout exists, that it affects performance and might even be expensive, beneath their words lurks an unspoken assumption: that burnout is somehow optional, a matter of attitude, something that sufficiently resilient people can just power through. I must admit, coming from a competitive sporting background myself, I was guilty of this assumption. I grew up with coaches telling me to harden up and that I could rest at the end.

The neuroscience says otherwise. Burnout is a physiological condition with measurable effects on brain structure and function. Chronic workplace stress literally changes the physical architecture of the brain. These changes explain the symptoms, the difficulty of recovery, and why telling someone to 'just push through' makes about as much sense as telling someone with a broken ankle to walk it off.

Selena Bartlett, renowned Professor of Neuroscience at Queensland University of Technology (QUT), makes the point that burnout recovery requires specific biological inputs to rebuild degraded neural structures. Sustained sleep, regular movement, social connection, and a sustained reduction in the chronic stressors that drove the degradation are essential. A two-week holiday cannot rebuild hippocampal volume, but months of modified conditions can.

Once you understand what's happening inside the skull of a burned-out employee, the conversation changes entirely. It stops being about attitude and starts being about brain health. And the focus moves in earnest towards the conditions necessary for recovery.

The brain under siege

The human brain handles stress through three main regions that work in constant communication: the amygdala, the prefrontal cortex, and the hippocampus. Understanding how these regions interact under stress is essential for understanding what burnout does to us.

The amygdala acts as an alarm system, detecting threats and activating the body's fight or flight response. When the amygdala perceives danger, whether from a predator or a passive–aggressive email from someone three levels above you, it triggers a cascade of physiological changes designed to help us survive immediate threats. The amygdala can't tell the difference between a lion and a calendar invite marked 'Urgent: important meeting'. It responds to both with the same ancient chemistry.

The prefrontal cortex manages reasoning, focus and emotional regulation. It's responsible for executive function: the capacity to plan, make decisions, regulate impulses, and engage in abstract thought. When we think about what makes humans distinctively human, we're largely thinking about prefrontal cortex functions.

The hippocampus stores memory and learning, helping us find meaning in our experiences. It's essential for converting short-term experiences into long-term memories and for contextualising present situations based on past learning.

Under short-term, acute stress, this system works beautifully. The amygdala sounds the alarm, the body mobilises resources, attention sharpens and reaction time improves. We deal with the threat, and then the system returns to baseline. This is our stress response working as it should.

Under chronic stress, the system breaks down. And this is precisely what happens in burned-out workers.

The cortisol cascade

Chronic stress drives persistent activation of the hypothalamic pituitary adrenal axis, the HPA axis, which regulates the stress hormone cortisol. Under normal conditions, cortisol follows a predictable daily pattern: high in the morning to help us wake up, gradually declining through the day, lowest during sleep.

In burned-out individuals, this pattern is disrupted. The body continues to produce cortisol in response to perceived threats, maintaining a state of physiological arousal even when there's no immediate danger. The Sunday evening dread, the racing mind at 2 am, the inability to relax even on holiday: these aren't personality traits, these are symptoms of a stress system that has forgotten how to switch off. Over time, this chronic elevation leads to what researchers call HPA axis dysregulation. This is when chronic stress turns the body's protective response into a source of harm.

Eventually, the HPA axis switches from producing high amounts of cortisol in response to stressors to abnormally low amounts, reflecting a burnout of the body's stress response itself. This burnout of the stress response has been observed in individuals with clinical burnout and it causes mild to moderate inflammation throughout the body.

This inflammation can lead to severe heart problems by contributing to the accumulation of plaque in arteries. When researchers say stress kills, they mean it literally.

The practical result is that a burned-out employee arrives on Monday morning already running on the physiological assumption that a threat is present, before anyone has said a word to them, before a single email has arrived, before the first meeting of seven. Their body has been preparing for danger all weekend.

Structural changes in the brain

Perhaps the most disturbing finding from neuroscience research on burnout concerns the prefrontal cortex. Studies using MRI imaging have found that patients suffering from burnout show more pronounced thinning in the medial prefrontal cortex compared to healthy controls.

Typically, the frontal cortex begins to thin as part of normal ageing. But in burned-out individuals, this thinning is accelerated. Meaning, the brain ages faster than it should. Other brain structures also show signs of wear: burnout patients appear to have shrinking in the caudate nucleus, a region central to motivation and to the brain's assessment of whether effort is worth making. Its shrinkage correlates directly with perceptions of workplace stress; the more pressure a person reports, the more pronounced the deterioration. This helps to explain something leaders often misread as attitude: the work that once felt meaningful, that now feels pointless, has not become so by choice. It is what happens when the part of the brain that generates the feeling of *this is worth doing* has been physically worn down.

Chronic exposure to uncontrollable stress causes loss of spines and dendrites in the prefrontal cortex, the brain region that provides top-down regulation of thought, action and emotion. The connections between neurons that allow for complex thinking, planning and emotional regulation are physically degraded by chronic stress.

This is measurable structural change. When we speak of burnout affecting someone's capacity to think clearly, make good decisions, or regulate their emotions, we're describing the consequences of actual physical damage to the brain regions responsible for these functions.

Read that again, slowly. When your employees are burned out, they are carrying something more serious than fatigue. The organ that does all the thinking, all the creating, all the problem solving you're paying for is being physically degraded by the conditions we've created.

The enlarged alarm system

As the prefrontal cortex shrinks, the amygdala grows. Long-term stress strengthens the brain's alarm circuits while weakening the parts that help us stay calm and think clearly. Research confirms this: participants in burnout groups show enlarged amygdalae and significantly weaker connections to the brain areas that regulate emotional distress (Golkar et al., 2014). In simple terms, the brain gets stuck in alert mode.

This explains why the burned-out version of yourself overreacts to minor frustrations, snaps at people you care about, and feels constantly on edge. The neural architecture has been physically remodelled by chronic stress. The alarm system has grown larger while the system meant to regulate it has shrunk.

The more stressed an individual reports feeling, the weaker the connectivity between the amygdala and prefrontal regions appears on brain imaging. Weaker connections between these two brain structures help explain why participants in burnout groups have more difficulty controlling their negative emotions.

This is the neurological basis for the emotional volatility that often accompanies burnout: the irritability, the crying, the difficulty maintaining perspective. Burned-out workers don't have weak characters. It's just that the brain regions responsible for emotional regulation are literally unable to do their job.

If you manage someone who has become emotionally volatile, who seems to overreact to small problems, who has lost the steady temperament they once had, consider the possibility that you're observing neurological damage rather than a character flaw. Also consider what conditions might have produced that damage.

The vicious cycle

The most troubling aspect of burnout neuroscience is the self-reinforcing nature of the changes. Researchers demonstrated this in a study that subjected rats to chronic stress over several weeks (Vyas et al., 2002). When they examined the animals' brains, they found something remarkable: the same stressor produced opposite effects in different regions. Neurons in the hippocampus had atrophied, their dendritic branches withering. But neurons in the amygdala had grown, their branches extending and multiplying. The stress was simultaneously dismantling the brain's capacity for memory and regulation while expanding its capacity for fear and threat detection.

The same pattern appears in humans. A Swedish study examining people with occupational burnout found not only enlarged amygdalae but significantly weaker connectivity between the amygdala and the prefrontal regions responsible for emotional control (Golkar et al., 2014). The researchers also documented what this looked like in daily life. Participants reported difficulty controlling negative emotions, heightened reactivity to minor provocations, and a persistent sense of being overwhelmed by demands that previously felt manageable. They described snapping at family members over trivial matters, bursting into tears in situations that wouldn't have concerned them before, and an inability to switch off even when the workday ended. Several reported lying awake at night, their minds cycling through work problems they could neither solve nor release.

This explains why burnout doesn't magically resolve when the external stressor is removed. The brain has been changed by the experience. Recovery requires active intervention to rebuild the neural pathways that have been degraded.

What this means for leaders

The neuroscience of burnout should change how every leader thinks about workplace stress. This is about brain health: the physical integrity of the very organ we depend on for every decision, innovation and competitive advantage our organisations produce. When we push employees past their breaking point, we are damaging the machinery of thought itself and creating conditions that will produce worse decisions, weaker creativity, and diminished capacity for the complex cognitive work that modern organisations depend on.

Think about the implications. That employee who used to generate innovative ideas but now just goes through the motions? Their prefrontal cortex may have been degraded to the point where creative thinking is physiologically difficult. That manager who used to handle pressure with grace but now flies off the handle? Their amygdala may have enlarged while their emotional regulation circuits weakened. That team that used to collaborate beautifully but now bickers constantly? They may all be operating from threat states that make cooperation neurologically challenging.

We wouldn't expect an athlete with a torn ligament to run faster. Yet we routinely expect employees with degraded prefrontal cortices to think better, decide faster and innovate more. Then we wonder why performance declines.

I reminded the audience of this fact when I opened CultureCon™ at the Sydney International Convention Centre in 2025 and referred to one of psychology's most quietly devastating studies. In 1973, John Darley and Daniel Batson recruited seminary students at Princeton, people who were training to become priests and whose professional identity was built entirely around service to others, and asked them to prepare a talk on the parable of the Good Samaritan. In that parable, a priest and a Levite walk past an injured man in the road. A stranger stops to help. Darley and Batson had arranged the same scene for the students. On their way to deliver their speech, each student passed a person slumped in a doorway, clearly in distress. The single variable that determined whether they stopped was not their personality, their religious conviction, or the fact that they were literally about to preach about helping strangers. It was whether they were in a hurry. Of those under high time pressure, only 10 per cent stopped. Among those with time to spare, 63 per cent did (Darley & Batson, 1973).

Stress did not make those who walked past bad people. It made them temporarily incapable of acting like the people they genuinely were. The part of the brain responsible for noticing, caring and responding had been crowded out by urgency. This is precisely what the neuroscience of burnout describes at a structural level, and it has direct implications for every organisation that runs its people at full tilt.

It's biology, not weakness. And when we create conditions for recovery, sustainable workloads, predictable schedules, psychological safety and rest, we are protecting the neural infrastructure that makes performance possible.

The hopeful truth

Again, there is good news buried in all of this: the brain changes associated with burnout are largely reversible.

In a 2009 study by Liston, McEwen and Casey published in the *Proceedings of the National Academy of Sciences*, medical students under intense pressure displayed functional brain changes in the prefrontal cortex. They showed disrupted attentional control, weakened connectivity in attention-shifting networks, and impaired cognitive processing. These patterns closely resembled the neural signatures seen in people with chronic burnout.

These alterations proved largely reversible. After the exam stress ended and the students had four weeks of recovery and relaxation, follow-up neuroimaging showed substantial restoration. Prefrontal function returned close to the levels of unstressed control participants.

Declan Edwards covers the science of what those conditions look like in practice in *How to Be Happy* (Wiley, 2026). The psychological conditions he identifies as foundational to happiness, including autonomy, connection, meaning and rest, are precisely the inputs neuroscience identifies as necessary for hippocampal regrowth, prefrontal cortex restoration, and HPA axis recalibration.

Neuroplasticity, the brain's capacity to change and adapt throughout life, works in both directions. Just as chronic stress can degrade neural connections, recovery conditions can rebuild them. The prefrontal cortex can regain function. The amygdala can return to normal size and the connections between brain regions can be restored.

But recovery doesn't happen automatically. It requires rest, reflection and connection. It requires conditions that allow the brain to repair itself. And it requires time; often far more time than organisations are willing to provide.

The Friday night social, as a solution to employee wellbeing, is what you get when the people designing the solution have never examined the problem. You can't rebuild degraded neural pathways with alcohol-fuelled social gatherings, a beanbag, a standing desk, or a 'bring your dog to work' day.

Bruce McEwen, a pioneering neuroscientist at Rockefeller University who spent decades studying how stress affects brain structure, found that chronic stress produces what he calls 'largely reversible, adaptive plasticity' in the hippocampus, amygdala and prefrontal cortex. The retraction of dendrites and reduced synapse density that occur under chronic stress may serve a protective function against permanent damage. McEwen's research confirms that acute and chronic stress-induced plasticity is reversible, at least in young adult brains, and doesn't constitute brain damage per se.

The brain can heal. But it needs the right conditions. And providing those conditions is a growing leadership responsibility.

The implications for your organisation

The same brain that breaks under chronic stress can heal under supportive conditions. Organisations that design for recovery will build workforces with the cognitive capacity to do the work that matters.

The leaders who understand this have a real advantage. They know that past a certain point, pushing harder produces less, and that the thinking power of the people inside an organisation cannot be bought on a balance sheet or replaced by a restructure.

What happens when these changes go unaddressed is the subject of the next chapter. The damage accumulates, and it does not stay in the brain. The damage is real, and so is the capacity to heal.

Incidental brain damage. Unintentional in almost every case. The predictable result of conditions most organisations have never examined.

CHAPTER 4

A slow motion crisis

> Wrong does not cease to be wrong because the majority share in it.
>
> —Leo Tolstoy, *A Confession* (1882)

I almost didn't write this chapter. The content is confronting. The neurological damage explored in the last chapter is only part of it. What I'm about to describe is medical evidence that burnout is killing people. When burnout gets past a certain point for some people, they can no longer cope with the emotional and neurological pressure, and they take their own lives.

Behind every one of those deaths is a family permanently altered and a workplace that rarely understood why. I've had the misfortune of having a handful of friends who chose to leave well before their time. In every instance the consequences to family and friends have been catastrophic. Children left without parents, partners suddenly isolated emotionally and financially and communities fractured forever. If life is about making our mark, then surely it's on us all to get in the way of this reality that causes such profound grief and loss.

While suicide is one of the more extreme impacts of unrecognised and untreated burnout, the physical toll across a range of health factors is dire. Workplace stressors contribute to approximately 120 000 deaths each year in the United States alone (Goh, Pfeffer & Zenios, 2016). That's a commercial airplane crashing every single day for a year.

We've built workplaces that can measurably reduce the lifespans of the people who work in them. If any other product or practice killed 120 000 people a year, there would be Congressional hearings or Senate inquiries, front page investigations and class action lawsuits. We would ban it. Instead, in large part, we treat it as the cost of doing business.

When we talk about building healthy, high-performing cultures, we are talking about something far more significant than engagement scores or productivity metrics. We are talking about human health and whether the people in our care will live full lives, or have those lives cut short by the conditions we create.

The cardiovascular catastrophe

Research shows chronic stress is linked to cardiovascular disease, with risk increasing by 40 per cent (Kivimäki & Steptoe, 2018). A landmark WHO and ILO study examining data from 194 countries found that working 55 or more hours weekly increases the risk of stroke by 35 per cent and death from heart conditions by 17 per cent, compared to a 35 to 40 hour week (Pega et al., 2021).

Chronic stress maintains elevated levels of cortisol and adrenaline, which increase heart rate and blood pressure. Over time, this constant cardiovascular load damages blood vessel walls, promotes the accumulation of arterial plaque, and increases the risk of heart attacks and strokes (Kivimäki & Steptoe, 2018).

The inflammatory response triggered by chronic stress further compounds the damage. Psychosocial stress stimulates systemic, low-grade inflammation even in the absence of infection or injury (Rohleder, 2014). This inflammation contributes to atherosclerosis, the hardening and narrowing of arteries, and makes existing plaques more likely to rupture, causing the acute events that kill people.

It's happening everywhere: office workers, retail employees, healthcare professionals, teachers. Anyone subjected to chronic workplace stress. The body doesn't distinguish between the stress of being chased by a predator and the stress of an impossible deadline or a toxic manager. It responds in the same way, and the damage accumulates in the same way.

When we talk about building cultures where people thrive, we're talking about preventing heart attacks and strokes, and the early deaths that result from overworked bodies. The stakes could not be higher.

The immune collapse

Chronic stress suppresses immune function, making burned-out workers more vulnerable to infections and slower to recover from illness. The same inflammatory processes that damage the cardiovascular system also impair the immune system's ability to respond effectively to threats.

This explains why burned-out employees take more sick days. Their bodies have lost the capacity to fight off the ordinary pathogens that healthy immune systems handle routinely. They are sick more often, and when they do get sick, they remain sick for longer, creating extended absences that compound the productivity losses from burnout.

But the immune dysfunction goes beyond infection risk. Chronic inflammation is implicated in a wide range of chronic diseases, from autoimmune conditions to certain cancers. The burned-out body progressively loses the capacity to maintain its own health.

I think about this when I see leaders dismiss wellness concerns as soft thinking (which as mentioned, is often). Try telling that to an immune system. The cultures we build either support physical health or undermine it. There is no neutral position.

The mental health spiral

The relationship between burnout and mental health conditions is bidirectional and devastating: burnout increases the risk of depression and anxiety; depression and anxiety increase vulnerability to burnout. The conditions feed each other in a spiral that can be extremely difficult to escape.

In 2026, burnout remains one of the workforce's biggest threats, with moderate to severe burnout, depression or anxiety affecting about half of US workers (Grow Therapy, 2025). More than three-quarters report some level of burnout, with 53 per cent at moderate to severe levels (Mind Share Partners via Grow Therapy, 2025).

Low psychosocial safety climate triples the risk of new depressive symptoms within a year (Afsharian et al., 2025). Improving it could reduce job strain by 14 per cent, depression by 13 per cent, absenteeism by 43 per cent, and presenteeism by 72 per cent (Safe Work Australia & Dollard et al., 2019).

The mental health consequences of burnout extend beyond the burned-out individual. Their suffering affects families, communities and the next generation. Children of burned-out parents are more likely to develop anxiety and depression themselves. Parental burnout reshapes the emotional climate at home in ways that affect children long after they leave it.

In my work with leaders on building healthy, high-performing cultures, I am often struck by how rarely they consider these ripple effects. The employee who goes home depleted every night is underperforming at work, and at home they are a different parent, a different partner and a different friend than they would be if their workplace supported rather than depleted them. Culture shapes what happens inside the organisation and what happens in every home that organisation touches.

The physical manifestations

Stress manifests in the body in ways that are immediately recognisable to anyone who has experienced prolonged workplace pressure: headaches, sleep disturbances, gastrointestinal problems, chronic pain and hypertension. Your doctor asks if you've been under stress lately. You laugh. It is the most you have laughed in months, which is its own data point. These are physical expressions of psychological overload (Schneiderman et al., 2005).

Feeling burned out leaves 44 per cent of US employees emotionally drained and 51 per cent feeling used up at the end of each workday (Gallup, 2024). These symptoms are directly related to withdrawal, diminished collaboration, and detachment from organisational culture. But they also signal physiological distress that, if ignored, can lead to more serious health consequences.

The body keeps the score, as trauma researcher Bessel van der Kolk reminds us. It records every episode of stress, every sleepless night, every meal skipped or eaten in haste, every hour stolen from rest and given to work. And eventually, it presents the bill.

Losses that cannot be undone

A study of US medical students found that those experiencing burnout were significantly more likely to report suicidal ideation (Dyrbye et al., 2008). Research on physicians found those experiencing burnout were also much more likely to consider taking their own lives, an association which operates in part through the heightened depression risk that severe burnout produces (Shanafelt et al., 2021). A meta-analysis examining suicide rates by occupation found that jobs characterised by high stress and low control carry markedly elevated risk (Milner et al., 2013).

The despair that accompanies severe burnout, the sense of being trapped, worthless and without hope, is the same psychological state that precedes many suicide attempts. When someone has lost the capacity to feel joy or meaning, when they feel they've nothing left to give and no way to escape their circumstances, they're at genuine risk.

I've seen this in my consulting work. Not often, fortunately, but more than once. Talented people, valuable contributors and beloved family members, destroyed by workplaces that asked too much, gave too little, and refused to see the warning signs until it was too late.

The decisions leaders make about workloads and cultures they create or tolerate, and the messages they send about what's expected, all carry consequences that extend far beyond any quarterly report.

The statistics I have cited here are derived from medical research and government data. What they cannot convey is what it looks like from the inside of an organisation when things have gone this far.

At The Culture Institute of Australia, our culture health investigations take us into workplaces at every stage of dysfunction. From teams showing early warning signs through to environments so broken that the harm being done is no longer deniable. What we find consistently is that suicide, when it appears in this context, is a shock but rarely a surprise. The warning signs were there. The conditions that produced them were often documented in complaint histories, exit interviews and performance records. Nobody had looked at them together until it was too late.

Work-related factors contribute to between 10 and 13 per cent of suicide deaths, according to analyses of suicide case investigations published in the *American Journal of Industrial Medicine* in 2024. The World Health Organization (WHO) estimates that in a company of 1000 employees, one worker will die by suicide every 10 years. For every one who does, between 10 and 20 more will have made an attempt. Workplace bullying carries nearly three times the suicide risk. Long working hours, between 45 and 52 hours weekly, carry nearly four times the risk. These are not exceptional outcomes. They are the statistically predictable consequences of conditions that too many organisations have normalised.

I raise this not to alarm but to be precise about what is at stake when we speak of culture as a strategic priority. The investigations we conduct are not abstract. They involve real people, real families and, in the worst cases, losses that cannot be undone. Every time a leader chooses not to address a toxic environment because it is uncomfortable, inconvenient or commercially awkward, they are making a choice with substantial and somewhat predictable consequences.

Burnout is killing people. The evidence of how and why is available. Organisations and the leaders within them will act on it, or find themselves answering questions from investigators and regulators about what they knew, when they knew it, and what they chose to do.

The normalisation of suffering

Perhaps what disturbs me most is how thoroughly we've normalised burnout. We speak of stress as if it were the weather, something to endure rather than something we create. We celebrate hustle culture and treat work–life balance as a quaint notion held by people who lack ambition.

We treat the people who burn out as failures rather than casualties. We have, quite remarkably, created a system that injures people and then blames them for bleeding.

This normalisation is itself a form of harm. When we tell workers that their exhaustion is their own fault, that they should have been more resilient, managed their time better and practised more self-care, we add psychological injury to physical harm. We make them feel ashamed of responses that are entirely predictable given the conditions we created.

Professor Selena Bartlett, whose 2026 research draws on three decades of neuroscience practice, is direct: applying the language of personal resilience to burnout is physiologically inaccurate, and it delays the recognition and structural response that recovery requires. When we frame a structural failure as a personal one, we guarantee the system stays broken.

And we let the organisations responsible for those conditions off the hook. Instead of asking why workplaces are generating such high levels of chronic stress, we ask why individuals aren't coping better.

I've spent 25 years fighting this normalisation. A leader describes burnout as a personal failing. An organisation responds to a mental health crisis with resilience workshops. Talented people are blamed for breaking under conditions that would break anyone. Each time, I am reminded of why my work matters.

Buddhism begins with *dukkha*, the honest observation that suffering is woven into human existence. But Buddhist philosophy draws a distinction between the suffering that arises from the nature of being alive, and the suffering we manufacture through avoidable choices. Loss, ageing, impermanence: these are *dukkha* we cannot design our way out of. A 70-hour workweek, a toxic manager, a workload no one could sustain, these are not. The burnout epidemic falls squarely into the second category. It is manufactured suffering built by people, sustained by systems and normalised by habit.

Culture as the determinant of health

The WHO recognises that the conditions in which people live and work are primary determinants of health outcomes. Workplace culture is a health intervention, whether we design it that way or not.

Every element of culture shapes physical wellbeing:

- The quality of relationships between colleagues affects stress levels and recovery capacity.
- The degree of psychological safety determines whether people can voice concerns before they become crises.
- The norms around workload and boundaries determine whether people have the time and space to maintain their health.
- The way leaders behave sets the tone for what's expected and permissible.

I've devoted my career to culture work. Building healthy, high performing cultures isn't separate from building healthy human beings. The culture *is* the intervention. Where we get it right, people thrive.

Where we get it wrong, we systematically damage the people in our care. There's no version of this where culture is somebody else's department.

The research on relational health reinforces this point. Bruce Perry, one of the world's leading trauma neuroscientists, found that the best predictor of a person's current mental health is their current relational health. Not their history or even their diagnosis. The best predictor is their connections, right now. Human beings are fundamentally social creatures. Our nervous systems are designed to co-regulate with others. When workplace relationships are characterised by trust, respect and connection, our stress response systems function more effectively. When those relationships are characterised by fear, competition and isolation, our stress response systems remain chronically activated.

The relational dimension of culture is essential. High performance without relational health is extraction. It produces short-term results at the cost of long-term capacity. High performance built on relational health is generative. It produces results that compound over time because the people producing them are growing rather than becoming depleted.

The moral weight of leadership

I've painted a grim picture and I offer no apology. The physical health consequences of burnout deserve to be faced squarely, without the euphemisms and minimisations that usually accompany discussions of workplace stress.

Every choice you make as a leader either contributes to the culture and health of your people or undermines it. Every norm you establish, every expectation you set, and every behaviour you model or tolerate becomes part of the environment in which human beings spend the majority of their waking hours. That environment shapes their bodies, their minds, their relationships and ultimately, their lifespans.

The responsibility is huge. Deloitte's 2024 research into human sustainability surveyed more than 3000 executives and workers across four countries and found that seven in ten workers want their executives to take significantly more responsibility for the human impact of how organisations are run. Eighty-two per cent of the C-suite agreed they need to be more accountable. And yet 81 per cent of those same executives admitted their organisation is not doing enough (Deloitte & Workplace Intelligence, 2024). Awareness without action is its own kind of failure.

The leaders I admire most are the ones who feel that weight and allow it to inform how they lead. Those who don't, by my definition, are not leaders.

Case studies from the field

Data indicates the scale and severity of the fire, but stories tell us what it feels like to burn.

We often speak of burnout in the abstract language of human resources: turnover rates, absenteeism and engagement scores. We sanitise the experience, converting visceral human suffering into neat rows on a spreadsheet or a red flag on a dashboard. But to truly understand the crisis we're facing, we must step out of the boardroom and into the quiet, desperate moments where careers and lives silently unravel.

The following stories are drawn from my years of consulting. Names and identifying details have been altered to protect privacy, but the essential truth of their experiences remains intact. These are the human faces of the strategic risks we manage every day.

The invisible weight: The middle manager

If there's a position in the modern organisation where burnout pressures converge most intensely, it's middle management. And if there's a story that captures what the statistics actually mean for real human beings, it's this one.

Rowan was a regional operations manager for a logistics company. He had been with the organisation for 11 years, promoted steadily through the ranks because he was reliable. That was the word everyone used: *reliable*. He kept the wheels turning. He solved problems before they reached senior leadership. He absorbed the chaos so others didn't have to.

When I met him, he was 43 years old and looked a decade older. He managed a team of 12, reported to a director who was rarely available, and served as the buffer between corporate targets and frontline reality. His days began at 5.30 am checking overnight reports and ended sometime after 9 pm when he finished responding to emails he hadn't had time to address during the day. He couldn't remember the last time he had eaten dinner with his family.

'I'm fine,' he used to tell me, the words automatic. As someone who profiles people for a living and is trained to gauge emotional intelligence, authenticity and cultural identity, I knew that Rowan was far from fine.

Most of the leaders around him were in the same position. Calling out a toxic system from inside it, without seniority, without political capital and without financial safety beneath you, is not a real option for most people. The privilege of doing what is right belongs to very few. For everyone else, absorbing the dysfunction and keeping the wheels turning is not a character flaw, it's survival.

So he absorbed everything. When the company cut headcount, he absorbed the extra work. When a direct report went on stress leave, he absorbed their responsibilities. When his company introduced a new reporting system that doubled his administrative burden, he absorbed the hours required to make it work. He was like a human shock absorber, and he was struggling.

(*continued*)

The signs were everywhere… He had gained 20-odd kilograms in three years. He told me that his marriage was functional but hollow and that he didn't really have any friends now, outside of work. In some ways, his world had shrunk to the dimensions of his laptop screen.

The turning point

Rowan didn't have a dramatic collapse. He just stopped. One Monday morning, he couldn't get out of bed. Not wouldn't. Couldn't. His body had finally refused what his mind had been demanding for years. His doctor signed him off for six weeks, then extended it to three months. The company, which had relied on him so completely, scrambled to cover his absence with three people.

The strategy for recovery

There was no role redesign, no executive coaching budget or sabbatical at a wellness retreat. He used the company's employee assistance program (EAP), saw a counsellor, and slowly rebuilt his boundaries. When he returned, he negotiated a reduced scope. Some colleagues saw this as a demotion.

For me, the interesting thing about Rowan was that no one had noticed he was drowning because he was too reliable to make waves. The organisation's systems had no mechanism for detecting his deterioration because those systems measured output, not cultural health. He was an engaged, high-performing employee right up until the moment he wasn't an employee at all.

There are thousands of Rowans in every organisation. Reliable. Invisible. Absorbing everything until there is nothing left to absorb. When they break, we call it unexpected, saying we had no way of knowing. Too often, we also had no incentive to find out.

The quiet cost: The corporate survivor

Dianne grew up in a regional town in Australia in a family where warmth was the default setting. Now, 30 years later, she is a group executive at a large multinational. She is commercially sharp, widely respected and, by most measures, at the top of her field. She is also one of the most naturally empathic leaders I have worked with. In another environment, that quality would be her greatest professional asset. In hers, it is something she has spent three decades learning to balance.

Dianne did not burn out, but survival inside a large corporation, when you are wired the way Dianne is wired, carries its own toll. The system she works in rewards a particular kind of leader: one who is decisive and risk averse, and who values process over people, and compliance above curiosity.

At the organisational level, the logic is simple and circular: the board interprets what shareholders want, strategy becomes a linear execution of that interpretation, and customer focus is bolted on as the acceptable face of growth. What never quite makes it into the equation is the person actually doing the work. The human being standing between the strategy and the customer, absorbing the gap between what the organisation promises and what it is resourced to deliver.

We explore this in depth in Chapter 8, but the short version is this: when that equation is out of balance, everything eventually falls. In most cases this is entirely unintentional. Nobody designed it this way. It accumulated, decision by decision, across years of leadership layers that each inherited the logic of the one before and rarely stopped to question it. In organisations like Dianne's, it has been out of balance for a long time. These systems have quietly engineered out the very thing they most need.

(*continued*)

Dianne can perform all of the things the system asks of her. But performing them consistently, across decades, in an environment where the leaders around her have largely stopped questioning whether the culture is worth questioning, requires a constant internal negotiation that nobody prepared her for and nobody acknowledges.

Nobody told Dianne that this was coming. There was no training for it, no conversation about what it costs to carry genuine values inside a system that does not formally reward them. She learned by doing, which mostly meant learning by absorbing.

What keeps Dianne functioning is not resilience in the way organisations mean when they run resilience workshops. It is identity. She knows who she is, and has a deeply supportive marriage and a clarity about her own values that most people in her position lost somewhere around Year 10. She rallies against the system in ways that quietly reshape it, though to many colleagues she appears to simply be part of it. In some respects she is. That is the only way the work gets done.

The toll is real, even if it is invisible on a performance review. Her broader social world has contracted in the way that senior leadership tends to contract it: the friendships that require time and presence, the community connections that need tending, and the version of herself that existed before the corporation became the dominant context of her life.

Dianne is a portrait of what sustained, values-driven leadership costs inside institutions that were not designed to support it. She is also the norm, not the exception. Many organisations are lucky enough to have a Dianne. Most have never thought seriously about what they are asking her to carry.

The identity trade: The consulting partner

I was in a meeting room on the top floor of a prestigious consulting firm. Tania and her fellow partners were working through their character profiles and working styles; the kind of structured self-reflection that firms like hers commission periodically to signal investment in their people. Tania noted the absence of altruism from her character profile with the same unemotional response she might have used to describe her preference for window seats. No discomfort or pause. No recognition that the room had just gone quiet.

For everyone else in that room, it was one of the most telling moments they had witnessed in a professional setting. Altruism is not a personality quirk. In a leader, it is the attribute that makes power safe for the people subject to it. Its absence, stated openly and without apparent concern, was less a character revelation than a cultural diagnosis. This was what the firm had selected for, rewarded, and ultimately produced.

The person who joins a prestigious firm at the beginning of a career brings something with them. Ambition, yes, but usually also a genuine desire to do good work, to be respected, to matter in some way beyond the title. What happens over years inside certain institutions is quiet and incremental: compromise becomes concession, concession becomes habit, habit becomes identity. At some point the person stops noticing the distance between who they were and who they have become, because the institution has provided a replacement self that comes with considerable rewards attached.

Tania had accepted that trade completely. Her sense of self was no longer her own. It belonged to the firm, to the title, to the

(*continued*)

floor she sat on and the clients she could name. She identified so thoroughly with the institution that any threat to it felt like a threat to her survival. This is where the toxicity originates: from a sense of self so thinly constructed that difference feels like threat, and autonomy in others feels like insubordination.

Her behaviour as a leader reflected it precisely:

- micromanagement dressed as standards
- exclusion operating as culture
- a visible disrespect for colleagues whose qualifications or approaches differed from her own
- political alliances built and broken with the efficiency of someone managing a portfolio rather than a relationship
- demands about office hours and physical presence that had nothing to do with performance and everything to do with control.

The people around Tania paid for this daily. The culture of her team was one of hypervigilance, where energy that should have gone into the work went instead into reading the room, managing her mood, and staying out of the line of fire.

Tania's own health suffered in ways she was unlikely to name. The relationships with her peers had corroded to the point of functional hostility. And the institution she had sacrificed so much of herself to serve would, in all likelihood, not remember her name 12 months after she left a 20-year career.

This is what happens when compromise is allowed to become concession, and concession is allowed to become identity. It requires only the absence of one question: what actually matters to me, and am I still living by it?

Most organisations have a Tania. The difference between Tania and Dianne is that Dianne never stopped asking that question, even when the system made it hard to do so.

We return to altruism as a leadership quality in Chapters 8 and 12, because its presence or absence turns out to be one of the most reliable predictors of whether a culture builds people up or quietly breaks them down.

Steve: The two-year exit

Steve was the kind of student schools build assemblies around. Top scores at a leading school, top scores at a leading university, the corner office trajectory mapped out before he had ever set foot in one. Bright and articulate, with the sensitivity that makes a good lawyer. He arrived at his desk on day one carrying everything in his head that the system had asked him to bring.

He lasted two years. Australian data shows that more than half of lawyers with one to three years' experience plan to leave their current firm (Momentum Intelligence, 2019). The American equivalent shows 44 per cent of associates gone within three years (NALP Foundation, 2017). Steve was on the curve.

What broke him was the gap between the work he expected and the work he was given. The case load he had trained for sat with senior lawyers who were not releasing it. The work he did was the work nobody senior wanted to do, and the only way to graduate from it was to demonstrate value by absorbing more of it. Self-determination theory, the most robust account we have of human motivation, names three conditions for psychological functioning at work: competence, autonomy and relatedness. Steve scored zero on all three. He could not feel competent on work he had not been trained for. He had no autonomy in choosing what he worked on, because work was distributed by partners protecting

(*continued*)

their own books. Relatedness collapsed inside a culture engineered around competition, where the colleague at the next desk was the person you were trying to outperform for the next file.

The litigation half of his work added a particular kind of pressure. Court deadlines have no flex. Negotiation is combative by design. A junior lawyer lives with the daily knowledge that a missed detail can produce a malpractice suit against them personally, and that fear sits underneath every billable hour. He pulled all-nighters and got paid the same as a normal day. He was back at his desk at nine the next morning. The firm catered for the extra hours with restaurant accounts and Friday drinks, all of which existed to keep volume high and partners visible to the juniors competing for their attention.

The class layer made it heavier. The top tier firms in Australia recruit predominantly from a narrow demographic: private school, sandstone university, white, Anglo. That demographic arrives with a pattern of competitive socialisation already wired in by school and family. Steve, sensitive and observant, recognised the ruthlessness required and decided he needed to leave. The alternative was suburban practice at a fraction of the salary, which to someone told for 15 years they were going to be a city lawyer felt indistinguishable from a public demotion. Richard Beasley's 2001 novel *Hell Has Harbour Views*, later filmed for the ABC, captured this exact pattern: the young senior associate chasing the corner office while quietly losing the person he started out as. Beasley wrote it from inside the profession because he was watching it happen.

Steve left at the two-year mark. He is now 55, a very well-respected associate professor at a leading university and an acclaimed legal academic and author. The profession he could not survive as a practitioner has become the profession he has spent decades thinking and writing about with the kind of care it withheld from him.

Conclusion

The medical research in this chapter explains what is happening inside the bodies and minds of people, at all levels of organisations, every day. It describes the cardiovascular load, the immune suppression, and the mental health spiral.

Most importantly, none of this is abstract: burnout has a face, a name, a family, and in the worst cases, a funeral. The normalisation of these conditions is a choice, made and remade across thousands of leadership decisions, in organisations that have simply never stopped to look at what they are producing.

Burnout is a shape shifter. It can be a cardiovascular event, a mental health spiral, a slow withdrawal, or a life cut short. What stays constant is the system that produced it.

Getting help

If this chapter has raised difficult feelings for you, please know that support is available:

Australia

- Lifeline: 13 11 14, available 24 hours, lifeline.org.au

USA

- 988 Suicide and Crisis Lifeline: call or text 988, available 24 hours, 988lifeline.org

UK

- Samaritans: 116 123, available 24 hours, samaritans.org

International

- Befrienders Worldwide: a directory that points readers to a crisis centre in their own country, befrienders.org

CHAPTER 5

The AI paradox

> Men have become the tools of their tools.
>
> —Henry David Thoreau, Walden (1854)

Artificial intelligence (AI) adds a volatile accelerant to an already dangerous fire. It promises to automate routine tasks, reduce workloads, and create space for more meaningful human work. What has arrived alongside that promise is a new category of anxiety, already significant, compounding the burnout crisis we mapped out in earlier chapters.

According to the Moodle State of Workplace Learning Report 2025, 13 per cent of US employees report that anxiety about how AI will impact their role is actively driving their burnout. A source of workplace stress that barely existed five years ago is now a significant factor for more than one in ten workers. That figure counts only those who consciously connect their burnout to AI. The broader anxiety runs deeper and wider than any survey cleanly captures.

The numbers outside the workplace confirm it. An Ipsos survey of 31 countries conducted in May and June 2023 found that 52 per cent of people agreed that products and services using AI make them nervous, a figure that had risen 12 percentage points since December 2021. In Australia that number reached 69 per cent, the highest of any country surveyed, while just 40 per cent of Australians said they were excited about AI, well below the global average of 54 per cent (Ipsos, 2023). By 2025, Ipsos's annual AI Monitor found global nervousness and excitement running almost level, at 53 and 52 per cent respectively, with the Anglosphere and high-income countries remaining consistently the most anxious.

I was in a tech client's office recently and a software engineer in his late forties described it to me this way: 'I spent 20 years becoming an expert. Now I watch junior developers use AI to produce in hours what used to take me days. I'm not being replaced yet. But I can see the replacement coming. And I've had to smile through meetings where we discuss how exciting it all is. I'm not sure my wife and kids would agree.'

The Moodle data puts AI anxiety in its proper context. Sixty-six per cent of American employees experience some form of burnout, driven by excessive workloads, lack of resources, economic pressure and labour shortages (Moodle, 2025). AI-related worry now sits alongside these as a measurable contributor, and unlike the others, it's accelerating. Workers are being asked to learn new tools, adapt to new expectations, and remain productive while carrying the genuine possibility that those same tools are making them redundant.

It's a reasonable fear: AI will eliminate some jobs and transform roles beyond recognition. What makes this particularly dangerous is the timing. The prefrontal cortex thinning documented in Chapter 3, the physical consequence of chronic stress, degrades precisely the cognitive capacity that navigating a major technological transition demands.

We're asking the most stressed workforce in recorded history to adapt to the most significant shift in the nature of work since industrialisation.

The anxiety engine

To understand the AI paradox, we must first understand what researchers call 'AI awareness': the extent to which employees perceive that their job could be replaced by artificial intelligence. This perception, regardless of whether replacement is imminent, triggers a cascade of psychological responses that feed directly into burnout.

Most organisations lean towards communication about AI that reassures, reframes and redirects. 'Upskilling programs' and other positive headlines, the language of opportunity.

The displacement is already in action. Graduate hiring in professional services, financial analysis, legal research, entry-level coding, and content production has contracted measurably since 2023. The World Economic Forum's Future of Jobs Report 2025 projects that by 2030, 170 million new roles will be created globally while 92 million existing positions will be displaced; a structural churn of 22 per cent of the formal workforce. The net figure is a gain of 78 million jobs. The equation paints what I consider to be a false positive. Displaced roles and emerging ones require different skills, exist in different geographies, and do not arrive on the same timeline. The people losing their jobs this decade are not automatically the people employed in the new roles next decade.

Younger employees feel the displacement most directly. The traditional career ladder assumes that entry-level roles exist, that competence is rewarded with advancement, and that the skills developed in early work translate into security over time. That ladder is being pulled up from the bottom while leaders tell the people who needed those rungs, to adapt and upskill. Adapting to what, exactly, and on whose time, is rarely specified.

As discussed, the body does not distinguish. Chronic uncertainty about whether your job category will exist in five years produces the same physiological stress response as chronic overwork. The HPA axis does not distinguish between 'My manager is unreasonable' and 'My profession may be obsolete'. Both activate the same cascade. Both degrade the same cognitive functions. Technological displacement operates at a scale that sits beyond any individual leader's control. The best leaders acknowledge it honestly, sit with the uncertainty alongside their people, and resist the pull towards corporate optimism that nobody believes anyway.

Workers who worry about AI displacement are paying attention. The leaders who acknowledge that, who say, 'I don't know exactly what this means for your role, but I'm committed to navigating it with you rather than around you', retain trust. The ones who deploy corporate optimism about exciting opportunities while quietly reducing headcount are building the conditions for the kind of disengagement that takes years to reverse.

A 2024 study published in *Humanities and Social Sciences Communications* found that AI adoption doesn't directly cause burnout. Instead, it operates through a mediating mechanism: AI adoption can increase job stress, and that elevated stress drives burnout.

The relationship isn't:

technology → burnout

The relationship is:

technology → anxiety → stress → burnout

Understanding this pathway is essential for intervention.

The same research identified a significant moderating factor: self-efficacy in AI learning. Workers who feel confident in their ability to learn and adapt to AI tools experience significantly less stress from AI adoption. Those who doubt their capacity to keep pace experience amplified anxiety that accelerates their path to burnout (see figure 5.1).

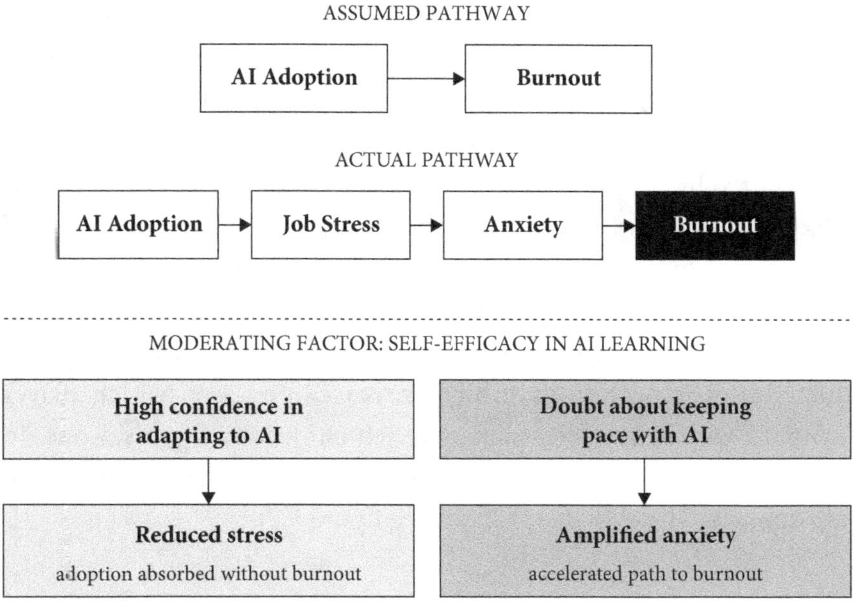

Figure 5.1 AI adoption and the path to burnout

Adapted from: Kim, BJ & Lee, J (2024). 'The mental health implications of artificial intelligence adoption: the crucial role of self-efficacy'. *Humanities and Social Sciences Communications* 11, Article 1561.

This finding has serious implications for how we build cultures. It suggests that the psychological impact of AI is shapeable. Leaders who invest in building their teams' AI confidence can buffer against the anxiety that AI naturally generates. Those who deploy AI tools without attention to the human dimension are, in my mind, pouring accelerant on an already burning fire.

Indian IT giants have reportedly reduced their workforces by more than 60 000 as part of AI-driven workforce reduction. Globally, the World Economic Forum's Future of Jobs Report 2025 projects that 39 per cent of existing skill sets will become outdated by 2030. Growing fluency with AI tools runs alongside a deepening fear of being replaced by them.

The productivity paradox

AI tools can increase productivity for many tasks. Studies consistently show that workers using AI complete certain tasks faster and produce better-quality results.

However, many organisations are using these gains to demand more output. If a tool lets you write a report in half the time, the reward is two reports. The worker who once had a reasonable task list now has an expanded one because AI makes more possible. The efficiency gains are captured by the organisation, and are not returned to the worker as reduced pressure or increased recovery time. In this respect, at least, AI behaves exactly like every other productivity tool in history: it makes the conveyer belt faster, not shorter.

This is the productivity paradox: technology enables more work, which raises expectations, which increases pressure, which drives burnout, which reduces capacity, which leads organisations to demand even more AI adoption to compensate for declining human performance. The cycle feeds itself (see figure 5.2).

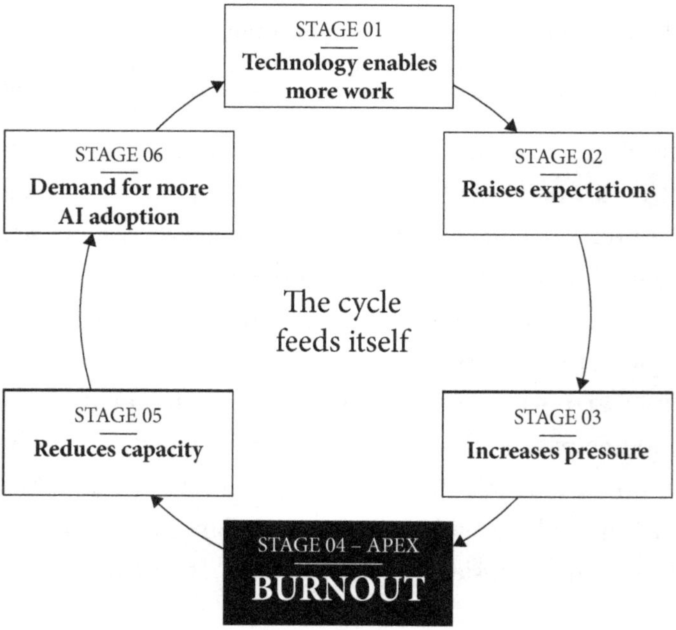

Figure 5.2 The productivity paradox

Microsoft's 2025 Work Trend Index documented a 42 per cent rise in what it calls 'digital exhaustion', driven not by any single tool but by 'tool sprawl', constant interruptions, and fragmented workflows. Workers aren't exhausted by AI specifically but by the multiplication of digital demands that AI has enabled. More tools. More inputs requiring attention. More outputs are then expected in return.

The promise of AI in handling routine tasks, freeing humans for higher order work, is a very appealing promise that speaks directly to dominant culture drivers like autonomy and self-actualisation. The reality is that AI has created new categories of routine tasks: reviewing AI outputs, correcting AI errors, feeding AI systems with prompts, integrating AI-generated content with human judgement. The work has changed but in everyday worklife, the burden has grown.

This is the universal reality for the organisations I work with. Leaders announce AI initiatives with great enthusiasm, projecting efficiency gains and competitive advantages. The change implications, specifically the anxiety of displacement and the cognitive load of constant adaptation, are typically not mentioned.

Organisations continue to treat AI as a technical project when it's fundamentally a culture project.

The cognitive dependence problem

A subtler dimension of the AI paradox concerns what happens to human capabilities when AI becomes embedded in daily work. Research from 2025 documents growing concern among workers about cognitive dependence: the erosion of human skills through reliance on AI assistance, often described as cognitive offloading, where frequent delegation of thinking tasks to AI tools leads to measurable declines in independent critical thinking, problem solving and analytical capacity (Gerlich, 2025).

Workers report that deep integration of AI tools is changing how they think. Critical thinking feels harder when AI can generate plausible answers. Creative capacity seems diminished when AI can produce endless variations. Problem-solving skills atrophy when AI handles routine challenges. And underneath all of it sits something more fundamental: human beings are wired to solve problems. The satisfaction that comes from working something out, from genuine intellectual effort, is central to our needs and to a rewarding working life. When AI handles the thinking, organisations count the efficiency and miss the cost.

This creates a distinctive form of anxiety that compounds traditional job security fears. Workers aren't just worried about being replaced by AI. They're worried about becoming less capable and less distinctively human in their contributions. Many fear a slow diminishment of the very qualities that made them employable in the first place.

Buddhist philosophy offers a useful lens here. Strong, independent identity doesn't depend on external circumstances, including professional success. People with a robust sense of self can think: AI might change what I do, but it doesn't change who I am. My job might evolve, but I remain. This kind of psychological grounding becomes essential when the nature of work is shifting beneath our feet.

However, cultivating such grounding is difficult when organisations offer little or no support for the transition, when workers are expected to adapt without acknowledgement of what adaptation costs, and the human dimensions of technological change are invisible to a leadership focused only on efficiency gains.

The surveillance paradox

AI has enabled new forms of workplace monitoring that create their own contribution to burnout. So-called 'bossware', which is employee-monitoring software powered by AI analytics, has proliferated as remote work has normalised. These tools promise to help managers understand productivity and identify problems early.

The psychological impact is the opposite of what organisations intended.

Research shows that AI-powered monitoring increases feelings of surveillance, reduces perceived privacy, and generates additional stress that compounds existing burnout risk (Kong et al., 2023; Park et al., 2024). Workers feel watched, measured and evaluated by systems they don't understand and can't appeal against.

This runs directly counter to what we know about human motivation. As Dan Pink has shown in *Drive* (2009), people perform at their best when three core drives are met:

- Autonomy: the desire to direct our own lives and work
- Mastery: the urge to get better at something that matters
- Purpose: the yearning to do what we do in service of something larger than ourselves.

Surveillance systems strip away autonomy at the most basic level, telling workers not just what to achieve, but exactly how, when, and for how long to move their mouse or type their keys. The result is a motivational collapse: extrinsic control replaces intrinsic drive, resentment builds, and culture health and engagement decline.

The paradox deepens when we consider exactly what that surveillance measures. Most monitoring tools track activity rather than outcomes: keystrokes per minute, mouse movements, and time spent in applications. These metrics capture busyness, not effectiveness. A worker staring thoughtfully out the window while solving a complex problem would trigger a red flag. A worker frantically clicking between tabs while accomplishing nothing would look like a model employee. In these instances, the system punishes thinking.

Worse still, surveillance reflects and reinforces a culture of distrust. The decision to monitor says: we don't trust you to work without oversight. The focus on activity metrics says: we don't trust you to manage your own time; and the implementation without worker input says: your experience of being monitored doesn't matter.

Some surveillance is legally required or is necessary for security. But organisations implementing monitoring should be honest about the tradeoffs. What do we gain in oversight? What do we lose in trust, autonomy and worker wellbeing? If the monitoring itself becomes a burnout driver, have we solved a problem or created one?

The alternative to surveillance is trust; building cultures where accountability operates through relationships rather than technology, and where what you produce matters more than how visibly busy you appear while producing it. It's these cultures where high performance organically emerges.

The disengagement connection

In the organisations I work with, disengagement from AI anxiety is rarely dramatic. Nobody hands in a resignation or makes a scene. What happens is quieter and harder to measure. People show up, complete what's required, and stop doing anything beyond that. The creative contribution, discretionary effort and genuine investment in outcomes recede gradually, until the organisation is running more on compliance rather than commitment.

Research confirms a direct pathway from AI anxiety to quiet disengagement. AI anxiety increases quiet quitting as a direct response to perceived job insecurity, with employees withdrawing effort and emotional investment as a protective mechanism rather than leaving outright. AI awareness, defined as the extent to which employees perceive their role could be replaced, directly undermines engagement, organisational commitment and job satisfaction (Bakir et al., 2025). The ADP Research 'Today at Work 2026' report, drawing on survey data from late 2025, found that only 19 per cent of workers globally were fully engaged, with AI-driven insecurity identified as a primary driver. ADP's own researchers described this as largely a leadership failure.

The visible cost of a poorly managed AI transition is eventual turnover. The invisible cost is the months or years before it, when workers have mentally departed while their bodies remain in the building.

The culture failure

The AI paradox is a failure of culture. The technology itself is neither good nor bad for human wellbeing. What matters is how leaders choose to implement it, communicate about it, and support workers through the transition it requires.

Most organisations have approached AI implementation as a technical project: selecting tools, integrating systems, and training users on its features. They have not approached it as a culture project: addressing fears, building confidence, restructuring expectations, and ensuring that efficiency gains translate into human benefit rather than more demands.

What organisations can do

This is what treating AI implementation as a culture project looks like in practice:

- **Start with honest communication.** Before deploying new AI tools, leaders have conversations with their teams about what the technology means for their work. Not corporate talking points about exciting opportunities, or the all-hands meeting where an executive uses the word 'transformation' 11 times while a room full of people silently calculate whether their mortgage can survive a redundancy, but genuine dialogue about concerns, uncertainties, and how the organisation will navigate them together. This requires psychological safety that many organisations have not yet built into their culture.

- **Invest in human development.** If AI is going to change the nature of work, workers need support in developing the capabilities that will remain valuable: complex problem solving, creative thinking, emotional intelligence, and relationship building. This means organisations need to deliver more than a training program, and instead ensure an ongoing commitment to human growth alongside technological advancement.
- **Redesign expectations.** If AI makes certain tasks faster, the appropriate response isn't automatically to pile on more tasks. Leaders should ask: what would it mean to use some of this efficiency gain to reduce pressure rather than increase output? What would it mean for people to have more time for the deep thinking and relationship building that AI can't replicate?
- **Address anxiety directly.** When workers are worried about their futures, pretending those worries are unfounded doesn't help. Leaders need to openly discuss the challenges of AI transition, acknowledge uncertainty about the future, validate the legitimacy of worker concerns, and create conditions where those concerns can be addressed rather than suppressed.
- **Build cultures where human value isn't reducible to task completion.** When workers understand that their worth comes from their own judgement, their relationships, their creativity and their humanity, technological change feels less threatening. When workers feel valued only for outputs that machines can now produce, technological change feels threatening.

What the best leaders do

Addressing the AI paradox requires interventions at multiple levels:

- **Acknowledge the anxiety.** Employees know that AI is changing their jobs. Pretending otherwise, or dismissing concerns as irrational, destroys trust and leaves anxiety to fester in silence. Leaders who openly discuss the challenges of AI transition create conditions where those concerns can be addressed rather than suppressed. This requires psychological safety that you may need to build first. If your organisation punishes vulnerability, start smaller with individual conversations rather than team discussions. Model the acknowledgment yourself before asking others to be vulnerable.

- **Invest in capability building.** Self-efficacy moderates the relationship between AI adoption and stress. Workers who feel confident in their ability to learn and adapt experience less burnout. This confidence requires sustained investment in training, support, and in opportunities to build competence in low stakes environments before high stakes application.
- **Return some efficiency gains to workers.** You may not control organisation-wide productivity expectations, but you likely have some discretion in how you allocate saved time within your team. Use that discretion visibly. If AI enables a task to be completed in half the time, consider whether doubling the task load is the appropriate response, or whether reduced work pressure might serve everyone better. Document the results. Build the case for broader change. The productivity paradox exists because organisations default to capturing all gains. A deliberate choice to share gains with workers breaks the cycle that turns efficiency into exhaustion.
- **Monitor for cognitive dependence.** As AI becomes embedded in workflows, periodically assess whether human capabilities are being maintained. Create opportunities for workers to exercise judgement, creativity and critical thinking without AI assistance. Augmentation that enhances human capability is the goal.
- **Use surveillance sparingly and transparently.** If monitoring is necessary, be transparent about what's being monitored and why. Involve workers in designing monitoring systems. Use data to support workers, not to evaluate them punitively. And

regularly assess whether the monitoring itself is contributing to the problems it's meant to identify.

- **Address identity explicitly.** Help workers understand that their value isn't reducible to tasks that AI can perform. Facilitate conversations about what distinctively human contribution looks like in an AI augmented workplace. Support the development of professional identity that can survive technological change.

The path forward

The AI paradox described isn't inevitable. Technology that could reduce burnout is currently amplifying it because of how we are choosing to implement it. Different choices would produce different outcomes.

The organisations that navigate this transition well treat AI implementation as a culture initiative rather than a technical one: they invest in psychological support alongside technical training; share efficiency gains rather than capturing them entirely; build confidence in their people rather than leaving anxiety to fester unaddressed; and they choose and develop leaders who think about people first. Technology-based change lands differently in those organisations. Better.

The burned-out workforce of today didn't have to happen. The AI-amplified burnout of tomorrow doesn't have to happen either. The paradox can be resolved. But resolution requires leadership that understands what's at stake and has the courage to make choices that serve people rather than short-term productivity metrics. The technology is here. The choice of how to use it remains ours.

People fear the unknown only a little less than losing their job. Be careful, your organisation may be asking them to live with both.

CHAPTER 6

The global landscape

> The customs and practices of life in society sweep us along.
>
> —Michel de Montaigne, *Essays* (1580)

The scale of the crisis is now clear. What the numbers cannot tell you is why the same underlying conditions produce such different outcomes in different places. While burnout is a global phenomenon it does not manifest uniformly. Cultural attitudes towards work, societal expectations around productivity, legal protections and economic structures all shape both the prevalence of burnout and the forms it takes. The best leaders understand this. They do not assume that what works in one context will land the same way in another, and they do not mistake local norms for universal truths.

Understanding these variations matters for several reasons. For leaders in multinational organisations, it illuminates how the same policies may have different effects in different locations. For all leaders, it demonstrates that current patterns aren't inevitable: different choices about work culture produce different outcomes. And for anyone interested in solutions, it provides a natural experiment in what truly works.

Japan: The culture that named death from overwork

Japan occupies a unique position in the world of burnout. It's the country that gave us *karoshi*, the word for death resulting from overwork, and *karojisatsu*, which is suicide caused by overwork. These are official categories recognised by the Japanese government, which compensates families when death is attributed to excessive work.

The cultural roots of Japanese work intensity run deep. After World War II, devotion to company and country fuelled economic reconstruction. The salaryman, the male office worker who dedicated his entire career to a single company, became an iconic figure. Working long hours was expected and celebrated as evidence of loyalty and dedication.

This culture produced rapid economic growth but at tremendous human cost. By the 1980s, *karoshi* cases were making headlines. Workers were literally dying at their desks, suffering heart attacks and strokes after weeks or months of excessive overtime. Others were taking their own lives after being crushed by work demands.

The government response was unusual in Western terms. Japan now sets a *karoshi* line at 80 hours of overtime per month, above which death from overwork becomes legally presumable. The threshold defines how much overwork is acceptable before it kills you, rather than asking whether that amount of overwork should exist at all. That distinction reveals a great deal about a culture that spent decades treating exhaustion as loyalty.

Yet the culture has been changing. Premium Friday initiatives encourage workers to leave early. More significantly, the Microsoft Japan experiment produced a 39.9 per cent productivity gain from a four-day week, which is notable not just for its magnitude but for where it occurred. That results like these could emerge from one of the world's most work-intensive cultures is worth noticing.

Japan's experience tells us two things at once:

1. Cultures that glorify overwork create conditions where people literally die from working.
2. Even the most deeply embedded cultural patterns can shift when evidence mounts that they're causing more harm than good.

I first encountered this in the early 2000s, when I was engaged to help a major Australian surf brand establish its culture and brand identity in Japan. I spent two weeks with their executive team, an interpreter named Jiro, and a group of Australian leaders, running a three-day seminar on what the brand meant, where it was going, and what the journey would require. I had done some reading on Japanese workplace culture before arriving, aware that direct challenge was not the norm. What I had not fully understood was the scale of what that looked like in practice.

For three days, a room full of senior managers nodded with what appeared to be enthusiastic comprehension. My read was that the message was landing. What was actually happening was that when I left the room, mild panic broke out and everyone worked furiously to make sense of what the tall Australian had been saying. The penny dropped on day three, when we asked the managers to present their transformation plans. They all presented in Japanese, and Jiro, I slowly realised, was translating diplomatically, softening, reframing, making sure I heard what I wanted to hear. Our own interpreter had been pulled by the same undercurrent (yes, a surfing analogy) as everyone else in the room. We regrouped, appointed a local manager with strong English to lead the process, and collaborated weekly for six months. It won't surprise you to learn that it worked better than my three-day seminar.

Five years later I was back in Japan, this time with a global healthcare company that had assembled its Asia Pacific executives for a regional program. In the room were Japanese, Korean, Chinese and Taiwanese leaders, all expected to conduct the program in English on the instructions of the German parent company, in the spirit, apparently, of collaboration. The first day made clear that this was not going to work. I stayed up most of the night rewriting the program so that managers could shape their actions in their own languages, framed by their own cultural logic. The results the following day were unrecognisable. The same people, the same material, the same room, but something had unlocked. There was a different level of respect.

Japan's work culture glorified overwork to such a degree that it was necessary to create a legally recognised category of 'death from overwork'. My experience there added something subtle to that picture: the difficulty of implementing change when the dominant cultural force runs beneath every visible surface, invisible to the foreigner standing at the front of the room and yet perfectly clear to everyone else in it.

The lesson from both trips was the same. The best leaders working across cultures do not arrive with answers. They arrive with questions, and they stay long enough to hear the real ones. Cultural humility can be the difference between a three-day seminar that lands nowhere and six months of genuine collaboration that produces something lasting.

The best leaders I have worked with since then carry something into every cross-cultural room that most leaders leave at home: a genuine willingness to be wrong about what they think they already know.

Germany: Structural protection through codetermination

Germany presents a different model: protection embedded in institutional structure rather than left to individual negotiation or company culture.

The German system of codetermination gives workers formal representation on company boards and requires 'works councils' in organisations above a certain size. These structures mean that worker interests are represented in decisions about working hours, working conditions, and organisational change. Workers have a seat at the table, not as a courtesy but as a legal requirement.

German law also provides strong protections around working hours. The *Working Hours Act* limits regular working hours to eight per day, extendable to ten only under specific conditions and with compensating rest. Rest periods between shifts are mandated. Sunday work is restricted. These aren't guidelines but enforceable requirements with consequences for violation.

The cultural attitude towards work reinforces these structures.

Germans generally separate work and personal life more clearly than workers in many other countries. The concept of *Feierabend*, the time after work ends, carries genuine cultural weight. There's a clear boundary between when you're working and when you're not. Answering work emails on evenings or weekends is less normalised than in Anglo American contexts.

As a result, Germany maintains one of the world's most productive economies while working fewer hours than most developed nations. German workers average around 1350 hours per year compared to nearly 1800 in the United States (OECD, 2024) and yet these shorter hours don't produce lower output. They produce more efficient use of time worked. Somewhere, an executive reading this just muttered, 'Yes, but we're different'. The data doesn't support that belief.

Burnout still exists in Germany, of course. No system eliminates it entirely. But the structural protections create conditions where healthy work is more achievable. Workers don't have to individually negotiate boundaries that are collectively guaranteed. The system supports rather than undermines human flourishing.

What's especially encouraging about the German model is how it removes the burden of boundary setting from individuals and places it in systems. In many workplaces, maintaining boundaries requires constant personal effort, and that effort itself is exhausting. The German approach recognises that structural solutions are more reliable than individual willpower.

The best leaders in any system treat structural protections as just the start line, not the end goal.

The Nordic model: Comprehensive protection

The Nordic countries, Denmark, Finland, Iceland, Norway and Sweden, consistently rank among the world's happiest nations and among its most productive. This isn't coincidental. The Nordic model demonstrates that worker wellbeing and economic performance are complementary.

Several elements define the Nordic approach. Strong unions negotiate wages and conditions across entire sectors, ensuring that competition happens on quality and innovation rather than worker exploitation. Comprehensive social safety nets mean that losing a job isn't catastrophic, reducing the anxiety that drives overwork. Generous parental leave policies support families without forcing choices between career and children.

Working hours in Nordic countries are among the shortest in the world. Denmark averages roughly 1380 hours per year (OECD, 2024). Flexible work arrangements are common and supported by policy. The right to disconnect outside working hours is increasingly protected by law.

Iceland has been particularly experimental. The country ran the world's largest four-day workweek trials from 2015 to 2019, covering more than 1 per cent of its working population. The trials reduced hours from 40 per week to 35 or 36 without salary reduction. Productivity remained stable or improved. Worker wellbeing increased substantially. Stress levels fell and work–life balance improved.

Following the trials, Icelandic unions negotiated reduced hours for a significant portion of the workforce. What began as an experiment became permanent change, driven by evidence that shorter hours produced better outcomes for everyone.

Critics sometimes suggest that the Nordic model only works in small, homogeneous societies. The principles themselves, of worker representation, social safety nets, reasonable hours and clear work–life separation, apply regardless of geography. They're choices that any society could make. The Nordic countries just made them earlier and more consistently than others.

Asia Pacific: The presenteeism challenge

Across much of Asia, workplace cultures share patterns that elevate burnout risk: strong expectations of physical presence, hierarchical structures that discourage challenging workload expectations, and cultural values that prize visible sacrifice.

In Singapore, a 2024 study found that over 40 per cent of employees reported high levels of burnout, with young workers particularly affected. The city state's competitive culture, high living costs and demanding work expectations create conditions where overwork is normalised and boundaries are difficult to maintain.

South Korea presents similar patterns. The term *gwarosa*, the Korean equivalent of *karoshi*, entered public discourse in the 2010s as death from overwork became a widely recognised social phenomenon. Despite government efforts, such as the 2018 reduction of the maximum weekly working hours from 68 to 52, cultural practices like *hweshik*, company drinking sessions that often extend workdays into late evenings, and strong expectations of presenteeism persist, undermining work–life balance and contributing to ongoing stress and overwork risks.

China's '996' culture, working from 9 am to 9 pm six days a week, became a subject of intense national debate in the late 2010s and early 2020s, when technology workers launched viral protests highlighting burnout, health crises, and overwork-related deaths. The practice, which totals around 72 hours weekly, was officially declared illegal by China's Supreme People's Court in 2021 as a violation of labour laws. Despite renewed government crackdowns in 2025, enforcement remains inconsistent, with average weekly hours still hovering around 48.5 in early 2025. Cultural expectations of dedication, low minimum wages, and workarounds like 'flexible' schedules often override legal protections, allowing intense overtime to persist in tech, manufacturing and startup sectors.

Australia and New Zealand: The contradiction

I've spent most of my career in Australia, and our global position on workplace mental health sits uncomfortably alongside the reputation we hold.

We have strong labour protections on paper. We have a cultural identity built around the 'fair go' and the idea that life should be about more than work. We have natural environments that invite outdoor living and active leisure. And yet, as noted earlier, we rank among the worst in the developed world for workplace harassment and bullying.

The Lloyd's Register Foundation data shows that nearly half of Australian workers have experienced workplace violence or harassment. That is a cultural feature of Australian working life. It reflects something about how our workplaces function, regardless of our cultural mythology about laid-back Australian attitudes.

I think this contradiction exists because we've relied too heavily on cultural assumptions and not enough on deliberate culture building. We assumed that being Australian would somehow produce healthy workplaces without the focus and effort that healthy workplaces require. We confused casual dress codes and first name basis with the CEO for genuine psychological safety. We mistook the fact that everyone calls each other 'mate' for evidence that everyone treats each other like one.

The organisations I work with that have healthy cultures have built them deliberately. They have not assumed that Australian informality would do the work for them but invested in the relationships, structures and leadership capabilities that a healthy culture requires. They have recognised that culture doesn't happen by accident, regardless of national context. There is never any luck involved in shaping intentional culture, not even for 'the lucky country'.

What the comparisons reveal

Examining burnout across different national contexts reveals patterns that transcend any single culture.

The most remarkable finding is that structural protections matter far more than cultural assumptions. Countries with enforceable limits on working hours, worker representation in governance, and social safety nets that reduce job loss anxiety, consistently show better outcomes than those relying on voluntary corporate wellness programs. Hope and good intentions, it turns out, aren't a policy framework.

Equally striking: shorter hours don't reduce productivity. The evidence from Germany, the Nordic countries, and organisations like Microsoft Japan consistently shows that reasonable hours maintain or improve output while substantially improving wellbeing. The assumption that more hours equals more production doesn't stand up.

Cultures can also change in ways that seem impossible until they happen. Japan, once the global exemplar of work-to-death culture, is shifting. The path is slow and incomplete, but the direction is unmistakeable.

And perhaps most importantly for you: individual organisations can create cultures that differ from national norms. Even in contexts where overwork is culturally expected, specific companies can establish different expectations. The culture you build within your team and organisation is determined by the choices you make, not by the country you happen to operate in.

Implications for leaders

For leaders operating across multiple countries, these variations demand attention. A policy that works well in a Nordic context may fail in an Asian one, not because the policy is wrong but because the surrounding culture and structures differ.

The best leaders develop cultural literacy: understanding not just what policies exist in different locations but how those policies interact with cultural expectations, enforcement patterns, and worker assumptions. What looks like the same policy may function entirely differently, depending on context.

It also requires willingness to create organisational cultures that may differ from surrounding norms. If local culture normalises overwork, a leader committed to high performance built on relational health must actively counter that norm within their organisation. This is harder than simply going with the cultural flow, but is essential if you want to build something different. It looks like this:

- **For leaders with board access.** Educate board members about these global patterns. Education is essential; the evidence that alternative approaches to work produce better outcomes is overwhelming.
- **For leaders without board access**. Understand that the cultural patterns you're fighting have structural roots. This knowledge is clarifying. It means you're not failing when you can't transform everything. Focus on what you can influence: your team, your direct reports, the microculture within your sphere.
- **For leaders in any single national context.** Learn from the global perspective; it offers a sobering reminder that without structural protection and cultural support, burnout risk remains high regardless of individual interventions. It also offers genuine encouragement. Other places have created conditions in which healthy, high-performing workers flourish. What they have done, others can learn from.

The burnout crisis is global. The responses that work draw on evidence from across borders and take their shape from local conditions.

The countries that protect their workers best, *decided to.*

PART 2

The Fuel

Understanding how we got here

Most leaders who read Part 1 recognise the crisis. They have seen it in their teams, felt it themselves, watched it spread. What they often lack is the explanation that makes change possible. Knowing that burnout is widespread does little to explain why and how your organisation produces it.

Part 1 mapped the furnace: its scope, its costs, and what it does to the brain and body. Part 2 goes inside to examine how it was built and who keeps it running.

CHAPTER 7

The accidental workplace

> In order that people may be happy in their work, these three things are needed: they must be fit for it; they must not do too much of it; and they must have a sense of success in it.
>
> —John Ruskin, *Pre-Raphaelitism* (1851)

When buildings collapse, we don't blame the people inside them. We investigate the design, the construction, and the engineering decisions that made collapse possible. We hold architects and builders accountable and change building codes to prevent future disasters.

When organisations burn out their workers, we tend to do the opposite. We typically (and silently) blame the burned-out individuals for their lack of resilience and send them to wellness workshops while leaving the conditions that burned them unchanged.

Dara Simkin's applied research with RMIT University's Behavioural Business Lab on playful work design demonstrates measurable gains in engagement and adaptability. These are real effects from investment in people. The same research confirms what this book argues from the structural side: that the interventions work where conditions support them. In organisations where the underlying structure remains extractive, the best human-centred programs are fighting a battle the individual cannot win.

Some companies offer fruit bowls and lunchtime yoga in buildings where the air conditioning has been set to the preferences of a man who left the company in 2019. They treat systemic dysfunction as personal failure.

The architecture of modern workplace culture has structural features that make burnout predictable. These are design choices, embedded in policies, systems and cultural assumptions. And they can and should be redesigned.

The myth of self-assembling culture

For too long, organisations have operated under the dangerous assumption that workplace culture will naturally evolve into something positive and productive if left to its own devices. This belief runs counter to everything we know about human group dynamics from anthropology, sociology and evolutionary psychology.

Human groups, when left without deliberate structure and guidance, tend towards dysfunction rather than harmony. This is our evolutionary inheritance, not a character flaw. Research in evolutionary psychology has established that humans naturally fragment into competing subgroups beyond approximately 150 people (Dunbar, 1992), and even small groups require deliberate social engineering to function effectively.

Culture doesn't happen by accident. The organisations that build thriving cultures do so deliberately. They define values and then hold people accountable to them. They create structures that encourage collaboration rather than competition. They invest in the ongoing work of cultural maintenance, recognising that disorder and decay are the defaults and that excellence requires constant effort.

When organisations fail to deliberately design culture, they get whatever emerges from the interaction of personalities, power dynamics and situational pressures. Usually, what emerges is dysfunction: silos, politics, mistrust, and the kind of toxic behaviour that drives burnout.

I can't overstate how fundamental this point is. Every other problem I discuss in this book flows from this original failure: *the belief that culture will take care of itself.* This dangerous assumption is the root cause of all cultural dysfunction. Until organisations begin truly understanding this and take steps to bridge this conceptual void, burnout and every other culture issue will continue to erode employee wellbeing and productivity.

The untrained leading the overwhelmed

In the UK, 82 per cent of managers are untrained in management or leadership (CMI & YouGov, 2023). In Australia and the USA, the overwhelming majority of leaders have never studied cultural leadership (how to create and manage team and organisational culture). The people most directly responsible for employee experience, workload management and burnout prevention have received very little, if any, preparation for these responsibilities. The promotion typically goes like this: someone is excellent at the work, excellent enough that a manager decides the best use of their competence is to take them away from the work and give them responsibility for 12 other people doing it. No preparation. No framework. A title change, a pay rise, and a new calendar full of one-to-ones they are not sure how to run. This is how the majority of the people most responsible for employee experience got the job.

What I'm describing is a design problem and a training problem. Organisations consistently promote individual contributors into management roles based on technical competence, then expect them to somehow intuit how to lead human beings. They're asking people to build, shape and nurture something they've no experience in.

The consequences are predictable. Managers who don't understand workload management overload their teams. Managers who don't understand psychological safety create cultures of fear. Managers who don't understand motivation rely on pressure and surveillance rather than autonomy and purpose. And when things go wrong, employees burn out, teams underperform and talented people leave, the untrained managers are blamed for failures that were virtually guaranteed by their lack of preparation.

We would never let someone perform surgery without medical training, or let someone fly a commercial aircraft without extensive certification. Yet we routinely place people in charge of other human beings without any preparation for that profound responsibility.

Every time I raise this in a boardroom, I see heads nodding. Everyone agrees in principle. And then nothing changes, because training managers properly, in cultural leadership, costs money and takes time, and there's always something more urgent. *There's always something more urgent.*

The HR illusion

When the topic of culture comes up in executive discussions, a predictable pattern emerges. Leaders look left and right, settling only when they lock eyes with the HR director, who they incorrectly believe is responsible for workplace culture. It's the corporate equivalent of a family looking around the table to see who will do the washing up. In most cases, they see organisational culture as someone else's job, a specialised function that can be delegated while they focus on what they consider to be real business matters.

This single misconception causes more cultural dysfunction than anything else I encounter.

The Global Workplace Happiness Report 2026 found that the strongest predictors of workplace happiness are inspiration and a sense of belonging. The weakest are workload management and role clarity. Organisations are investing most heavily in the things that matter least to how people actually feel, and neglecting the things that matter most.

Culture isn't created or owned by HR. It's created through policy, process and the daily behaviour of leaders. It is shaped in break rooms, video chats and corridor conversations, and transmitted through eye contact, small nods and the daily accumulation of moments that make up working life. Each team and department develops its own version, shaped more by what its leader does every day than by any values document. HR can support culture work. They can provide tools, training and frameworks. They can measure and report on cultural indicators. But they can't own culture because culture is owned by everyone, and most importantly, by the leaders whose behaviour sets the tone.

This isn't a criticism of HR professionals. Many understand these dynamics better than anyone and are frustrated by the limitations of their mandate. Some of the most effective culture advocates I've worked with sit in HR functions, fighting daily to expand what's possible within structures that constrain them. The criticism is aimed at how organisations have structured accountability for culture in ways that let operational leaders off the hook while setting HR up to fail.

In Australia, the UK and the USA, we love to repeat the line 'the board sets the tone at the top for culture'. It's a comforting idea, but it doesn't match reality. When it comes to culture, we have to deal with reality, not aspiration. The board does have a formal mandate for performance and risk oversight, which includes responsibility for culture governance. In practice, though, it's the CEO and executive team whose day-to-day behaviours, priorities and unspoken expectations truly shape the culture. This effect is then amplified further down the line by team leaders. Their communication, decision making, and how they respond to pressure all determine what people experience and accept as normal.

Real culture change requires leaders to recognise that *they are the culture*. Their behaviour is the culture. Their priorities become the team's priorities. Their tolerance for toxic behaviour defines what's acceptable. Delegating this to HR is a clear sign that a leader doesn't understand their primary role.

There is a concept in Buddhist thought called *samsara*, the cycle that perpetuates itself. Organisations that burn through their people tend to replace them with people who will also burn out, under the same conditions, producing the same results, while leadership commissions the same engagement survey and reads the same findings with the same expression of surprised concern. The cycle is driven by the failure to see the cycle. Interrupting *samsara* requires stepping back far enough to notice the pattern. Most organisations never do or just can't. Typically, the urgency of the next quarter makes that kind of seeing feel like a luxury.

The always-on prison

Digital technology promised to liberate workers from the constraints of time and place. Instead, in many cases it has imprisoned them in a perpetual workday that never ends.

One in four US employees works outside of their scheduled hours most of the time or every day, while 63 per cent work outside those hours sometimes (Mind Share Partners, 2025). The boundary between work and life has dissolved entirely for a majority of the workforce.

The brain requires recovery time to consolidate learning, restore depleted resources and regulate emotional balance. When work intrudes into every waking hour, and increasingly into sleeping hours through late-night emails and early-morning notifications, the recovery process is disrupted and burnout becomes inevitable.

The architecture of always-on work is embedded in technology, but is enabled by culture.

Organisations that expect immediate responses at all hours create cultures of permanent availability. Leaders who send emails at midnight signal that midnight work is expected. The technology provides the capability. Culture determines whether using it at midnight becomes an expectation.

Across hybrid workplaces, digital overload, constant notifications, excessive meetings and lack of focus time are emerging as modern burnout drivers. Workers are drowning in communication while starving for concentration. They respond to everything and concentrate on nothing. Deep work, contemplative thought and general task quality are the casualties.

I often ask leaders a simple question: what message do you think you send when you email your team at 11 pm? They usually say something about not expecting a response, about just clearing their inbox, about people knowing they can reply whenever. Then I ask them what message they received when their boss emailed them at 11 pm early in their career. The answer is always different. They felt pressure to respond, and that their availability was being tested and their commitment measured. Even the recognition that an email from their boss was sitting unattended in their inbox creates pressure.

The message you intend to send and the message you actually send are rarely the same. And in cultures without explicit norms, people default to the most anxious interpretation.

The mindless meeting culture

If you want to understand why knowledge workers are exhausted, look at their calendars. Research shows that professionals now spend an average of 21.5 hours per week in meetings (Reclaim.ai, 2023), with time spent in meetings having increased 252 per cent since 2020 (Microsoft, 2022).

For many, that's more than half their working hours. Most of those meetings could be emails. And most of those emails could be nothing.

But the meetings themselves are only the visible portion of the damage. What the calendar doesn't show is the work that surrounds every meeting like scaffolding around a building.

First, preparation. The average professional spends 69 minutes preparing for each meeting they attend (ViewSonic, cited in Flowtrace, 2025). That is agenda review, preparatory reading, slide decks, background research, the anxious mental rehearsal of what you are going to say. For status update meetings alone, employees spend four hours a week preparing (Rev, cited in Flowtrace, 2025). *Four hours.* To prepare for meetings whose sole purpose is to tell people what they are already doing.

Second, the void. Sixty-two per cent of workers regularly attend meetings where the goal was never stated in the invite, and 54 per cent leave unclear about what was decided or who is responsible for what (Atlassian, 2024). The meeting happens. Nothing follows.

Third, and this is where it becomes truly perverse, the meetings that do produce an outcome. Atlassian's research found that 77 per cent of meetings end in a decision to schedule another meeting. The primary output of meetings is more meetings. Each of which requires its own hour of preparation, its own calendar block, its own follow up that either doesn't happen or spawns yet another meeting. The cycle is perpetual and endlessly expanding.

Let's do the arithmetic for a professional attending seven meetings a day, a conservative number in most corporate environments. That's seven hours of preparation work alone. Add the meetings themselves, typically 30 to 60 minutes each. Nearly two thirds of those meetings will produce nothing. And the ones that do produce something will mostly produce another meeting tomorrow, which requires another hour of preparation tonight.

The total meeting burden, meetings plus preparation plus the administrative trail, regularly exceeds 50 hours per week. More than a standard working week consumed entirely by meetings. The actual work, the thinking, the creating, the problem solving, the things the organisation is supposedly paying for, gets done in whatever time remains. Which increasingly means evenings. Weekends. The hours that were supposed to belong to recovery.

This is how you can get an entire workforce that looks busy while producing questionable value. Every calendar is full. Every inbox is overflowing and every person is exhausted. And yet the question in most boardrooms remains: why isn't productivity improving?

Meetings have spread from occasional coordination mechanism to the default mode of work. Calendars are blocked solid from morning to evening (back-to-back), leaving no time for the deep focus that complex work requires. Workers attend meetings about meetings, schedule meetings to discuss the outcomes of previous meetings, and spend the time between meetings preparing for upcoming meetings.

In many instances, this is theatre, not true collaboration. The appearance of work substituted for actual work. As a consultant, I often have to fall into line with our client's operating rhythms and cultural patterns. At times that can be frustrating. It is also valuably illuminating. I get to see firsthand how meeting cultures vary across organisations; and the correlation between meeting load and burnout is unmistakeable.

The structure of modern workplaces incentivises this theatre. Visible busyness is rewarded; invisible thinking isn't. Presence in meetings signals engagement; absence signals disengagement. The result is calendars packed with variable-value gatherings while high-value work happens in stolen moments: early mornings, late nights, weekends.

The best leaders confront meeting culture directly. They redesign how coordination happens. Every recurring meeting should be eliminated unless someone can articulate precisely why it must exist. Every new meeting should require justification. The default should be no meeting, not a meeting. Every meeting that survives this test should be able to answer a few simple questions:

1. What decision will this produce?
2. Who is it for?
3. Can this decision be made by two people in five minutes?

If the answer to the last question is 'It can', the meeting is already cancelled. You're welcome.

The inbox that never empties

Meetings consume the calendar. But what fills the space between meetings? The answer, for most knowledge workers, is email. And what fills the space between emails is notifications. And what fills the space between notifications is the anxious anticipation of the next notification. That's the whole day.

The average professional now receives 121 emails per day. McKinsey estimates that we spend 28 per cent of our working week reading and responding to email alone. That is 11.2 hours, or nearly 1.5 full working days, every week, dedicated to a tool that was supposed to make communication faster.

If meetings are the scheduled destruction of productive time, email is the unscheduled kind. It arrives without warning, fragments whatever thought you were in the middle of, and demands a response that feels urgent regardless of whether it actually is.

The cognitive cost is severe. Gloria Mark at the University of California found that it takes an average of 23 minutes and 15 seconds to return to a task after an email interruption. Not 23 seconds, 23 minutes. Workers who are constantly interrupted report significantly higher stress, frustration and mental workload, and produce work under conditions that make sustained thinking functionally impossible. We have, without any formal decision or policy, built a communication system that works directly against the cognitive capacity we're paying for.

But email is only the first layer. The modern knowledge worker receives an average of 65 notifications per day across platforms: Slack messages, Teams alerts, app pings, calendar reminders. Each one triggers the same interruption, the same 23-minute recovery, the same erosion of the sustained attention that complex work requires. One widely cited industry estimate, which is almost certainly conservative, is that collectively, context switching between communication channels costs the global economy an estimated US$450 billion annually. That number is so large it feels abstract. Let me make it concrete: it is roughly the GDP of Argentina, lost every year because we cannot stop interrupting each other.

The deepest irony is why we tolerate it. Email and messaging have become proxies for visibility. Responding quickly signals engagement. Being available signals commitment. A full inbox signals importance. We have confused the appearance of responsiveness with productive work, and the confusion is costing us dearly.

The day that never ends

If the inbox consumes the working day, the smartphone ensures the working day never ends. The Slack Workforce Index, drawing on data from more than 10 000 desk workers globally, found that employees who feel obligated to work after hours are 20 per cent less productive than those who log off at the end of the day. The always-on employee produces less than the one who goes home.

This finding should stop every leader who sends emails at 10 pm in their tracks. But the data gets worse. Fifty per cent of workers rarely or never take breaks during their working day, and those non-break-takers are 1.7 times more likely to experience burnout. Meanwhile, workers who do take regular breaks report 62 per cent higher work–life balance, 43 per cent better ability to manage stress, and 13 per cent higher productivity.

Breaks make people better at their jobs. The absence of breaks makes them worse.

In 2024, Slack ran an experiment where they forced employees to take breaks and disconnect after hours. The results were almost comically clear: productivity increased by 21 per cent and stress management improved by 230 per cent. They had to force people to stop working to prove that not working made them better at working.

Ninety per cent of American workers say a right to disconnect law would be beneficial to their wellbeing. Several European countries have already enacted such legislation. Australia's own right to disconnect provisions, effective from August 2024, reflect a growing global consensus that the always-on expectation is not a feature of modern work but a failure of it. And yet the cultural pressure persists because in most organisations, the person who responds to the late-night email is still perceived as more committed than the person who doesn't. Quite often we reward the behaviour that the evidence tells us destroys performance.

The office designed to destroy concentration

We need to talk about the open plan office. Not because it is the most important contributor to burnout, but because it is the most visible demonstration of how organisations make decisions about the way people work. The open plan office was sold to us as a collaboration catalyst. Tear down the walls, the thinking went, and people will share ideas, build relationships, and innovate spontaneously. The logic was intuitive, while the evidence was nonexistent.

A landmark study of more than 40 000 workers across 303 office buildings, published in the *Journal of Environmental Psychology*, found that enclosed private offices outperformed open plan layouts on every single measure of occupant satisfaction, including ease of interaction. The very thing that open plan was supposed to improve, it made worse. Workers in open offices don't collaborate more. They collaborate less, because they've learned that every conversation is overheard and every interaction is an interruption to someone else.

The productivity losses are staggering. Sound consultant Julian Treasure estimates, drawing on his consultancy research, that workers in open plan offices are 66 per cent less productive than those with private workspaces (Treasure, 2014).

A study from the *British Journal of Psychology* showed that conversational distractions alone waste 21.5 minutes per person per day. In an open plan office, where interruptions are constant, the mathematics of concentration become impossible. There simply aren't enough protected windows of time in the day for anyone to do deep work.

Employees know this. A 2018 survey by Bospar found that 76 per cent of employees hate open plan offices. *Three quarters.* That's three quarters of a workforce telling us that the physical environment designed for them is making their work harder, while leadership continues to build that environment because it is cheaper per square metre and because the word 'collaborative' is a recognised, foundational aspect of healthy culture.

The open plan office persists for the same reason so many burnout-producing practices persist: it optimises for what's visible, not for what's valuable. Open plan offices look productive. Rows of occupied desks photograph well for company websites. The energy of a bustling floor feels dynamic to the executive walking through on the way to their private office. The executive who designed the open plan office has a door.

The appearance of collaboration and the reality of concentration are not the same thing, and we have built our workplaces around appearance.

The hierarchy of harm

Let's move on to the area of culture where I spend most of my time, both in research and practice: toxic behaviour. Toxic workplace behaviour is the biggest single predictor of burnout: employees in toxic climates are *eight times* more likely to burn out (McKinsey & Company, 2022). A workplace that tolerates toxic behaviour is a machine for producing burnout with industrial efficiency. Toxic management behaviours explain 60 per cent of burnout variance globally.

This toxicity cascades through organisational hierarchies. Executives pressure senior leaders who pressure middle managers who pressure frontline workers. Each level absorbs stress from above and transmits it downward, often amplified by the pressure of competing demands. The worker at the bottom of the hierarchy receives accumulated pressure from every level above.

The hierarchy of harm is structural, not personal. Even well-intentioned people, placed in poorly designed systems, transmit toxicity. The executive who works 80-hour weeks models destructive behaviour regardless of what they say about work–life balance and the manager who forwards urgent requests without filtering creates urgency cascades regardless of their personal kindness.

Addressing burnout requires redesigning hierarchies to buffer rather than amplify pressure. The best leaders at every level see part of their role as protecting the people below them from the chaos above. The hierarchy should function as a series of filters, each level transforming chaotic demands into manageable work.

If you're in the middle of a hierarchy that amplifies rather than buffers pressure, you face a choice about what kind of node you will be. You may not be able to change what flows down from above, but you can change how you transmit it. This is buffer leadership: absorbing chaos so your team doesn't have to, translating impossible demands into prioritised work, pushing back where you can and absorbing what you can't.

Buffer leadership is exhausting. It requires emotional labour that goes unrecognised and energy that could be spent elsewhere. But it's also one of the most important things a mid-level leader can do. Your team may never know what you shielded them from. That's the point. The chaos stops with you, transformed into something workable before it reaches them.

No individual can indefinitely absorb systemic dysfunction. But while you work to change the system, or assess whether it can be changed at all, buffer leadership protects the people who depend on you. It's a form of care that operates through what you don't pass along.

Culture pyromaniacs

Every fire needs someone to light it. Burnout, like any fire, has a source. It is built by people, and in most organisations where burnout is endemic, specific individuals are actively accelerating it. They are what I call 'culture pyromaniacs', and understanding them is essential to understanding why the fire keeps burning even when everyone claims to want it out.

Culture pyromaniacs come in two forms: the pyromaniac leader and the pyromaniac employee. The three leader types that follow these two forms reveal the distinct psychological profiles that drive the pyromaniac leader's behaviour.

The pyromaniac leader

The pyromaniac leader is usually capable, sometimes charming, and almost always politically skilled. What distinguishes them is what they do with the authority they have been given. They deploy accelerants: demands calibrated beyond what is sustainable, metrics designed to extract rather than develop, policies that signal that the organisation's needs will always exceed any individual's capacity to meet them. They build the conditions for burnout systematically and do it in the language of excellence. The vocabulary sounds very much like leadership, but isn't.

Underneath the performance, something more personal is usually operating. The pyromaniac leader has almost always lost the thread back to a life that exists outside their role. Work has become the sole source of their identity, their status, their evidence of worth. The intensity they demand of others is the intensity they depend on themselves, because without it, the question of who they are becomes very difficult and uncomfortable to answer. This isn't an excuse for the damage they do, it's an explanation of why they keep doing it even when the evidence of that damage is right in front of them. They can't afford to slow down. Slowing down would require confronting what is waiting in the silence outside the office.

The pyromaniac leader is almost always invisible from above and catastrophic from below. They manage upward with extraordinary skill. Boards see strong numbers. Shareholders see returns and senior executives see a leader who delivers. None of them see the mechanism of delivery: the extraction, the fear, the accumulated exhaustion of teams running at a pace that cannot be maintained. The pyromaniac leader controls the information that reaches the top. The fire is always below the floor they're standing on, invisible from the boardroom until the structure gives way.

This is what makes them so difficult to remove and so costly to retain. They survive performance reviews because they measure what the pyromaniac leader is expert at managing: the appearance of results. The human cost of those results, the attrition, the burnout claims, the quiet departures of the best people, gets attributed elsewhere. The team wasn't resilient enough, the market was difficult, the talent wasn't there. The pyromaniac leader is rarely in the room when the consequences of their accelerants are discussed and are rarely associated with the consequences.

Organisations that want to identify their pyromaniac leaders should look in the gap between how a leader is described by their superiors and how they are described by the people who have worked for them. The pyromaniac leader typically generates very different accounts from those two directions. Upward: results driven, decisive, high standards. Downward: exhausting, impossible to satisfy, a leader whose team is always under pressure and never quite good enough. The gap between those two descriptions is the smoke. And where there's smoke …

The pyromaniac employee

The pyromaniac employee has made work-life suffering a competitive sport, and like the pyromaniac leader, the reason is almost identical: the loss of a meaningful identity outside of work. When the organisation becomes the primary, and sometimes the only, source of meaning, status and self-worth, the toxic conditions that burn others out become the very conditions that make them feel purposeful. They are first in and last out, driven not by what the work demands but by what leaving would require them to face: a version of themselves that exists without the title, the urgency, the feeling of being needed. Strip away the job and the question of who they are does not have a ready answer.

Pyromaniac employees broadcast their sacrifice. They make boundaries look like laziness and recovery look like disengagement. They are not doing this cynically; they believe it, which is precisely what makes them so effective at keeping the temperature high. The pyromaniac employee is so enmeshed with their work that any challenge to the pace of that work is experienced as a challenge to the self. They cannot support a healthier culture because a healthier culture would require a healthier relationship with their own identity, and that's work that hasn't been done.

Both the pyromaniac leaders and employees are frequently drawn to each other. The leader who demands everything finds in the employee a willing mirror, someone who reflects their values back and makes the extraction feel like culture. The employee finds in the leader someone who finally appreciates the full depth of their commitment. The relationship looks like loyalty but it functions as an accelerant. Together they raise the ambient standard to a level that makes everyone around them either match an unsustainable pace or feel inadequate for failing to.

Pyromaniacs at any level are hard to name because organisations rarely want to look at people who, by conventional metrics, appear to be among their strongest performers and ask a different question: at what cost, and to whom? The pyromaniac's results are often substantial. As is the damage beneath them. Organisations that choose to see only the results have already decided about whose experience counts. That decision compounds, and it shows up eventually in the data, in the departures, and in the culture survey that hopefully catches the board's attention.

The structural work of tackling burnout matters. But you can redesign the building all you like. If the pyromaniac still has the keys, the smoke alarm will go off again. And again.

Pyromaniac leaders share the same observable output: they accelerate the fire. The psychological engine producing that output differs, and the difference matters because it determines what, if anything, can be done. Two profiles account for most of what organisations encounter. Importantly, there are of course others: the passive-aggressive, the performatively helpless, the anxious leader, the narcissistic leader and the sociopathic leader are the most common. Between them they account for the majority of the cultural damage this book describes.

The three most common faces of pyromaniac leaders

More than two decades working with senior leaders has taught me that most pyromaniac leaders are unaware of their penchant for a blowtorch. They come in different forms, each shaped by personal histories that remain uncovered through the recruitment process.

The damage caused by each stems from wildly different psychological origins: an anxious leader is the byproduct of unmanaged insecurity; the narcissistic leader's damage flows from an internal life organised around self-interest; and the sociopathic leader lacks the empathic circuitry to register it as damage at all.

A landmark analysis by Donald Sull and colleagues at MIT Sloan Management Review synthesised 11 separate meta-analyses, each drawing on thousands of studies of toxic workplace behaviour. Across every dimension examined, a single factor emerged with consistent dominance: leadership. Leadership behaviour and the norms it establishes are ten times more highly correlated with whether employees experience their culture as toxic than any demographic variable such as age or seniority (Sull et al., 2022).

Read that against what we already know from Gallup: managers account for 70 per cent of the variance in team engagement. The same variable, the character and behaviour of the leader, is responsible for both the best and worst organisational outcomes. The lever is the same.

The neuroscience makes the mechanism visible. Research on inter-brain synchrony shows that when people are in the presence of a leader, their neural activity begins to couple with that person's. A regulated leader creates the neurobiological conditions under which a team can think clearly and collaborate. A dysregulated one activates threat responses that narrow thinking, reduce creativity and undermine the collaboration the organisation is counting on.

The question of how leaders are selected sits at the heart of this, and we will return to it in detail later.

The anxious leader

The anxious leader arrives looking like high standards, strong conviction, decisive management and an uncompromising commitment to excellence. Underneath all of that is anxiety in a suit.

The anxious leader has one primary, almost existential need: control. The micromanagement, the need to be in every decision, the intolerance of ambiguity, the rage when things happen without their knowledge or approval, all of it is about self-regulation. The leader who must control their environment is a leader who cannot tolerate their own internal state without external evidence that everything is under control. The team becomes a prop in the management of their manager's anxiety.

I've sat across from this leader in boardrooms on five continents. I've experienced it directly, early in my career and again years later when I should have known better. What struck me then, and still strikes me now, is how little awareness these leaders tend to have of the damage they're producing. They believe the fear they generate is respect. They interpret the silence in the room as agreement, and mistake self-preservation for buy-in. For me personally, I was never fearful, more sympathetic. I could see through their performative demands to someone who didn't believe in their own worth. Someone who was scared and needed therapy more than a big title.

The psychological signature is consistent. Insecure leaders tend to lack curiosity about the people around them, because curiosity requires acknowledging that others might know things you don't, which threatens the internal architecture they've built to feel safe. They tend towards certainty in proportion to their anxiety. The more frightened they are, the more absolute their positions become. And they tend to surround themselves with people who confirm rather than challenge, which means the information they receive gets progressively more distorted until the gap between their perception and reality becomes dangerous.

The damage flows directly into the teams below them. A leader who manages their anxiety through control creates a team that manages its anxiety through compliance. Compliance looks like alignment from the outside and functions as a slow extinction of discretionary effort, honest communication, and creative risk taking from the inside. The team learns what gets rewarded and what gets punished. They optimise accordingly. The brilliant ideas stop being voiced. The early warnings stop being raised. The problems get managed sideways rather than upward, because upward is not safe. By the time something goes visibly wrong, the information that could have prevented it has been withheld for months.

The other universal characteristic of anxious leaders is their distinct lack of perspective. They tend to overidentify with their role, with their station, and quite often with money. As a result, many things matter to them more than they should. Their fear of being exposed, of not measuring up to the version of themselves they project, distorts reality in ways that make sustained proximity difficult for most people and untenable for others.

For burnout specifically, controlling leadership is among the most reliable predictors. The burnout is not simply caused by overwork or unclear expectations, though those are symptoms. It is caused by the chronic stress of operating in an environment where your judgement is distrusted, your autonomy is constrained, your honest observations are unwelcome, and your safety depends on pleasing someone whose definition of pleasing shifts with their mood. The human nervous system will tolerate that for a while, but not indefinitely.

This anxious, controlling and insecure leader is usually not a bad person. They are generally a person in pain, whose pain has been given institutional power. Insecurity is part of being human. The tragedy is that organisations routinely promote people into positions where their unaddressed anxiety becomes everyone else's working conditions.

Anxious leaders that can examine what drives their behaviour can change. The journey from control to genuine confidence, the kind that has no need to prove itself through dominance, is available to anyone with enough self-awareness to begin it. Those who are not willing, or not capable, are culture pyromaniacs of a different kind, they are the narcissist and the sociopath.

The narcissistic leader

Thomas Erikson, in *Surrounded by Narcissists* (2022), opens with an observation that resonates well beyond the self-help shelf: narcissism is no longer rare. Clinical narcissistic personality disorder affects somewhere between 1 and 2 per cent of the population. The behaviours associated with it, narcissistic traits, the self-absorption, the reluctance to find empathy, the need for admiration and the willingness to exploit others to get it, show up in an estimated 20 per cent. Most of the narcissists causing damage in organisations have never been diagnosed with anything

Social media, hyper-individualism and the rewarding of self-promotion have created conditions in which narcissistic behaviour not only thrives but is actively selected for. Psychologists Twenge and Campbell documented this trajectory in *The Narcissism Epidemic* as far back as 2009. The trend has accelerated.

In leadership specifically, the numbers are worse. Research published in *The Leadership Quarterly* found that narcissists reach CEO positions faster than their peers (Rovelli & Curnis, 2021). The selection processes that fill senior roles reliably favour traits that overlap with narcissism: confidence, decisiveness, charisma, the compelling narrative of personal achievement. Organisations have built a selection process that is excellent at identifying people who want power and largely indifferent to what they intend to do with it.

I have worked with narcissistic leaders across multiple industries and continents, and the experience is consistently the same in the early stages. They are often the most engaging person in the room. Funny, confident, apparently interested in you. There is a quality of energy around them that feels like momentum. They generate a sense of direction and certainty that organisations, particularly anxious ones, find deeply comforting. Early on, it is easy to see why boards choose them and why teams initially follow with enthusiasm.

Look closer and the picture shifts. The interest they show in you is calibrated, rarely genuine. It lasts precisely as long as you are useful to them. Their certainty is not the product of good thinking; it is the product of an internal life organised entirely around their own centrality. Every conversation has an invisible subject that is always the same: them. Every decision passes through a single filter: what does this do for me?

The research on their specific behaviours is consistent. Narcissistic leaders take credit and distribute blame. They recast themselves as victims when challenged. They are exquisitely sensitive to criticism while deploying it freely against others. They identify vulnerabilities in people around them quickly and use what they find. They surround themselves with people who mirror their views back rather than challenge them, which means the information reaching them becomes progressively more distorted over time. They manage upward with skill and treat those below them as instruments.

What makes them genuinely dangerous at the organisational level is the compounding effect. Stanford research found that once narcissistic leaders assume positions of power, their effects become hugely magnified, and that they tend to consolidate that power by removing those who challenge them (O'Reilly, Chatman & Doerr, 2014). Research on narcissistic CEOs shows they tend to shape the composition of those around them over time, surrounding themselves with people who share their tendency to mistake boldness for wisdom and gradually neutralising those who don't (Zhu & Chen, 2015). By the time the damage is visible from the outside, the internal architecture protecting it is usually well established.

The culture they leave behind follows a predictable pattern. Collaboration collapses because trust does. The people with the most to offer, and enough self-awareness to recognise what is happening, leave first. Those who remain have either adapted to the climate or lack the options to escape it, and the organisation gradually fills with people in the narcissistic leader's own image

Unlike the anxious leader, who can, when pushed, examine what drives their behaviour, the narcissistic leader almost always lacks the self-awareness that examination requires. Feedback does not land in the way it is intended. Coaching conversations become performances. Development frameworks designed for people who want to grow are simply not the right tool for people whose primary concern is how they appear to be growing.

The intervention is structural. Genuine 360-degree accountability. Boards that weigh cultural evidence alongside financial results. Reference processes that reach below the people a candidate has chosen as referees. Selection tools that measure degrees of empathy and altruism against power-seeking and competitive traits, because the gap between those dimensions is one of the most reliable indicators of how a leader will use the authority they are given. And the institutional courage to act on what the evidence shows, before the compounding begins.

The sociopathic leader

The anxious leader can, in their better moments, be reached. They can examine what drives their behaviour. Some do. The sociopathic leader cannot, and this is not a moral failing. It is a neurological one.

Clinical estimates suggest that somewhere between 4 and 6 per cent of the general population meet the criteria for antisocial personality disorder. In corporate leadership, that figure is considerably higher. The selection processes that fill boardrooms and C-suites reliably favour traits that overlap with sociopathy: decisiveness under pressure, emotional detachment, comfort with risk, the capacity to make hard calls without apparent distress. Organisations mistake these traits for strength. Sometimes they are. The same detachment that allows a leader to restructure without sentimentality can, in the absence of any counterweight, allow them to burn through people without registering it.

The sociopathic leader can be very hard to recognise because they're not always the one who shouts. More often they are the one who smiles. They are frequently the most compelling person in the room: articulate, confident, and interested in you right up until the moment you are no longer useful. The charm is not performed. It is a learned mechanism, developed over a lifetime, and it works. Boards see it. Shareholders see it. The people reporting to them see (and feel) something else entirely.

What distinguishes the sociopathic leader is the absence of empathy, not suppressed or crowded out by pressure, simply absent. The burnout they produce is substantial: the exhausted teams, the toxic culture, the attrition, the human cost. But the leader experiences none of it as a problem they are responsible for. They experience it, if they experience it at all, as a management issue. A communications issue. A talent acquisition issue.

I have sat across from this leader too. What is striking is not the damage they cause, which is visible in the data and in the exit interviews and in the faces of the people around them, but how untroubled they are by it. Not suppressing distress. Simply not having any. That is not something coaching addresses. It is not something feedback reaches. The self-awareness frameworks in this book are not designed for leaders who lack the basic empathic architecture those frameworks assume.

This matters for organisations because the intervention is different. You do not develop this leader into a better version of themselves. You build governance structures that constrain the damage a single person can cause: genuine 360-degree accountability, boards that weigh cultural evidence alongside financial performance, and the institutional courage to act on what that evidence shows. The most important thing an organisation can do for a sociopathic leader is ensure they do not hold unchecked power over other people's working lives.

The compassionate framing is this: they cannot do any better. That is true and worth recognising, because it prevents the anger from becoming the point. But compassion does not require leaving them in a position where their limitation causes harm at scale. The most humane response to a leader who cannot help what they are is to ensure the system around them can.

The altruistic leader

The single quality that separates the best leaders from the other types described in this chapter is altruism.

Robert Greenleaf, whose servant leadership model has been the subject of sustained empirical research since its introduction in 1970, identified altruism as the first precept of effective leadership: the genuine desire to place the worth of others above the self. Greenleaf's model names the qualities that altruism generates: listening, empathy, healing, awareness, commitment to the growth of people, and the building of community. These qualities are expressions of a single underlying disposition rather than separate skills to be acquired independently.

Dan Pink's research identifies the conditions under which people perform at their best: autonomy, mastery and purpose. The altruistic leader creates those conditions because they are genuinely interested in what makes the people around them grow. Curiosity about others is a downstream consequence of actually caring whether people are well. The altruistic leader is curious because they are invested. They are present because the person in front of them matters. They are generous because their internal economy is not built on scarcity or competition.

The inter-brain synchrony research adds something important here. A regulated, altruistic leader is a biological input to the people around them. Their settled internal state creates the conditions under which others can think clearly, take creative risks, and do their best work. The character of the leader is the primary environmental variable shaping the brain health of everyone who reports to them.

Structural problems and their solutions

The dangerous leaders described in this chapter, the anxious, the narcissistic, the sociopathic, are real people and they cause real damage. But focusing only on the people misses something important.

Remove a pyromaniac leader from a broken system and the system will, in time, produce another one.

The structures that shape how work gets done, how leaders get selected, how performance gets measured, how communication flows, and how presence gets rewarded, are not neutral. They have their own logic, their own momentum, and their own capacity to produce predictable outcomes regardless of who is sitting in the chair.

Most of the structural problems described in this section were not designed to harm anyone. They were designed for efficiency, scale, control, and for the appearance of rigour. The open plan office was meant to encourage collaboration. The performance review was meant to drive accountability. The always-on expectation was enabled by technology that was supposed to make life easier. None of it was designed with human beings in mind in any deep sense, and that absence, repeated across enough decisions over enough years, is what produces the conditions I have spent a career trying to reverse.

The best leaders understand this. They do not simply try to be good people inside broken structures. They look at the structures themselves, name what those structures are producing, and work to change them. The best leaders do this intuitively.

The selection problem

Most organisations select leaders using processes that reliably favour the people most likely to cause the problems described above. Remarkably, the confidence, decisiveness and compelling personal narrative that perform well in an interview panel are among the traits most consistently associated with narcissistic personality. The qualities that win a room full of interviewers are frequently the qualities that should concern them most.

Research from Stanford, INSEAD and the University of Georgia converges on this finding: narcissistic individuals are disproportionately drawn to leadership roles, and conventional hiring processes are poorly equipped to detect them. We have built a system that is very good at identifying people who want power and largely indifferent to what they will do with it once they have it.

The minority who are narcissists tend to move faster through organisations than their peers, because the traits that raise red flags in a healthy culture are often the traits that get rewarded in a destructively competitive one. Speed, certainty and self-promotion read as leadership from the outside. The selection process, built around presentations and panel interviews rather than how a person treats the people below them, cannot see what it was never designed to look for.

The single most reliable predictor of how a leader will treat their team is how they have treated previous ones. Reference processes that reach below the people a candidate has chosen as referees, structured questions that probe for specific past behaviours rather than hypothetical responses, and cultures that treat exit interview data as a genuine hiring signal rather than a farewell formality: these are available to any organisation that chooses to use them.

The middle manager squeeze

Middle management is where the pressures described in this chapter converge most intensely. These are the people caught between strategic demands from above and operational realities below, expected to implement decisions they had no voice in making while maintaining the morale of teams that are increasingly stretched.

Research confirms that middle managers now report the highest burnout rates of any organisational level, with 71 per cent reporting burnout symptoms (meQuilibrium, 2025), reversing earlier patterns where frontline workers bore the greatest burden. Nearly half said they were likely to quit within a year due to the stress of the role (UKG, 2023).

Many middle managers are in their late thirties to early fifties, the life stage when they are most likely to have children at home and ageing parents requiring care simultaneously. Twenty-nine per cent of all caregivers fall into this sandwich generation category, and among caregivers under 50, that number rises to 47 per cent

(AARP & NAC, 2025). The professional demands sit on top of that personal load without acknowledgement or adjustment.

Middle managers are expected to translate strategy into execution, motivate teams while enforcing policies they may not agree with, deliver results on metrics they had no voice in setting, remain visible to those above and accessible to those below, and do all of this while also managing their own workload. The pandemic added coordination complexity across distance. Many organisations added these responsibilities without removing others, treating remote management as a simple extension of in-person management rather than a fundamentally different skill.

The expectation that middle managers absorb organisational stress without showing strain is perhaps the most costly of all. They are supposed to remain calm when executives are anxious, positive when workers are demoralised, and confident when the path forward is unclear. This emotional labour is invisible in job descriptions and uncompensated in performance reviews, and it depletes reserves just as surely as any visible demand.

Organisations typically design support systems for executives, who matter strategically, and for frontline workers, who matter legally and reputationally. Middle managers fall between those two groups: too senior to qualify for protections designed for vulnerable workers, too junior to access resources reserved for leadership. They are expected to cope because coping is their job. Recognising that this tier faces unique pressures requiring specific support, including coaching resources, peer networks, protected thinking time, and realistic workload assessment that accounts for emotional labour, is the minimum that the role demands.

The distributed work dimension

The early pandemic narrative around remote work was hopeful. Without commutes, workers would have more time. Personally, I calculated saving 7.5 hours a week, a whole working day, by working from home. Without office distractions, focus and productivity improved. Without rigid schedules, work and life integrated more naturally. Mine was an unusual case.

Remote work dissolved the boundaries that physical offices had enforced. For many people when work happened at home, home became work. The daily commute, however unpleasant, had provided transition time between roles. The office, however imperfect, had been a place you could leave. Working from home meant never fully leaving and never fully arriving, existing in a state where work was always potentially present.

Research consistently shows that remote workers work longer hours than their in-office counterparts (Microsoft, 2025). Some of this is visible overtime. Much of it is invisible: checking email before officially starting and working through lunch and dinner because for many people, there is no social reason to take a break. The flexibility that remote work provides often becomes flexibility to work more rather than flexibility to live better.

Remote work removes the visibility that burnout detection depends on. When workers are not visible, their struggles are not visible either. In an office, a manager might notice that someone looks tired, seems withdrawn, or is staying late every night. At a distance, these signals disappear. Workers can spiral towards burnout without anyone noticing until they are already there.

Hybrid arrangements add their own complexity. Workers shuttling between home and office lose the routines that either pure arrangement might provide, facing the boundary erosion of remote work and the commute burden of office work simultaneously. Coordination becomes difficult when team members are in different locations on different days.

Most organisations implemented distributed work hastily during the COVID-19 crisis and without reckoning with what it requires. Policies designed for office-based work persist unchanged. Expectations calibrated for visible workers apply to invisible ones. The human needs that physical workplaces accidentally served, social connection, routine and the separation of work from life, are left unmet without anyone quite noticing. Distributed work needs to be designed from the ground up rather than grafted onto assumptions built for a different era. The questions are straightforward:

- What routines will create boundaries when physical separation does not?
- What practices will surface struggling workers when visual cues are unavailable?
- What will replace the informal social connection that offices provided?

The performance review problem

The annual performance review emerged from military management practice during World War I, designed to identify soldiers suitable for officer promotion. It was adopted by corporate America in the 1950s and has not been substantially redesigned since. Like almost all aspects of war, this also needs to be retired.

Most organisations still run annual reviews that rank employees, differentiate performance levels, and distribute rewards accordingly. The logic seems sound. You need to identify your best performers and address underperformance, and you need some mechanism for allocating limited rewards fairly. It's the execution that creates burnout.

For months leading up to review season, employees are anxious about how they will be rated. They perform not for genuine value creation but for visible achievement that will impress whoever is evaluating them. They compete with colleagues who should be collaborators. They avoid risks that might lead to failures that could hurt their rating. The review itself is often an exercise in mutual discomfort. Managers struggle to deliver difficult feedback constructively. Employees struggle to receive it without defensiveness. The formal rating rarely matches the employee's self-perception, producing either complacency or resentment.

Those rated highly feel pressure to maintain their status. Those rated lower feel demotivated and start looking elsewhere. Those rated in the middle feel invisible. The organisation has sorted people into categories and improved nobody's performance.

Stack ranking and forced distribution make everything worse. When managers must identify a certain percentage of their team as underperformers regardless of actual performance, someone must be sacrificed to the bell curve. The knowledge that this is coming creates a fear that permeates the entire review period.

I have watched organisations where talented people spent more energy managing their performance reviews than doing their actual jobs. Where innovation disappeared because trying new things meant risking visible failure.

The practice is so normalised it has become invisible as a problem. Nearly every organisation does some version of annual reviews. The culture costs rarely get counted alongside the supposed benefits: the anxiety, the political behaviour, the damaged relationships, the risk aversion, the time spent preparing documentation and calibrating ratings rather than doing productive work.

Gallup's 2023 research found that only 14 per cent of employees strongly agree their performance reviews inspire them to improve. Eighty-six per cent experience the review as somewhere between irrelevant and demoralising. A 2023 Bonusly survey found that 95 per cent of managers are frustrated with their own performance review systems. Research by Scullen, Mount and Goff (2002) demonstrates that 62 per cent of the variance in performance ratings reflects the rater's own biases rather than the actual performance of the person being rated. More than three-fifths of your rating is a measure of your manager. SelectSoftwareReviews found in 2023 that 85 per cent of employees would consider quitting after an assessment they perceived as unfair. The annual review actively drives anxiety, burnout and attrition.

In my experience, the organisations that have replaced the annual review haven't lost accountability. They've found more of it. Gallup's data shows that employees who receive meaningful feedback weekly are four times more likely to be engaged than those who receive it annually. The annual review takes the single most powerful lever managers have for developing their people and compresses it into one anxiety-laden, bias-distorted, backward-looking conversation per year. More frequent, lighter-touch feedback conversations, evaluation based on team outcomes rather than individual comparison, development focus rather than rating focus, and separation of feedback conversations from compensation decisions: these approaches maintain accountability without creating the annual trauma cycle. If your performance review system creates more anxiety than development, encourages competition over collaboration, and consumes disproportionate time and emotional energy, it is part of your burnout problem.

The architecture can be rebuilt

Most leaders want their people to thrive. The gap between that intention and the reality documented in this chapter is simply a design gap.

Every policy, every process, every norm in the structures described above was introduced by someone who believed it would help. The open plan office was meant to encourage collaboration. The performance review was meant to drive accountability. The always-on culture was enabled by technology that was genuinely supposed to make life easier. The road to the burnout crisis was paved with reasonable assumptions that nobody tested against the evidence.

The structures that produce burnout are not laws of nature. They are choices, accumulated over decades, that can be unmade and rebuilt. In Australia, the UK and across the European Union, this is no longer only an ethical question. Employers are legally required to identify and manage the psychosocial hazards. The question of whether to build healthier cultures has, for many leaders, already been answered by their regulators.

Workplaces and cultures created by accident are filled with leaders and circumstances that lead to burnout. Culture cannot be left to chance when the result is almost always workplace wildfires.

CHAPTER 8

Stoking the furnace

> From craving springs grief, from craving springs fear. For one who is wholly free from craving there is no grief, nor any fear.
>
> —Dhammapada, verse 216 (3rd century BC)

In some boardrooms of the world, a single imperative is preached with religious intensity: *more*. More growth. More productivity. More shareholder value. More hours. More output. More, more, more, without apparent limit or end.

I was once at a conference in the US where the global CEO started a chant: 'Make more money. Make more money'. I thought it was a joke. Sadly, no.

This imperative has become so pervasive that questioning it seems almost blasphemous. We want growth, productivity, and to maximise returns. What kind of leader would want less?

But the relentless pursuit of *more* is killing us. It has created workplaces that extract human life as fuel for quarterly earnings. And if we're to extinguish the burnout crisis, we must confront it.

The drive for *more* undermines the very performance it claims to pursue. Sustained intensity degrades cognitive capacity. Accountability applied without trust erodes innovation. Drive without recovery burns through the discretionary effort that excellence depends on.

In the short term, gains produced by the relentless pursuit of *more* can be significant. The problem is what tends to follow. Capability erodes gradually, often invisibly. Cultures built on sustained pressure tend towards compliance over creativity, conformity over quality, and internal competition over collaboration. The metrics can look healthy long after the foundations have begun to weaken, and the full cost rarely lands on the people who set the conditions. Leadership moves on. The consequences? Not so much.

The arithmetic of diminishing returns

The long-hours equation is burnout culture's most cherished myth. We celebrate the executive who works until midnight, or the team that pulls the all-nighter. We tell stories of founders who slept under their desks as though sleep deprivation were a badge of honour rather than a cognitive impairment. These stories are culturally dangerous.

Economist John Pencavel of Stanford University studied the output of munitions workers during World War I and found that productivity declined sharply after 50 hours per week. At 55 hours, the decline accelerated. At 70 hours, total output was identical to what the worker would have produced at 55 hours. Those additional 15 hours, more than two full working days, produced literally nothing. That data applies to employees today: the employee is present but the work is not being done.

A study of 4197 Korean workers found the exact point at which output starts its collapse: those working 52 or more hours per week experienced productivity losses between 5.1 and 6.6 per cent, which, when you calculate the cost across a large workforce, represents a staggering waste of human capacity and organisational investment (Lee et al., 2020). And the World Health Organization (WHO) puts the human cost in even starker terms: employees working 55 or more hours per week face a 35 per cent higher risk of stroke and a 17 per cent higher risk of dying from heart disease. We are not merely wasting people's time. We are shortening their lives.

The Slack Workforce Index confirms this in the modern context. After-hours work doesn't just fail to improve outcomes; it actively degrades them. Employees who work after hours show 20 per cent lower productivity scores and are twice as likely to report burnout as those who maintain boundaries. Every hour worked beyond a reasonable threshold makes the next hour less productive, and the hour after that less productive still, until the worker is just occupying space, generating the appearance of effort while producing nothing of value.

More hours. Less output. More presence. Less performance. More sacrifice. Less result. We have the evidence and we ignore it, because hours are visible and the quality of thought is not.

The invisible epidemic

If the cult of long hours wastes time, presenteeism creates an even more fundamental problem by giving the illusion that occupied desks mean productive work. Every organisation tracks absenteeism. How many days did people take off? What is our sick leave rate? These numbers appear on dashboards, are discussed in board meetings, and trigger HR investigations when they rise. Absenteeism is visible, countable, manageable. Surprisingly, it is, comparatively, a trivial problem.

The Global Corporate Challenge (2015) studied nearly 2000 employees using methodology validated by the WHO and found that the average worker is absent for approximately four days per year. The same worker is physically present but functionally unproductive for 57.5 days per year. Four days absent. Fifty-seven and a half days present but not working. The problem we obsess over is a rounding error compared to the problem we ignore entirely.

Presenteeism costs the US economy approximately $1.5 trillion per year. Absenteeism costs approximately $150 billion. Ten to one.

The UK Institute for Public Policy Research puts it at £25 billion against £3.7 billion. A global study published in PMC confirmed the ratio holds across eight countries regardless of industry, culture or geography.

Presenteeism costs organisations between five and ten times more than absenteeism, everywhere, every time.

And yet walk into any HR department in the world and ask what they track. Sick days. Leave balances. Absence rates. Unplanned absences. Return-to-work interviews. The infrastructure for monitoring absenteeism is elaborate and well-funded, while the infrastructure for understanding presenteeism is, in most organisations, nonexistent. We have built an entire management apparatus around monitoring whether people show up, and almost nothing around understanding whether they are working when they do.

This is the fundamental error that underlies every practice this chapter examines. We measure what is visible: occupied chairs, logged hours and physical presence. Engaged minds, productive hours and cognitive presence are invisible. And so we optimise relentlessly for the visible instead of the valuable.

Buddhist philosophy identifies *tanha*, craving or grasping, as a root cause of suffering. The endless wanting that characterises modern work culture is precisely this: an insatiable hunger that grows stronger with each feeding. We achieve the target, and immediately there's a new target. We hit the number, and the number increases. The wanting never stops because it has no natural endpoint. This is the very predictable path to exhaustion.

The quarterly cage

Modern capitalism operates on quarterly time horizons. Public companies report earnings every three months. Executives are evaluated on quarterly results. Investors make decisions based on quarterly performance. The entire apparatus of contemporary business is oriented towards 90-day cycles.

This creates a fundamental misalignment between what benefits organisations over the long term and what appears beneficial over the short term. Employee wellbeing, culture development, capability building: these generate returns over years, not quarters. They require investment that may not show results until long after the current executive team has moved on.

Extracting maximum effort from employees, on the other hand, shows immediate results. Push people harder, and output increases, temporarily. Cut wellness programs, and expenses decrease, temporarily. Eliminate slack in schedules, and utilisation increases, temporarily. The long-term costs of these short-term gains, including burnout, turnover, knowledge loss and cultural degradation, show up in future quarters.

This is the predictable result of how modern markets operate: doing exactly what they're designed to do, maximising short-term returns. The failure is in our assumption that short-term returns are what we should be maximising. When burning people out becomes a rational strategy, the system has already failed.

The Buddhist concept of *anicca*, impermanence, offers perspective here. It was the word my dad used to open and close every meditation retreat he ran. *Anicca* simply means everything changes. The quarterly results that seem so urgent today will be forgotten next quarter. The executive who sacrificed their team for this month's numbers will eventually move on. The organisation itself may not survive the damage done in pursuit of temporary gains. The best leaders recognise and understand impermanence and ask better questions:

- What are we building that will last?
- What matters beyond this quarter?
- What legacy are we creating?

Only then can we truly begin shaping culture that delivers, every quarter.

The limits of shareholder primacy

Burnout is the predictable output of a particular interpretation of corporate purpose: that companies exist to maximise shareholder value, and all other considerations, including employee welfare, community impact and environmental health, are subordinate to this primary obligation.

This damaging interpretation only became dominant in recent decades. For most of business history, corporations were understood to serve multiple stakeholders and purposes. The elevation of shareholder value to supreme status began in the 1970s, and with it came an increasing tendency to view employees primarily through the lens of cost rather than capability.

Workers became costs to be minimised, not people to be developed. Their welfare matters only to the extent it affects productivity and retention. When squeezing employees harder increases short-term returns, the logic of shareholder supremacy compels the squeeze.

But an excessive focus on short-term shareholder returns is self-defeating even on its own terms. There is no evidence that running people into the ground increases long-term shareholder value. There is, however, considerable evidence that it destroys it.

What began as a legitimate focus on accountability to shareholders has, in too many organisations, evolved into a short-termism that undermines the very returns it claims to protect.

When extraction destroys value: Boeing

Boeing provides a stark illustration of how shareholder primacy can backfire catastrophically. Between 1998 and 2018, Boeing returned US$61 billion to shareholders through buybacks and dividends, representing 81.8 per cent of its total profits over that period (Lazonick & Sakinç, 2019). Between 2013 and 2018 alone, the company spent US$41.5 billion on stock buybacks while capital expenditure fell to less than 2 per cent of sales by 2018, half of what rival Airbus typically spent (Robison, 2024).

This created high-pressure environments among engineers and staff who faced relentless demands to cut costs and accelerate production. Rather than invest the US$7 billion required to design an entirely new aircraft to replace the ageing 737, Boeing chose to re-engineer the existing model and save the money, an amount that matched what it was spending annually on buybacks at the time (Lazonick & Sakinç, 2019).

The culmination was the 737 MAX crashes in 2018 and 2019, which killed 346 people and were linked to design flaws produced under these conditions. The crashes resulted in the grounding of the fleet, over US$20 billion in direct costs, a stock price collapse of more than 50 per cent at its lowest point, a 2024 guilty plea to fraud charges, and long-term reputational damage. Harvard Business School's analysis found that the decisions made in the name of shareholder value ultimately cost Boeing's investors US$87 billion since 2018 (George, 2024).

The shareholder-value playbook produced exactly the opposite of what it promised. The short-term gains were dwarfed by the long-term losses, and 346 people paid for the difference with their lives.

When returns come before the business: Toys R Us

The collapse of US toy retailer Toys R Us exemplifies how shareholder-driven extractive practices that prioritise payouts over operational health led to environments with high burnout

(*continued*)

risk, suppressed wages, reduced productivity, and ultimately to value destruction.

In 2005, private equity firms KKR, Bain Capital and Vornado acquired the company in a US$6.6 billion leveraged buyout, loading it with more than US$5 billion in debt to finance the acquisition (SEC, 2005). This debt burden forced aggressive cost cutting: stagnant wages and chronic understaffing. The capital that could have modernised e-commerce and maintained store quality went to debt servicing. The workforce was understaffed and underpaid, working under the conditions this book documents as reliable predictors of burnout. The results showed in the stores and eventually in the company itself (Miranda, 2018; Dayen, 2018).

The shareholder-first playbook yielded short-term gains for the private equity firms: over US$470 million in fees alone. By 2017, the debt and operational neglect triggered bankruptcy, closing all US stores and eliminating 33 000 jobs. It destroyed employees and the company alike. Everyone lost except those who structured it, who took their fees and moved on.

When investment creates value: Example A – Unilever

Unilever, while under former CEO Paul Polman's leadership from 2009 to 2019, offers a clear case of long-term stakeholder focus outperforming extractive short-termism.

Polman shifted the company towards a multi-stakeholder model with the Unilever Sustainable Living Plan in 2010, committing to decouple growth from environmental impact, improve social outcomes, and invest in fair wages, supplier health, and community wellbeing. He explicitly rejected quarterly earnings obsession and share buyback priorities.

Despite initial Wall Street criticism, this approach delivered strong results: 290 per cent total shareholder return over his tenure, outpacing many peers, expanded market share, and enhanced resilience through loyal customers and engaged employees. By prioritising purpose-driven innovation over cost slashing, Unilever created lasting value, showing that stakeholder investment fosters innovation, brand strength and superior long-term returns, while pure shareholder primacy often leads to fragility and underperformance over time.

When investment creates value: Example B – Costco

Costco and Walmart's Sam's Club operate in the same market, sell comparable products, and compete for the same customers. They made fundamentally different decisions about the people doing the work.

Costco pays its workers approximately 40 per cent more than Walmart, provides comprehensive health and retirement benefits, resists layoffs, invests heavily in training, and grants employees substantial autonomy to solve problems. This is not philanthropy. It is a deliberate business strategy built on the calculation that the cost of treating people well is lower than the cost of replacing them.

The results confirm the calculation. Costco's annual employee turnover runs at approximately 8 per cent, against an industry average of 60 per cent (Ton, 2024). The cost of recruiting and retraining at Walmart's turnover rate is substantial; Costco avoids most of it. The company generates US$21 805 in operating profit per hourly employee, compared with US$11 615 at Sam's Club, despite paying significantly higher wages (Cascio, 2006). Costco's membership renewal rate consistently exceeds 91 per cent, a direct

(*continued*)

reflection of what happens when people who feel valued serve customers.

Wall Street initially criticised Costco co-founder Jim Sinegal for paying employees too well. His response was consistent for decades: he could not afford to pay them less. The turnover, the lost productivity, the recruitment costs, and the institutional knowledge walking out the door were expenses the model simply could not carry. Treating people well was not a cost. It was a competitive advantage that extractive models could not replicate because, to replicate it, they would have to become a different kind of organisation.

Costco has outperformed Walmart in shareholder returns by a substantial margin over the past decade. The company that chose investment over extraction delivered better results for everyone: employees, customers and shareholders alike.

What if you are not the CEO?

The examples above share something in common: they describe decisions made at the very top of organisations. Paul Polman could reject the quarterly earnings obsession because he was the CEO. Jim Sinegal could pay his people 40 per cent above the industry average because he co-founded the company and answered to no one who disagreed. The private equity firms could load Toys R Us with debt because they owned it. The Boeing board could prioritise buybacks over engineering because they controlled capital allocation.

Most leaders reading this book aren't in those positions. You may report to executives who have internalised the imperative for *more*.

You may work within incentive structures you didn't design, or face quarterly targets that leave no room for the approaches this chapter advocates. You may agree with everything I've written, while feeling powerless to act on any of it.

Pretending otherwise would limit the usefulness of this book to the people who need it most.

The sphere of control

Drawing on Stephen Covey's framework from *The 7 Habits of Highly Effective People*, your working life can be divided into three categories: what you control, what you influence, and what you cannot change.

What you control includes your own behaviour, how you communicate with your team, the micro decisions you make daily about workload distribution, the way you respond to pressure, and the example you set. No one can take these from you. Even in the most extractive environment, you control how you treat the people who report to you.

What you influence includes decisions made by peers and immediate superiors, team norms that develop through collective behaviour, and the evidence you can gather about what works. Influence operates through relationships, credibility and persistence. It's slower than control but wider in scope.

What you can't change, at least not directly or quickly, includes shareholder expectations, board-level strategy, market pressures, and the fundamental economics of your industry. Fighting these directly is usually futile and often career-ending.

Wisdom lies in knowing which category each challenge falls into and responding accordingly. Wasting energy trying to control what can only be influenced, or trying to influence what can't be changed, leads to frustration and burnout. Focusing energy where it can truly make a difference, even if that difference is smaller than you would like, leads to impact.

Buffer leadership in practice

Buffer leadership was introduced in Chapter 7 in the context of middle management. The principle extends to any leader caught between a system they cannot immediately change and the people who depend on them. If you can't change the system, you can still change what the system feels like for the people you lead.

Buffer leadership means translating impossible demands into prioritised work. When everything is urgent, nothing is, so you decide what's urgent and protect your team's focus. It means filtering communication, sharing what's necessary, and shielding your team from noise that would only add anxiety. It means taking the heat for decisions, and representing your team's constraints upward even when that's uncomfortable.

Buffer leadership is exhausting precisely because it works by absorption. You're taking on stress so others don't have to. This isn't sustainable indefinitely, which is why it must be paired with the other strategies below.

Coalition building

A single leader pushing for change is easy to dismiss. A coalition raising the same concern is not.

If you believe the current approach is damaging, you're probably not alone. Others in your organisation are likely seeing the same warning signs: turnover, burnout, declining engagement, lost institutional knowledge. Finding these people and building relationships with them creates the foundation for collective advocacy.

A useful example: when Microsoft Japan's leadership wanted to test a four-day working week, they did not attempt to change company policy unilaterally. They built internal support, documented the business case, ran a contained experiment, and presented the results. Productivity increased by 39.9 per cent. The data did what individual advocacy could not. The experiment became the evidence.

Evidence building

Burnout culture persists partly because its costs are invisible while its benefits are measured. You can change that equation within your sphere by making the costs visible:

- Track what happens in your team.
- Document turnover and its costs.
- Note the correlation between crunch periods and sick leave.
- Measure the time lost to rework from errors made under exhaustion.
- Bring data alongside your principles when you advocate for different approaches.

Evidence also means running experiments where you can. A leader I worked with in one of Australia's tech unicorns began protecting two hours of uninterrupted focus time each morning for her team of eight, blocking the calendar and setting a team norm that no meetings or messages required responses before 11 am. Within six weeks, project completion rates had improved and two team members who had been flagged as disengaged had visibly re-engaged. She documented it, presented it at her leadership team meeting and within a quarter, the practice had spread to two adjacent teams. She did not change company policy. She changed what she could, measured it, and let the results make the case.

When to stay and when to leave

There's honour in staying within a flawed system and making it better from inside. There's also a point where staying becomes complicity, and the gap between your values and your environment becomes unbridgeable.

Only you can judge where that line is. But consider:

- Are you making any difference?
- Is the trajectory improving, even slowly?
- Is the cost to your own health and relationships acceptable?
- Are you becoming someone you don't want to be?

If the answers suggest you should leave, that isn't failure. Some systems can't be changed from within. Some organisations don't deserve you or your effort. Walking away can be the most powerful statement you make, and it may be necessary for your own survival. I have done it, and I have spent precisely zero seconds regretting it. The jobs not taken, the toxic cultures not absorbed, the compromises not made: these shape a life and a career as much as anything pursued. Many of the rewards in life come from what we choose not to do.

The best leaders create pockets of sanity within extractive systems, demonstrate alternatives that work, and contribute to the slow accumulation of evidence and pressure that eventually tips the balance. Although that isn't everything, it still matters.

The measurement problem

British economist Charles Goodhart observed in 1975 that any statistical regularity collapses once it becomes a target for control. Anthropologist Marilyn Strathern later distilled it: when a measure becomes a target, it ceases to be a good measure (Strathern, 1997).

Modern workplaces have built their entire performance infrastructure on exactly this error. Hours are measurable, so hours become the target. Presence is visible, so presence becomes the proxy for commitment. Email response time is trackable, so responsiveness becomes the definition of engagement. None of these things is productivity. All of them are easier to measure than productivity, and so they have become what organisations optimise for.

The consequences run directly through everything this chapter has documented. The open plan office that looks productive from the outside. The meeting culture that fills calendars while emptying the hours available for actual thinking. The always-on expectation that generates visible activity and invisible exhaustion. The presenteeism data that shows 57.5 days of physical presence producing nothing of value. These are not separate problems. They are the same problem: a system that measures what it can see and then wonders why what matters keeps declining.

Human resources: the language of extraction

Consider the language we use: human resources, human capital management, headcount, FTEs, talent acquisition, performance management. Every term reduces humans to instruments, resources to be allocated, capital to be deployed, heads to be counted, units to be managed. Imagine introducing yourself at a dinner party as a unit of headcount. Imagine telling your children you're a resource being optimised. The language is absurd when you say it aloud, which is why nobody ever does.

Language shapes perception, and the language of human resources shapes how leaders perceive the people they lead. When workers are resources, their welfare matters only to the extent it affects resource performance. When workers are headcount, reducing headcount becomes a straightforward optimisation problem. You're not firing a person with a mortgage and two children approaching school age. You're rightsizing.

The burnout culture requires this linguistic distance. It would be difficult to celebrate burning out actual human beings. It's much easier to celebrate optimising resource utilisation. The abstraction creates moral space between decisions and their human consequences. Nobody holds a press conference to announce they're eliminating people.

They announce they're 'optimising their organisational footprint' or 'rightsizing to meet market conditions' or, my personal favourite from a recent ASX announcement, 'recalibrating their human capital architecture'.

The human beings are people with families, aspirations, health problems and finite lifespans. They're people whose nervous systems weren't designed for chronic stress, whose brains are physically damaged by the conditions we create. When we speak of human resources, we mean these people. Us. And we deserve language that acknowledges our humanity.

I've started using different language in my own work. I talk about people, not resources. I talk about teams, not headcount. I talk about colleagues and collaborators, not talent. The language feels awkward at first because it goes against decades of business convention. But that awkwardness is revealing. It shows how deeply the extractive mindset has shaped even how we speak.

The executive bubble

The pressure for *more* is applied most fervently by those who experience it least directly. Executives and senior leaders often inhabit a bubble of privilege that insulates them from the conditions they create.

Many have assistants who manage their calendars and filter their communications, flexible schedules that often allow them to attend children's events and take proper holidays, and compensation packages that remove financial stress from their lives. They have status and autonomy that, in part, protect them from the kinds of pressures their workforce faces.

Burnout statistics confirm this perception gap. Associates and entry-level employees are the most likely to report reduced engagement due to burnout, 62 and 61 per cent respectively, compared to just 38 per cent of C suite leaders (DHR Global, 2025). The people making decisions about workload are the people least affected by those decisions.

Breaking through this bubble requires deliberate effort. The best leaders seek out the truth about working conditions, knowing that the truth will be uncomfortable. They create channels for honest feedback that bypass the filtering that normally sanitises bad news. They remember what it was like before they had assistants and autonomy, and they make time to listen to those who can tell them.

Customer first, people last

Customer obsession is one of the most powerful organising principles in modern business. The financial case for it is substantial, the strategic logic is sound, and the organisations that have embedded it deeply tend to outperform those that haven't. This section accepts that logic but completes it.

The doctrine of customer obsession has a clear origin. In his first letter to Amazon shareholders in 1997, Jeff Bezos established a principle that would reshape global business thinking: start with the customer and work backwards. Customer obsession became the first of Amazon's 16 leadership principles, placed first deliberately. In the 23 shareholder letters Bezos wrote as CEO, the word 'customer' appeared 443 times, more frequently than the word 'Amazon' itself. He told shareholders directly that there was never any misalignment between customer interests and shareholder interests.

The philosophy spread. Within a decade it had colonised business schools, consulting frameworks and board decks on every continent. Within two decades it was the dominant organising principle of commercial enterprise. NPS scores. CSAT dashboards. Customer journey mapping. Voice of the customer programs. An entire industrial apparatus pointed, with extraordinary rigour, in a single direction.

Boards embraced it because the financial case appeared overwhelming. In 2023, Forrester Research found that customer-obsessed organisations report 41 per cent faster revenue growth, 49 per cent faster profit growth and 51 per cent better customer retention than their peers.

Its modelling showed that a large manufacturer halting its customer obsession investment would forfeit US$771 million over 12 years. A large financial services firm would lose US$862 million.

The strategy is right. It's the implementation and culture that is frequently incomplete.

It measures, with extraordinary precision, what the customer experiences. It builds dashboards, feedback loops and strategic plans around that question. What it rarely asks, with anything approaching equivalent rigour, is what the person experiences who is serving that customer. The employee is present in the model as an instrument, a delivery mechanism for customer value, but not consistently as a variable that determines whether that delivery is possible at all.

That gap is expensive.

Gallup's research across thousands of organisations and decades of data shows that companies in the top quartile for employee engagement outperform bottom-quartile peers by 23 per cent higher profitability, 18 per cent higher productivity, and 10 per cent higher customer loyalty and retention (Gallup, 2022). MIT's Center for Information Systems Research, studying more than 200 organisations, found that companies in the top quartile for employee experience were 25 per cent more profitable than those in the bottom quartile and generated twice the innovation revenue (Dery & Sebastian, 2017). IBM's Smarter Workforce Institute found that organisations with superior employee experience achieve 2.5 times greater revenue growth over time (IBM, 2016). The financial performance of customer-facing businesses is downstream from the experience of the people doing the work.

Eagle Hill Consulting reported in 2025 that 64 per cent of US workers say the employee experience directly impacts their ability to serve customers. That figure belongs on every customer experience dashboard in every organisation running a customer-obsession strategy. More than six in ten of your customer-facing employees believe how you treat them determines how they treat your customers. Yet fewer than 40 per cent of organisations place significant importance on employee experience. The gap between what employees say matters and what organisations measure is where customer obsession leaves value on the table.

Gallup confirms it: employees experiencing frequent burnout are far less likely to believe their organisation delivers on its customer promises. When the Society for Human Resource Management (2019) tallied the cost of toxic workplace cultures in the United States, it reached $223 billion over five years, dominated not by absenteeism but by turnover; the departure of people who could no longer give what was being demanded of them. MIT Sloan's analysis of 34 million employee profiles found that toxic culture is more than 10 times more powerful than compensation in predicting whether an employee leaves (Sull et al., 2022). A customer obsession strategy that neglects the people doing the serving creates the conditions that undermine the very outcome it is trying to achieve.

Forrester, the research firm most associated with championing customer obsession, acknowledges in its own definition that true customer obsession requires a continuous eye on your employees. The qualifier is rarely given equal weight. The measurement apparatus points at the customer.

Organisations that want to lead on customer experience over time are those that invest in their people with the same rigour, because the employee experience is the infrastructure through which customer experience is delivered.

Genuine attention to what customers need, what they experience, and what would make their lives better is exactly the kind of orientation healthy organisations should sustain. The question is whether that attention can be delivered by depleted people. Depleted people can follow a script, hit a metric and complete a transaction. They can't reliably do what creates loyalty: the quality of human attention that makes a customer feel seen, valued and worth coming back for. That requires something in reserve. Building that reserve is the difference between basic customer service and customer obsession.

A different measure

The organisations that have consistently led on customer experience are the ones that completed the equation: they made their people the primary investment and let the customer experience follow as a result.

Richard Branson has championed this for decades. Virgin does not put the customer first. Employees are the company's top priority, customers second, shareholders third. The position sounds counterintuitive only if you believe customer experience is something an organisation points at. Branson's view was simpler: if the person working at your company is not appreciated, they are not going to do things with a smile. No amount of customer journey mapping fixes that. Virgin Atlantic became one of the most recognised service brands in the world by treating that principle as an operating system rather than a slogan.

Herb Kelleher built Southwest Airlines on the same logic and produced one of the more unusual outcomes in modern commercial history: more than 35 consecutive years of profitability in an industry notorious for thin margins and endemic bankruptcy. His formula was simple and he repeated it for decades. Your employees come first. If you treat them well, they treat your customers well, your customers come back, and your shareholders are happy. At the centre of Southwest's success, he said, were its culture and its people.

Both Branson and Kelleher arrived at the same insight from opposite ends of the business world. Customer experience is downstream of employee experience. You can't engineer it from the customer end. You build it from the inside and it arrives at the customer as a consequence. When organisations reverse that sequence, naming the output as the strategy, they optimise for the wrong variable and then wonder why the numbers keep telling them something is broken.

The organisations that lead on service understand the sequence correctly. They invest in their people with the same rigour they invest in their customer experience infrastructure. They understand that engagement, discretionary effort and care are not manufactured by NPS dashboards. They are the product of people who feel seen, trusted and valued as the source of performance rather than merely as the mechanism of its delivery. Customer obsession and employee investment are not in tension. The second enables the first.

Summary

Burnout culture is destroying human beings and, in the long run, destroying the organisations that embrace it. From my experience, most executives either don't see this or have decided not to.

The evidence in this chapter makes a compelling commercial case. Costco outperforms extraction on every measurable dimension while paying its people 40 per cent more than its direct competitors. Unilever delivered 290 per cent total shareholder return under a leader who explicitly rejected quarterly earnings obsession. Southwest Airlines built 35 consecutive years of profitability in an industry notorious for bankruptcy by putting its people first. The organisations that invest in their people do not sacrifice performance for principle. They produce better performance because of it.

The best leaders understand this and are not waiting for permission to treat their people well. They have read the data and are building the organisations that will still be standing when the ones running on extraction have burned through everything available to them.

Insisting that work should serve life rather than consume it is commercially rational. The organisations doing it are already proving it.

***More!* and *Customer, Customer, Customer!* are not strategies. They're what some leaders say when they've run out of ideas.**

CHAPTER 9

Just one more email

Beware the barrenness of a busy life.

—Socrates

If you've read this far, you understand that burnout is an epidemic, its costs are staggering, and the workplace we have built is destroying value while claiming to create it. You may be ready to do something different. But there is something you may need to face first: the possibility that your mental model of high performance is itself the problem.

Most leaders carry assumptions about what creates excellent results. These assumptions feel like common sense and they feel validated by experience: the two things humans tend to rely on to determine facts and make decisions.

US General Stanley McChrystal encountered exactly this in Iraq. When he took command of Joint Special Operations Command in 2004, his force had overwhelming advantages: superior numbers, equipment, technology, training and funding. They were losing. Al-Qaeda in Iraq operated as a decentralised network that moved faster than the coalition's hierarchical structure could respond. Every traditional metric said McChrystal should be winning. The battlefield said otherwise.

The performance model his force ran on was the one most organisations still use: efficiency, hierarchy, control, need-to-know secrecy, centralised decision-making. Applied with discipline and commitment, those principles were making his force slower and less effective than a decentralised enemy with a fraction of his resources.

In *Team of Teams* (2015), McChrystal described what he built instead. Radical transparency replaced compartmentalised secrecy. Trust networks replaced siloed operations. Decision-making authority moved to those closest to the action. The model that had served militaries for centuries was replaced with something that looked far less like control and far more like culture.

When his force finally located Abu Musab al-Zarqawi, the unit commander launched the strike without asking permission. McChrystal's reflection on that moment captures what he had built: the commander had not asked permission and did not need to. Trust was the system.

That force, in that environment, learned what the evidence keeps confirming and organisations keep resisting: pressure, control and hierarchical command fail precisely when they matter most. What works is culture: shared consciousness, radical trust, and empowered people aligned around common purpose.

The control instinct in all of us runs deep and Industrial-era thinking still casts a long shadow over many leadership practices, with predictable results.

The illusion of control

The belief that control ensures quality reflects a fundamental misunderstanding of how quality actually emerges in complex work. For routine tasks with clear specifications, close monitoring may catch errors. The assembly line inspector who checks every widget serves a real function. But most valuable work isn't routine. It requires judgement, creativity, and adaptation to circumstances. This kind of work can't be controlled into excellence. It has to be enabled.

When you monitor people closely, you get compliance. They do what they think you're looking for. They optimise for the metrics you measure and become skilled at appearing productive in the ways you have defined productivity.

What you lose is everything else: the discretionary effort that goes beyond the minimum, the creative insight that emerges from psychological safety, the honest feedback that surfaces problems early, and the ownership that comes from autonomy.

Control also consumes enormous resources. Every hour a manager spends monitoring is an hour not spent enabling. Every system built for surveillance is a system not built for support. The overhead of control crowds out the investment in capability that would make control unnecessary.

The organisations that produce the highest quality work hire well, develop their people, create clarity about what good looks like, and then trust people to deliver. Control is seductive because it creates the illusion of certainty. But complex work always involves uncertainty. The attempt to eliminate it through control amplifies it by suppressing the human judgement that navigates uncertainty well.

The cost of internal competition

The belief that competition drives excellence ignores what complex organisations require in order to succeed. It's true that individual competition can motivate individual effort, and the sales contest that rewards the top performer may produce more sales activity. But there are significant second-order effects.

When people compete against their colleagues, they stop helping one another. Knowledge hoarding moves in quietly, occupying the space where collaboration used to live. The insight that could help a colleague, the shortcut discovered last quarter, and the contact who could solve their problem become assets to protect rather than resources to share. The collaboration that complex work relies upon gets replaced.

Competition also distorts behaviour in ways that damage organisations. People optimise for the metrics that determine winners and losers, even when those metrics don't capture what really matters. They take credit for shared successes and deflect blame for shared failures.

And competition selects for a particular kind of person: those who thrive in zero-sum environments, who are comfortable advancing at others' expense. This may not be the kind of person your organisation needs and it's certainly not the kind of person that shapes a healthy culture and delivers excellent work.

The research on psychological safety, pioneered by Amy Edmondson at Harvard Business School, demonstrates repeatedly that teams outperform where people feel safe to take interpersonal risks. That safety is incompatible with intense internal competition. You cannot simultaneously compete against someone and trust them enough to admit uncertainty or ask for help.

The brainstorming delusion

This particular belief is so universally held that questioning it feels absurd: if you want creative ideas, gather people in a room and brainstorm. The facilitator writes the prompt on the whiteboard, reminds everyone that there are no bad ideas, and waits for the magic to happen. I'm often that facilitator and very rarely do I see any form of magic.

Brainstorming was invented by an advertising executive called Alex Osborn in 1953. He believed that deferring judgement during idea generation would increase creative output. He was wrong. Research has known this for decades. Brainstorming persists for the same reason the five-day week persists and the performance review persists: once something becomes the way a thing is done, the evidence that it does not work tends to circulate in academic journals while the practice continues regardless.

In 1991, Mullen, Johnson and Salas published a meta-analysis of more than 800 teams comparing group brainstorming with individuals working alone and then pooling their ideas. The individuals outperformed the groups on both the number and quality of ideas generated. Across 38 separate experiments, independent workers consistently beat equivalent groups. The larger the group, the worse the effect: groups of nine produced fewer ideas per person than groups of six, which produced fewer than groups of four. The very activity we use to generate ideas is the activity that generates the fewest of them.

The reasons are well understood:

- **Production blocking is the primary culprit.** In a group, only one person can speak at a time. While that person speaks, everyone else is waiting, and while they wait, they forget their own ideas or unconsciously edit them to align with what has already been said.
- **Social loafing compounds the problem.** In groups, individuals exert less effort because responsibility is diffused.
- **Evaluation apprehension adds another layer.** People censor themselves, afraid to voice unusual ideas in front of colleagues or superiors, regardless of how many times they are told there are no bad ideas.
- **Status management operates alongside all of this.** People read the room rather than commit to the idea. They watch how the most senior person in the room responds before deciding whether their contribution is worth making. The idea gets filtered through the question of how it will land rather than whether it is any good.

Why does brainstorming persist? Because it feels democratic and inclusive, and embodies values we want to believe in. And no one has bothered to check whether embodying those values and achieving those outcomes are the same thing. They aren't. Brainstorming was invented in 1953. So was instant coffee. Neither is anyone's first choice.

There is a concept in Buddhist philosophy that describes *right* action, as distinct from maximised action. *Right* action means action that is appropriate to the situation, proportionate to the need, and guided by clear seeing rather than compulsion. The obsession with *more*, more hours, more meetings, more brainstorming sessions, is compulsive action masquerading as strategy. The evidence consistently shows that *less*, done with full attention, produces more. Every contemplative tradition has known this.

The return-to-office illusion

If brainstorming is the sacred cow of creative process, the return-to-office mandate is the sacred cow of organisational control. Since 2023, a parade of major corporations have demanded that employees return to the office full-time, citing collaboration, culture and productivity. I've had to listen to this from clients myself. The evidence does not support these claims.

Stanford economist Nicholas Bloom ran a randomised controlled trial across 1612 employees at Trip.com. Hybrid workers showed no difference in performance grades, promotion rates or lines of code written compared to their fully in-office counterparts, and were 33 per cent less likely to resign (Bloom, Han & Liang, *Nature*, 2024). A University of Pittsburgh analysis of S&P 500 companies found that return-to-office mandates did not improve financial performance or firm value, while employee satisfaction declined significantly. The same analysis found that companies were more likely to impose mandates after their stock prices dropped, meaning RTO was a response to underperformance, not a cause of recovery (Ma et al., 2024).

A Baylor University study tracking more than three million employee profiles across 54 major technology and financial firms found that RTO mandates accelerated the departure of high-performing, senior and diverse employees at disproportionate rates, precisely the people organisations can least afford to lose (Ding et al., 2025). A King's College London analysis of more than one million observations in the UK Labour Force Survey found that by late 2024, 55 per cent of women said they would seek a new job if required to return full-time, and a further 9 per cent said they would simply quit (Chung & Yuan, 2025). The US Bureau of Labor Statistics found a positive relationship between growth in remote work and total factor productivity across industries. The industries that expanded remote work fastest also saw faster productivity growth (BLS, 2024). The Flex Index found that fully flexible companies grew revenue 1.7 times faster than mandate-driven firms between 2019 and 2024.

Amazon's five-day mandate, which took effect in January 2025, became the most closely watched experiment in modern workplace policy. An internal Slack survey leaked in October 2024 found that 91 per cent of respondents were unhappy with the policy, with average satisfaction rated 1.4 out of 5. When the mandate took effect, Amazon did not have enough desks in at least seven cities.

Gartner's research confirmed what followed: full-time office mandates produce no measurable productivity improvement and cause measurable declines in morale and trust.

A BambooHR survey of 1504 US employees, conducted in March 2024, found that one in four VP and C-suite executives admitted they hoped RTO mandates would trigger voluntary departures, using office attendance as a managed exit strategy rather than a productivity measure. The mandate was, for some, a managed exit strategy dressed as a culture initiative.

A 2024 KPMG CEO Outlook survey found that 83 per cent of CEOs expect a full return to office within three years. The gap between what the evidence shows and what leaders believe is astounding. CEOs are making workforce decisions based on instinct, tradition, and the need to justify expensive real estate leases, rather than on research freely available to anyone who cares to read it.

The structure we never questioned

Of all the assumptions embedded in the modern workplace, the five-day working week may be the most deeply entrenched and the least examined. We accept it the way we accept gravity: as a fact of nature rather than a choice made by people in a particular time for particular reasons. Henry Ford popularised the five-day week in 1926. He also published a virulently antisemitic newspaper, was awarded a medal by the Nazi government, and believed jazz was a Jewish conspiracy to corrupt American youth. We kept the five-day week. We let the rest go. Progress, as ever, is selective about what it carries forward.

A century later, we apply the same temporal structure to knowledge work, creative work, strategic work and caring work. The economy of 2026 bears no resemblance to the assembly line economies of 1926. However, the standard Western working week remains.

Between 2015 and 2019, Iceland ran two large-scale trials of a reduced working week across more than 2500 workers, approximately 1 per cent of the country's entire workforce. Workers moved from 40 hours to 35 or 36 hours per week with no reduction in pay. The results, analysed by Autonomy and the Association for Sustainability and Democracy, remained the same or improved across the majority of trial workplaces, while worker wellbeing increased dramatically across every measure tracked including stress, burnout, health and work–life balance. By 2022, 86 per cent of Iceland's workforce had moved to shorter hours or gained the right to do so as a result of the trials (Haraldsson & Stronge, 2021).

The UK followed with its own pilot in 2022, involving more than 60 companies. Ninety-two per cent chose to continue with the four-day model after the trial concluded. Absenteeism fell by 65 per cent. Staff turnover fell by 57 per cent. Revenue held steady or grew (Autonomy/4 Day Week Global, 2023). Microsoft Japan trialled a four-day week in 2019 and productivity increased by 39.9 per cent (Microsoft Japan, 2019).

These are not marginal improvements achieved by small, unusual companies. These are transformative results replicated across countries, industries and organisational sizes.

The five-day week persists for the same reason every practice in this chapter persists: because we have always done it, because changing it requires courage, and because leaders fear that fewer visible hours will mean less visible output. Fewer hours, when implemented thoughtfully, produce better concentration, lower burnout, reduced turnover, and equal or greater output.

The selection effect

There is a deeper problem with cultures built on hours, pressure, control and competition. They don't create resilient, high-performing people. They filter for the narrow demographic that can temporarily tolerate a particular kind of stress.

Think about who thrives, or at least survives, in such environments. It's typically the young. Without significant caregiving responsibilities. Healthy. From backgrounds that prepared them for this particular kind of pressure. And typically, privileged enough to have options if it becomes too much.

That is a subset of human talent, and not necessarily the most capable subset. The brilliant engineer who also cares for elderly parents can't take a role requiring full-time, on-site attendance. The creative problem-solver who thinks best with adequate rest can't perform under chronic pressure. The collaborative leader who builds strong teams can't thrive where competition is the dominant mode.

Burnout cultures select for tolerance of extraction, and tolerance gets mistaken for excellence. The people who remain have adapted to the conditions. They look capable and committed because they are, because surviving those conditions requires both.

When you build cultures that work for a wider range of people, you access a wider range of talent. That is a proven and substantial competitive advantage. McKinsey's *Diversity Matters Even More* report, in analysing more than 1265 companies across 23 countries, found that organisations in the top quartile for gender and ethnic diversity on executive teams were 39 per cent more likely to outperform their peers financially (McKinsey, 2023). The relationship between diverse talent and financial performance has strengthened in every McKinsey report since 2015.

What high performance actually requires

If the myths are wrong, what is right? What produces sustained high performance in complex work?

The answer emerges from understanding what knowledge work demands: cognitive capacity, discretionary effort, creative risk-taking, collaborative coordination and customer attunement:

- **Cognitive capacity** means having the mental resources to think clearly, solve problems creatively, and exercise sound judgement. This capacity is depleted by chronic stress and restored by recovery.
- **Discretionary effort** means contribution beyond the minimum required. It only emerges when people feel valued, when they believe in what they're doing, and when they trust that their contribution matters.
- **Creative risk-taking** means being willing to try new approaches and experiment with solutions that might fail. This is impossible in environments where failure is punished, where appearing competent matters more than being competent.
- **Collaborative coordination** means working effectively with others whose contributions complement your own. This integration fails when competition dominates and trust is absent.

- **Customer attunement** means understanding and caring about the people your work serves. Depleted, cynical, disengaged workers can't and don't extend genuine care to customers. What they can do is follow emotionally hollow scripts.

Notice what enables these requirements: people who have capacity, who are engaged, who feel safe, who trust each other, who have something left to give. People who haven't been burned out by their workplace.

High performance requires healthy people.

Professional care

Here we arrive at a concept that makes many leaders uncomfortable: care.

When I introduce care in leadership conversations, I often see resistance flash across faces. Leaders imagine something that feels foreign to their understanding of professional effectiveness, becoming everyone's therapist, holding hands through difficult conversations, accepting poor performance in the name of kindness.

Researchers studying compassion in organisations across the past two decades have produced a consistent finding. Leaders who combine genuine care with high standards produce the strongest results. Care alone produces happier employees who underperform. Standards alone produces results that do not last. The combination is what builds sustained excellence. The research names this *professional care*, and the data shows it outperforms every alternative leadership stance studied.

This resistance rests on a confusion between personal care and professional care. Personal care is what you offer to friends and family. It is unconditional. It prioritises the relationship itself and says: I value you regardless of what you produce.

Professional care is different. It is care expressed through the design of conditions, investment in capability, and accountability for results. Professional care says: I am committed to creating an environment where you can do excellent work, and I will hold you to high standards while providing support to meet them. Professional care may be the most demanding form of leadership.

Professional care by design

Professional care by design means understanding what people need to do their best work and systematically providing it: adequate resources; clear expectations; reasonable workloads; psychological safety to raise concerns; and recovery time to sustain effort. The leader who cares professionally doesn't *hope* conditions will be adequate. They *ensure* they are.

Jane Dutton and her team at the University of Michigan have spent over a decade studying what they call compassion architecture in organisations. Their 2014 synthesis published in *Annual Review of Organizational Psychology* examined how the structural design choices leaders make (work systems, role clarity, recovery time, psychological safety) enable people to do excellent work. The research shows that compassionate design is not soft. It is the deliberate construction of conditions for performance, and organisations that build it outperform those that rely on individual effort to overcome poor design. The leader's care becomes visible through what they build into the system.

Professional care as an investment

Professional care as an investment means asking what this person could become with the right conditions: feedback designed to build capability, stretch assignments paired with support.

William Kahn at Boston University coined the term 'psychological presence' in 1990 to describe the quality of attention and investment leaders bring to their people. His research showed that employees in genuinely developmental relationships demonstrated significantly greater capability growth than those in transactional ones. The investment is the specific act of seeing potential in a person and pairing stretch with support designed for them.

Professional care as accountability

Professional care as accountability means that the leader who cares professionally can say: This isn't meeting the standard, and I know you can do better, what support do you need? Care without accountability is abdication. The worker whose poor performance goes unaddressed isn't being protected. They're being denied the feedback that would help them improve.

The most direct evidence for this comes from Lilius and colleagues at Harvard and the universities of Michigan and British Columbia, published in *Journal of Organizational Behavior* in 2008. They specifically compared leaders who showed compassion alone against leaders who combined compassion with high performance standards. Compassion alone produced happier employees who underperformed. The combination produced 23 per cent higher engagement, 19 per cent lower turnover, and statistically significant performance gains. Holding the standard while providing support is itself the act of care. Letting the standard slide protects neither the person nor the team.

What professional care is not

Professional care is not therapy, not friendship, and not the avoidance of difficulty. It holds high standards while providing support to meet them. That combination is both rare and devastatingly effective.

Peter Frost at the University of British Columbia studied leaders who collapse the distinction between personal and professional care. His *Harvard Business Review* research described the toxic handler pattern, leaders who absorb personal distress without role-appropriate boundaries. They burn out within two years and produce worse team outcomes than leaders who maintain the professional frame. The distinction is not coldness. It is the discipline that allows care to be sustainable across years rather than collapsing into either friendship or exhaustion.

Lasting residue: The marketer

Susan is one of Australia's leading marketers. Before she became that, she spent several years inside one of Australia's most respected investment banks, an organisation whose brand carries the kind of market trust that makes its name shorthand for credibility. From the outside it's a high-performance institution doing high-quality work. From the inside it is something else.

Susan describes a culture where people cried at their desks because they could not absorb the pressure and yet they were also proud to be there. They consoled one another in the toilets between meetings. Pride and consolation existed simultaneously in that culture. It's what a strong external brand will allow you to do to your people for longer than it should.

Much of the pressure came from how senior leaders spoke to the service functions inside the bank. The marketing and communications people, who supported the deal makers, were addressed as a tier below the people generating the revenue, treated as second-class citizens whose role was to receive instruction. Presentations to senior leadership ran on a particular dynamic: high pressure, sharp counter feedback, with no trust banked beforehand. The research on this is well established. People can only receive feedback constructively when they feel psychologically safe with the person delivering it. In the absence of that safety, feedback gets internalised and starts to interfere with everything that comes after.

Susan watched a team leader, who was excellent at her work and well loved by her people, lose her job a month before she was due to go on maternity leave. The reasoning, dressed up in commercial language, was that she put her people before her deadlines. She still delivered the results. She simply delivered them with care, and care was read as a deficit of performance edge. A month before maternity leave is a particular kind of timing. It cannot be a coincidence, and it is also impossible to prove.

Susan's trust calibration had been broken. For years after she left the bank, in cultures markedly warmer than the one she had escaped, Susan still expected senior leaders to be looking for the shortcut in her work or the example they could make of her. She second guessed herself in meetings where nobody was second-guessing her. The skill she had lost was specific and consequential: the ability to disagree with someone in a way that strengthened the working relationship, and to commit to a decision after the interrogation rather than retreating from it. The investment bank had taught her, week by week for years, that disagreement meant danger.

Susan is thriving now. The bank still has its market reputation, and another cohort of bright people is currently moving through it. Some of them are presenting to senior leaders next week. They are about to receive feedback they have not been given the trust to absorb. They will absorb it anyway, and some of that will sit with them for years after they leave the building, and make it into a book about what not to do when it comes to corporate culture.

Curiosity as competitive advantage

Alongside professional care, curiosity is a defining characteristic of cultures that sustain high performance. In my experience, successful culture transformation does not happen without leaders and employees choosing to become more deliberately curious.

The research shows why it matters commercially. Only 24 per cent of workers feel curious at work on a regular basis, and 70 per cent say they face active barriers to asking questions (Gino, 2018). Curiosity is scarce. Organisations that build it are operating in space most competitors have not entered. The gap between executive perception and employee reality makes this harder than it sounds: 83 per cent of executives say they encourage curiosity at work. Only 52 per cent of employees agree (Harrison, Pinkus & Cohen, 2022). Closing that gap is itself a competitive act.

Curiosity enables accurate perception

Curious leaders ask questions. They investigate before concluding and remain open to the possibility that their understanding is incomplete. Their decisions are more likely to produce intended outcomes because they are made about the world as it actually is.

Gino's research found that curiosity reduces the systematic errors that fixed frameworks produce. Curious leaders approach decisions with more open questions and are measurably less susceptible to confirmation bias (Gino, 2018).

Curiosity drives innovation

Innovation requires exploring beyond current practice.

Gino's 2018 research across thousands of employees and multiple countries found that organisations rated high on curiosity culture produced significantly more innovative ideas and cross-functional collaboration than peers (Gino, 2018). A 2023 study of 563 firms found that CEO curiosity directly drives firm innovation through actively seeking ideas outside existing frameworks. The effect is moderated by organisational inertia, curiosity at the top requires structural support to translate into organisational outcomes (Li et al., 2023).

Curiosity builds collaboration

Curiosity about others, their perspectives and expertise, creates the foundation for effective collaboration. A curious leader listens differently. They ask questions that surface someone else's expertise rather than asserting their own.

Lievens, Harrison, Mussel and Litman's 2022 review of the accumulated workplace curiosity literature found that social curiosity, the subtype focused on understanding others, consistently predicts collaborative outcomes. Teams led by socially curious leaders draw on collective expertise more effectively and produce higher quality decisions (Lievens et al., 2022).

Curiosity supports learning

Organisations that learn from experience outperform those that don't. Learning requires treating failures as information.

Amy Edmondson at Harvard Business School has spent 25 years studying how organisations learn. Her central finding is that psychological safety, the condition curiosity in a leader helps create, determines whether teams surface failures at all. Teams in psychologically safe environments surface significantly more failures. They feel safe naming what went wrong. The failure becomes information rather than liability (Edmondson, 1999).

Gino's research adds a finding directly relevant to this book's argument: curiosity is associated with reduced stress and burnout. Curious workers forge stronger connections, perform better and maintain higher wellbeing, because curiosity reframes uncertainty as a source of interest rather than threat (Gino, 2018). The case for curiosity is not separate from the case against burnout. It is the same case.

Professional care and curiosity create results

Modern work is too complex for solo effort. Professional care creates the trust that collaboration needs. And curiosity about other perspectives makes integration possible.

The professional care model produces achievement that deepens over time. People grow through the process rather than become depleted, developing capabilities that make the next challenge more achievable. Innovation requires psychological safety because creativity involves risk. And when professional care creates safety, people bring their ideas forward. Curiosity makes exploration welcome, so that people can venture beyond established patterns.

Critically, customer centricity flows from care. The depleted, cynical worker cannot extend genuine care to customers. When people are cared for, they have capacity to care for others. When curiosity is cultivated internally, it extends externally. The organisation that invests in its people creates people capable of investing in customers.

The choice

The high-performance myths persist because they contain partial truths overgeneralised into damaging practices. Pressure can sharpen focus, briefly. Competition can motivate effort, narrowly. Control can catch errors, sometimes. Hours can produce output, temporarily.

The alternative is not softness or lack of ambition. Professional care and curiosity are demanding disciplines. They require rigorous attention to conditions, sustained investment in people, accountability for results, and continuous examination of how work happens. This is far harder than simply demanding more hours and applying more pressure.

But it works. It produces sustainable achievement rather than extractive spikes. It enables innovation that fear-based cultures can't generate. It builds collaboration that competitive cultures can't sustain. It creates customer centricity that depleted workforces can't deliver.

The choice is not between performance and care. That framing is itself a problematic, over-subscribed myth. The choice is between two performance models: one that extracts until exhaustion and one that invests towards compounding returns. The best leaders build capabilities competitors cannot replicate and attract talent extractive cultures cannot keep. High performance myths persist because everyone repeats them. Professional care and curiosity are the source of sustained high performance.

Sustained high performance is built from care and curiosity. The myths that replace them are burnout, rebranded.

CHAPTER 10

The Great Forgetting

Alas for those that never sing, but die with all their music in them!

—Oliver Wendell Holmes, *The Voiceless* (1858)

Have we forgotten what life is for? At its core, the burnout epidemic reflects a profound loss of purpose, a forgetting of what matters, that allows work to grow until it overtakes every other aspect of our lives.

Buddhist philosophy has shaped my professional practice for more than 30 years. I've maintained a daily meditation practice through every phase of my career. It hasn't made me a perfect leader but it has helped me see more clearly what I was doing and what it was costing. It has helped me recognise when I was burning bright and burning out. It remains the practice I return to when I need to assess how I am going, and it continues to help me find *The Middle Way* between too much and too little. The observations I draw from Buddhism are practical, from a philosophy that has been refined over centuries and shared across traditions. They address human behaviour, attention and effort, and they help explain why we keep building workplaces that make people miserable.

If the word 'Buddhist' makes you wary, I understand but encourage you to read on. I'm sure you'll find it interesting.

The delusion of permanence

Buddhist philosophy begins with a fundamental observation: everything changes. All phenomena, including our bodies, our thoughts, our circumstances and our organisations, are impermanent. The previously discussed Pali term *anicca* describes the constant flux that characterises all conditioned existence.

Modern work culture operates under the opposite assumption: that the current situation will persist indefinitely and must therefore be maximised. Many of us work as though we will always have our current job, our current career, current life. We sacrifice present wellbeing for future rewards as though the future is guaranteed.

But nothing is permanent. The job you're burning yourself for may be eliminated tomorrow. The career you're building may become obsolete. The organisation you're sacrificing for may cease to exist. Even if these things persist, you won't. Your health, your relationships, your finite time on Earth is being consumed by work that will continue long after you're gone.

Recognising impermanence isn't depressing, it's liberating. When we understand that everything passes, we can hold our work more lightly. We can ask whether what we're doing is worth the price we're paying in this moment, rather than deferring the question to a hypothetical future.

I think about this often when I work with executives who have sacrificed decades for their careers. Some have achieved remarkable things and feel genuine satisfaction. Others arrive at senior positions and discover that the destination doesn't feel the way they imagined it would. The relationships they neglected can't be resumed. The health they damaged can't simply be restored. The years they traded are gone.

The recognition of impermanence doesn't mean abandoning ambition or refusing to work hard towards meaningful goals. It just invites a lighter grip on them. The journey shapes you as surely as the destination does, but the person you become along the way outlasts any title you ever hold.

The best leaders understand impermanence. They resist sacrificing their people for quarterly earnings that will be forgotten next quarter and they hold cultures steady as targets change.

Attachment to outcomes

The Buddha's second insight concerns *dukkha*: suffering, or more precisely, the dissatisfaction that pervades human experience. This suffering, he taught, arises from *tanha*: craving, attachment, the endless grasping after what we want and pushing away of what we don't. Most of us know them as cravings, attachments and aversions.

Modern work is a factory for generating attachment. We become attached to outcomes: the project that must succeed, the bonus that must be earned. We become attached to identity: I'm a successful executive, a valued contributor, an important person. We become attached to the future: when I achieve this goal, *then* I'll be happy.

The chapters before this one ask organisations and leaders to examine what they have built. *Dukkha* and its source, *tanha*, are different. They live inside the individual, beyond the reach of any policy or performance review. The relationship each of us holds with craving, attachment and aversion is ours to examine and ours to change.

These attachments drive the behaviours that produce burnout. The executive attached to their identity as a high performer works 80-hour weeks to maintain that identity. The worker attached to job security accepts impossible demands rather than risk appearing inadequate. The leader attached to outcomes pushes their team past breaking points to deliver on commitments.

I see this pattern constantly. The leader who can't let a project fail, even when failure is the rational response to changed circumstances. Failure, called early, is the organisation's most useful signal. It shows what the changed circumstances require and frees the resources to respond. The executive who can't accept feedback that challenges their self-image, even when that feedback would make them more effective.

Buddhist practice involves loosening these attachments by holding outcomes more lightly while continuing to care about them. You can work towards goals while remaining free of dependence on their outcome. You can perform your role while knowing you are more than it, and you can prefer certain outcomes without your wellbeing depending on them.

This loosening creates space for better performance. Western psychology calls this 'quality psychological flexibility': the capacity to experience thoughts and feelings fully and still act on what matters. A longitudinal study by Bond and Bunce, tracking 412 workers across 12 months, found that this capacity predicted both mental health and job performance one year forward, independently of job control, personality, and locus of control. The causation ran in one direction. Flexibility shaped outcomes. Randomised controlled trials have since confirmed that building it reduces burnout, increases innovation potential, and improves mental health.

From my experience, the highest performing individuals, from national sporting teams and politicians through to CEOs, understand this intuitively. They care deeply about results and carry that care with equanimity. They compete with full commitment and know the outcome is never entirely theirs to command. A qualitative study of senior leaders completing a ten-week mindfulness program found that leaders reported greater balance and reduced emotional reactivity in the months that followed (Rupprecht et al., 2019).

The Middle Way

The idea of *The Middle Path*, or *The Middle Way*, originates in Buddhism and is simple: there is a pace between punishing yourself and giving up that you can actually sustain.

Modern work culture has largely abandoned *The Middle Way*. The organisational answer to *The Middle Way* is to run people hard, then gesture towards recovery. The pace itself is rarely questioned. *The Middle Way* in work means effort that can be sustained: working hard enough to accomplish meaningful things, but not so hard that we destroy ourselves in the process. It means rhythmic engagement: periods of focused work followed by rest.

Finding *The Middle Way* requires honest assessment of where you are right now. This is harder than it sounds. In 2024, neuroscientist Wolfram Schultz showed that dopamine neurons require progressively greater stimulation to produce the same reward signal. In a chronically high-pressure working environment, the nervous system recalibrates upward. Anna Lembke, Medical Director of Addiction Medicine at Stanford, describes the brain's pleasure and pain pathways as a balance that tilts with sustained overstimulation. The habituated brain reads its own calm as deprivation. This is why rest feels threatening to the people who most need it.

The results speak for themselves. Marc Benioff, CEO of Salesforce, integrates practices like meditation into his leadership and company culture, balancing aggressive business growth with employee wellbeing, while avoiding overwork. He credits these principles for fostering empathy, ethical decision-making, and innovation that lasts.

Novak Djokovic, holder of a record 24 Grand Slam singles titles and widely regarded as the greatest tennis player of his era, credits daily meditation and mindfulness for his mental resilience and balanced approach to elite competition. He emphasises recovery and moderation in training and has built a career on the principle that sustainable performance requires sustainable preparation.

These examples show how balance supports excellence across sport and high-stakes leadership. *The Middle Way* is based on doing what matters in ways that can be sustained.

The lost art of enough

Buddhist practice cultivates *santutthi*: contentment, the capacity to be satisfied with what one has. Importantly, *santutthi* doesn't represent resignation or passive acceptance of injustice. It's the wisdom to recognise when striving has become suffering, and when pursuing more has become an obstacle to wellbeing and performance.

Contemporary business culture doesn't make contentment easy. The signals around us, from performance metrics to social comparison to quarterly targets, tend to emphasise what's next rather than what's here. There's always another milestone, another benchmark. The question of *Enough?* rarely gets asked, partly because, for many, asking it feels like admitting defeat.

Yet endless striving carries real costs. Energy directed towards perpetual wanting is energy unavailable for living. The promise of future satisfaction can crowd out present engagement. And the behaviours that chase *more* sometimes produce the very exhaustion they were meant to overcome.

Learning to say *enough* is countercultural, but it means recognising a point of sufficiency: this meets my needs; this allows me to live well. Declan Edwards, in *How to Be Happy* (Wiley, 2026), names the four conditions the research identifies as foundational to genuine contentment: autonomy, connection, meaning and rest. These are the inputs. Enough is what you have when they are present.

A compelling example comes from Brian Chesky, CEO of Airbnb. In 2022, after the company's explosive pandemic-era growth and IPO, Chesky deliberately slowed aggressive expansion, recognising the business had reached a point where unchecked scaling might create more problems than it solved. He capped headcount, cut underperforming initiatives, and refocused the business on product quality, profitability, and an employee base he had not burned through. Airbnb posted its first consecutive profitable years in 2023 and 2024, with net income of approximately US$2 billion and US$2.6 billion respectively, after a decade of losses. Chesky chose *enough*. Not less. Not retreat. A deliberate decision that *more* wasn't automatically better.

Right Livelihood

Buddhist philosophy offers a practical framework for living called the Noble Eightfold Path. It covers ethics, attention and wisdom. One element addresses work specifically: *Right Livelihood*, meaning work that does not harm ourselves or others. This concept extends beyond avoiding obviously harmful occupations. It invites us to examine the relationship between work and life, between effort and what that effort is costing us.

Through this lens we might ask whether any work that depletes us serves our deeper interests, regardless of its prestige or compensation. Work that damages health, strains relationships, or erodes our sense of self raises questions worth sitting with, even when it offers rewards and serves purposes.

Right Livelihood points towards work as service: contribution that offers value to the world while allowing the contributor to flourish. It involves matching capabilities to needs, finding meaningful contribution, and maintaining conditions that make sustained contribution possible.

This can sound like idealistic dreaming, particularly for those navigating constraints around income, responsibilities and limited options. Yet many people do find work that serves this description, and the concept offers a useful compass even when the path isn't straightforward.

I've worked with leaders who made significant changes once they examined their work through this lens. Some realised they were in the right work but the wrong organisation. Some realised they were in the right organisation but the wrong role. Some realised they needed to change nothing external but everything internal about how they related to their work. I remember working with a former political leader, an incredible leader, who arrived at these realisations through the lens of *Right Livelihood*. He examined it as a Christian, through the idea of vocation: that work is not merely economic activity but a calling aligned with one's gifts and contribution to the world. He described feeling like a caged eagle, a person whose talents and gifts were being curtailed by the culture and constraints of the organisation around him.

The examination itself is valuable, regardless of what it reveals. Most of us have never, or at least rarely, asked whether our work is sustaining us or slowly taking us apart. Typically, we inherit assumptions about what success looks like and pursue those assumptions without question. When I work with senior leaders and teams, *Right Livelihood* is session one.

The meditation on death

Buddhists practise *maranasati*, or mindfulness of death, as a form of practical wisdom. Acknowledging that life ends has a way of clarifying what matters.

Imagine yourself at the end of your life, looking back. Perhaps you're on a balcony looking back over all of your years. What will have mattered? The extra hours worked, or the time spent with people you love, the experiences that shaped you, and the person you became along the way?

Most of us do not contemplate mortality deliberately. We bump into it in a hospital waiting room or on a flight through turbulence. The Buddhist tradition treats this accidental encounter as too important to leave to chance. When people face mortality directly, their own or that of someone close to them, they often report a shift in perspective. Priorities that seemed urgent reveal themselves differently. The relationship between time and what we spend it on comes into sharper focus.

I experienced this myself when my father passed. In the acknowledgements of this book, I noted that he never wrote a book because he said it would take too much time away from helping his patients. At the end of his life, I don't think he regretted that choice. He knew what mattered to him, and he organised his life accordingly

The question *maranasati* raises is whether such clarity is available before crisis demands it. Whether remembering our finite nature while fully alive might reshape how we work and what we work for.

I'm not suggesting you spend your workdays contemplating mortality. I'm suggesting that occasionally connecting with the reality that your time is limited can bring useful perspective to decisions that otherwise get made on autopilot. The email that feels urgent at 10 pm may feel less urgent when held against the finite hours you have with your family. The career advancement that requires you to sacrifice your health may look different when you remember that your career will end but you will still have to live in your body.

Mindfulness in the boardroom

These contemplative insights translate directly into corporate leadership. In my view, they belong in boardrooms as much as, if not more than, in monasteries.

Mindfulness practice, the deliberate cultivation of present moment awareness, offers leaders a practical tool for clearer perception and wiser decision making. When we practise mindfulness, we're better positioned to see situations accurately, with less distortion from anxiety or wishful thinking. We become more able to perceive what's truly happening in our organisations. We notice gaps between stated values and actual behaviour, our own included.

Regular contemplative practice builds capacity for this clearer seeing. A 2024 systematic review synthesising neuroimaging research across mindfulness and meditation found consistent evidence of neuroplasticity: increased cortical thickness in the prefrontal cortex, reduced amygdala reactivity, and improved connectivity between the regions responsible for emotional regulation and cognitive control (Calderone et al., 2024). The brain, it turns out, responds to contemplative practice the way it responds to any other form of deliberate training. Beyond the neurological benefits, mindfulness creates space for wiser choices. In the pause between stimulus and response, we can choose rather than react. We can consider consequences before making demands.

Summary

The 'great forgetting' that this chapter addresses is about the perspective we've abandoned. Somewhere along the way, some of us stopped remembering that work exists to serve life, that human beings have needs beyond productivity, and that the purpose of economic activity is human flourishing rather than the accumulation of wealth for its own sake. The forgetting happens so gradually that most of us forget that we forgot.

The questions explored in this chapter, around impermanence, attachment, *The Middle Way*, contentment, *Right Livelihood* and mortality, point towards a different relationship with work than the one our culture typically offers. They suggest that the burnout crisis may involve not just structural and economic factors but something deeper: questions about meaning, purpose, and what a life well lived looks like.

These aren't questions with easy answers, and different people will answer them differently. But they're worth exploring as we turn to practical solutions in Part Three.

Better policies matter. Structural changes matter and so does the underlying orientation we bring to work itself.

PART 3

The Phoenix

Building healthy, high-performing cultures

You have seen the scale of the crisis and the systems that create and sustain it. Part 3 is about what you do with that. Leaders who shape healthy cultures recognise their role in designing their team's experience and hold relational health as a professional and moral obligation.

CHAPTER 11

The leader's journey from capacity to care

What do we live for, if it is not to make life less difficult to each other?

—George Eliot, *Middlemarch* (1872)

For a psychologist, my father offered very little advice. He understood that people learn through their own exploration, and he trusted the process enough to leave me to mine. There was one exception I can recall: I asked him once about fulfilment and career choices, and he said simply, 'Do what moves you'.

I spent most of my life only partially understanding that. It sounds like the kind of advice that works better if you don't have a mortgage. But I've come to think it points at something more precise than passion. It points at the question of what, when you encounter it, you *cannot* and *will not* walk past.

For me the answer has always been the same: I can't walk past unkindness. I can't watch a person with power use it to diminish someone without power and file it under 'the cost of business'. I don't have a neutral response to that. I've tried. I'm apparently not built for it. Instead, I'm built to draw attention to injustice and the perpetrator.

This book is a product of that same intolerance, dressed up in research and frameworks because that's what it takes to get organisations to listen. But underneath the data and the frameworks, the driver is much simpler: I believe human beings deserve to go to work and come home undamaged; that leaders have a responsibility to make this possible; and that leaders who can't or won't meet that responsibility shape cultures that damage people, whether they intend to or not. None of this should be a controversial position, but in many organisations it still is.

Before we examine the practical strategies for addressing burnout, we must confront a more fundamental question: Why do so many leaders fail to act even when the evidence of suffering is right in front of them? And if you're a leader reading this, the evidence is now right in front of you.

I've spent over two decades watching leaders navigate workplace crises. Some respond with genuine concern and effective action. Others remain curiously unmoved. The difference has nothing to do with intelligence, experience, or even character in the conventional sense, it lies in a developmental journey that many leaders have never undertaken. A journey from merely having the capacity to understand others to deeply caring about them in ways that inspire behaviour change. Without that journey, every strategy in this book becomes just another initiative that sounds good and changes nothing.

For high-performing leaders, this journey isn't optional. Leaders who skip this developmental work will most likely implement burnout reduction programs in the same way they implement expense reporting systems: technically correct and ultimately ineffective. The journey that changes this moves through the six stages described here (see figure 11.1).

The leader's journey from capacity to care

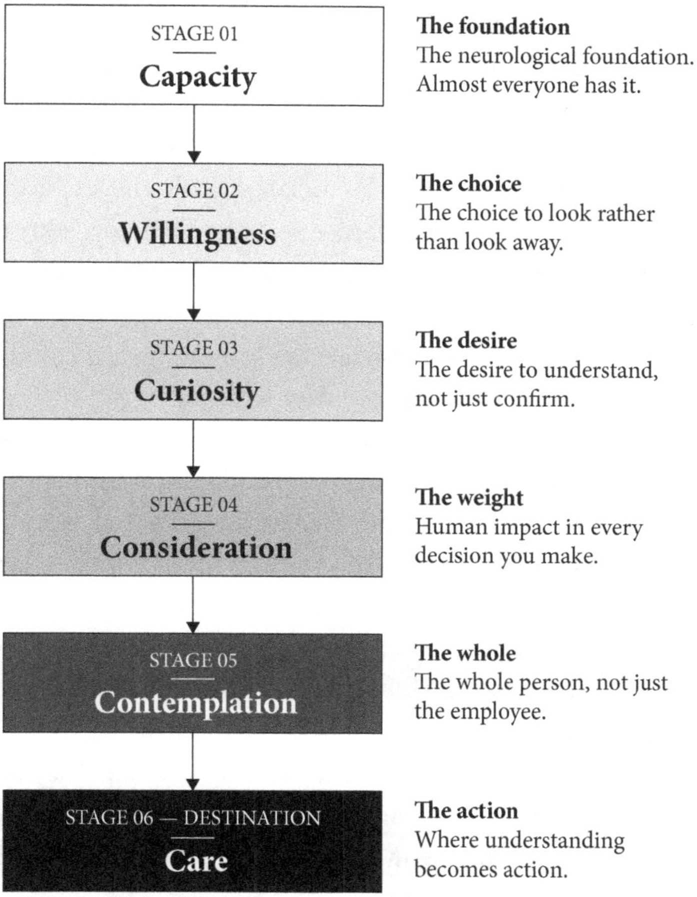

Figure 11.1 The leader's journey from capacity to care — six stages of development

Stage 1: The capacity to see

Encouragingly, the neurological capacity for empathy is nearly universal. Mirror neurons, theory of mind, emotional contagion: these are standard equipment in the human brain. Researchers like Simon Baron Cohen have mapped these systems in detail, and neuroscientists including Andrew Huberman have brought this work to wider audiences.

With rare exceptions involving specific neurological conditions, most people possess the basic machinery for understanding what others experience.

This capacity is remarkable. When you observe someone in pain, the regions of your own brain associated with the experience of pain activate. When you watch someone experience joy, your reward circuits respond. The human brain is literally wired to resonate with the experiences of others.

However, the neuroscience also teaches something less comfortable: capacity alone changes nothing.

Child psychiatrist Bruce Perry, whose work on trauma and development has influenced how we understand the brain, captures this with a phrase worth remembering: 'Genetics is potential; relationships are how potential is expressed'. The same principle applies here. We may be born with neural architecture capable of empathy, but that architecture requires activation through experience, attention and practice. Biology provides the foundation. What we build on it depends on something else entirely.

Far more people could run a marathon than ever do. They have the legs, the lungs, the cardiovascular architecture. Fewer than 1 per cent of people will ever complete one in their lifetime. The gap between those who could and those who do is vast.

The same is true for empathy. Most leaders walk past exhausted employees every day. They sit in meetings with people who are clearly struggling. They receive resignation letters from talented people who cite burnout as their reason for leaving. The information is available. The capacity to process it exists. And often, nothing happens.

Why? Because capacity is merely the first step on a longer journey. Having the ability to understand others says nothing about whether you will use it, direct your attention towards others' experiences, or allow what you perceive to affect your decisions.

I've worked with and consulted to many leaders who believed they were empathetic because they had the capacity for empathy. They could, in theory, understand what their employees experienced. In practice, their calendars were built around what the system rewarded: the visible performance of high performance. Mostly strategy meetings and financial conversations. The calendar of someone who has confused looking serious with being serious.

Stage 2: The willingness to look

The second stage of the journey is willingness. This is the decision to use your capacity, to direct your attention towards what others experience, to look at what's happening around you rather than remaining focused exclusively on tasks and targets.

Willingness sounds simple, however looking at suffering is uncomfortable. When you see that your employees are exhausted, your workplace is damaging people, you face an uncomfortable choice. You must either do something about what you've seen or live with the knowledge that you're choosing not to act.

Many leaders unconsciously choose not to look, because looking would demand a response. They develop what might be called 'strategic blindness', an ability to walk through their organisations without seeing what is happening. They focus more on dashboards and metrics, reducing human experience to numbers that can be analysed without emotional engagement. They schedule back-to-back meetings that leave little time for conversation and build executive bubbles that insulate them from the reality of many of their employees.

This blindness is protective. The human psyche has limited capacity for distress. If you fully absorbed the suffering of everyone around you, you would be overwhelmed. Some filtering is both necessary and healthy.

Some leaders feel the weight of suffering so acutely that awareness itself becomes the problem. I know this from my own experience. Small Giants Academy, founded by Berry Liberman and Danny Almagor, is an incredible education and leadership initiative dedicated to climate action and social justice. Serving on its board, I found myself almost too present to the scale of what needed fixing. Knowing it, sitting with it, carrying it in and out of board meetings, left me at times unable to do anything useful with it at all. Psychologists call this compassion fatigue: the emotional cost of sustained exposure to others' suffering. Interestingly, the capacity for empathy, turned up without regulation, can become its own form of incapacity.

However, some leaders have filtered too much. Some have insulated themselves so thoroughly that they no longer perceive the human reality of their organisations. They make decisions with enormous human consequences while remaining disconnected from those consequences. They speak of workforce optimization, and restructuring, and rightsizing without ever confronting the exhausted faces, the damaged health and destroyed families that these words represent.

Developing willingness means choosing discomfort. It means deliberately removing the filters, stepping out of the executive bubble and creating space in your calendar for real conversations. It means asking questions like: How are you really doing? What's your actual experience of working here? What am I not seeing?

And then it means staying present with the answers, even when those answers are painful to hear. And critically, it means taking action.

One CEO I worked with decided to spend one day a month working alongside frontline employees. Not observing from a distance; *actually doing the work*. The results were dramatic. Within three months she had overhauled policies she previously considered reasonable. The willingness to look had shown her things she couldn't unsee.

One of my favourite clients is Reece Group, the Australian plumbing and bathroom supplies company. Before any executive takes up a position at head office, including the CEO, they spend six months working in a branch. They call it 'branch time'. You serve customers and stock shelves. You learn what it costs to do the work that corporate decisions will eventually affect. By the time leaders reach head office, they carry a deep, lived understanding of branch life. Reece has made the willingness to look part of the architecture itself.

Stage 3: The curiosity to understand

The third stage is curiosity: the genuine desire to understand, not just to confirm what you already believe. While willingness opens the door to perception, perception alone can mislead. Leaders who are willing to look may still misunderstand what they see, interpreting others' experiences through their own assumptions and filters. This is where curiosity comes in.

Curiosity is harder than it sounds. When we observe behaviour that puzzles us, our first instinct is usually to explain it in terms we already understand: the employee who seems disengaged must be lazy; the team that misses deadlines must lack commitment; the person who pushes back on workload must not be a team player.

Psychologists call this the fundamental attribution error (FAE): the tendency to attribute others' behaviour to their character while underestimating situational factors. We see someone struggling and conclude there's something wrong with them, rather than asking what circumstances might be shaping what we observe. It's one of the most consistent findings in social psychology, and one of the most damaging patterns in leadership.

Research published in *Development and Learning in Organizations* found that FAE compounds over time. When leaders repeatedly read situational struggle as character failing, their teams become progressively more cynical and less willing to share knowledge. Each cycle of misattribution makes the next one more likely. A 2024 study in the *Journal of Economic Psychology* found a related pattern: leaders tend to credit good outcomes to themselves while attributing poor group performance to their teams. That scapegoating effect accumulates, eroding trust and learning capacity over time.

FAE is stubborn because it is rewarding. Humans default to instant explanations. They feel satisfying because they confirm our existing worldview. They block true understanding by replacing the complex reality of another person's experience with a simple label that requires no further investigation.

Curiosity means holding your explanations lightly, and recognising that your first interpretation is probably incomplete. Stephen Covey's advice to 'seek first to understand, then to be understood', captures this well. Many leaders do the opposite, entering conversations with their conclusions already formed, and looking for confirmation rather than information. They listen just long enough to find an opening for their own perspective.

Curious leaders ask different questions: they ask about people's *experience* of what happened, not just about the events; they ask about *how people see something*, not just what they think; and they ask about *what would make things work* for them, not just what they need.

They also ask questions of themselves: What am I assuming here? What might I be missing? How would this situation look from a completely different perspective? Why might another person experience this differently than I do?

Curiosity requires intellectual humility, acknowledging that your perspective is limited, that others possess information and insight you lack, and that understanding requires ongoing effort rather than a single conversation. Leaders who believe they already understand something don't bother to investigate further, mistaking their assumptions for knowledge.

In my advisory capacity, I often ask leaders to describe the typical day of their frontline employees. The answers reveal how much or how little curiosity has been operating. Some leaders can describe in detail the challenges, frustrations and small victories their people experience. Others offer vague generalisations that reveal they've never really wondered what life is like for the people who work for them.

Stage 4: The consideration of others

You probably already know your team is under pressure. That's not the same as knowing that the developer on your left has not slept properly in four months because of the project timeline you signed off, or that the account manager three desks away cried in the car park on Tuesday and came back in because she couldn't afford not to. Understanding without consideration is academic. You can know intellectually what others experience without allowing that knowledge to influence your decisions. The fourth stage of the journey is consideration: factoring others' experiences into the choices you make.

I've sat across the table from leaders who were genuinely distressed by what I'd just told them about their team, and who approved the very initiative that caused it. There is often a barrier between reflection and ownership, and while it stands, the same decisions keep getting made.

Consideration is what closes that gap. It means deliberately bringing human impact into decision making. For every significant choice, one question: what will this mean for the people who have to live with it?

This doesn't mean human impact trumps all other factors. Business realities are real, and sometimes difficult decisions are necessary. But consideration means human impact is always part of the equation, always weighted in the balance, never invisible or irrelevant.

The discipline of consideration requires structural support. Most decision-making processes don't include human impact assessment. Business cases include financial projections, risk analyses and implementation timelines. They rarely include systematic consideration of what the decision will mean for the people affected.

Leaders who want to build consideration into their practice can start by adding a simple question to every major decision: Who will be affected by this, and what will their experience be? This single question, asked consistently, can transform how and when decisions are made.

Consideration also requires courage. When you consider human impact, you often discover that expedient decisions have substantial human costs. You then face a choice: ignore what you've discovered or adjust your approach. Many leaders prefer not to consider, because consideration often demands a response.

Importantly, leaders who skip consideration pay a price. Their decisions often generate resistance they didn't anticipate. Their initiatives fail because they overlooked how people would respond. Consideration is both ethical and practical.

Stage 5: The contemplation of lives

My clinical psychotherapist father used to speak of two broad types of people: those who naturally contemplate the inner lives of others, and those who do not. He observed this throughout his working life, and the distinction stayed with me.

Peter Fonagy's concept of reflective functioning describes the capacity to understand others through their inner mental states: what they feel and what drives them. Research confirms that people vary substantially in this capacity. Some are naturally drawn towards what Fonagy calls rich mentalising, noticing what others carry beneath the surface. Others read behaviour at face value.

Trapnell and Campbell's research established that this reflective disposition is a stable, individual difference. Some people have it by nature, while others build it through practice. Part of my work, and the work of this book, is to help others build it.

Consideration often remains shallow because it focuses on immediate impacts. The fifth stage, contemplation, goes deeper. It involves reflecting on the whole lives of the people we lead: not just their work performance or immediate circumstances, but their broader existence. This may sound strange in a business context. Why should leaders contemplate the lives of their employees beyond what's relevant to work?

The answer is that people don't segment as neatly as organisational charts suggest. The employee you see at work is the same person who goes home to a family, who carries hopes and fears that shape everything they do. Work affects life in ways most organisations have never accounted for. Decisions that look sensible in isolation can create harm when the larger context is invisible.

The crisis at home and the crisis at work are rarely separate. Australian Bureau of Statistics figures show family and domestic violence offenders rose by 8 per cent in 2024–25, the largest annual increase since national recording began. These statistics describe people who arrive at work every morning.

Contemplation is the practice of holding the whole person in mind. It means considering not just deliverables but circumstances; wondering about what someone goes home to, what pressures they carry, and what aspirations they hold. Seeing them as a complete human being rather than a function.

This awareness transforms how you lead. When you know that someone is caring for an ageing parent, you understand their distraction differently. When you know that someone is navigating health challenges, you can adjust your expectations accordingly, and when you understand the life context within which work happens, you make better decisions about how to support people in doing their work.

Buddhist philosophy speaks of seeing *with the eyes of compassion.* This doesn't mean being soft or avoiding difficult conversations. It means perceiving accurately, without the distortions that come from treating people as instruments.

Contemplation takes time. It requires slowing down enough to actually see people, to wonder about their experience, to reflect on what their lives are like.

The most common response when I raise this with leaders is: 'I don't have time'. I've heard it often enough to take it seriously, and to question it equally often. Most leaders have more discretionary time than they claim. The real question is what they have decided it is for. Contemplation rarely appears on those lists because most leaders have never consciously decided that understanding the people they lead is a legitimate use of their time. Once they do, the time tends to appear.

Research by Gloria Mark at the University of California, Irvine, found that the average time people spend focused on a single screen before switching dropped from two and a half minutes in 2004 to just 47 seconds in recent years (Mark, 2023). The digital environment we inhabit is designed to fragment attention, and leaders aren't immune to these forces. Between the pace of modern organisations, the volume of competing demands, and the constant pull of notifications and devices, the conditions for contemplation have become scarce.

Writer John Koenig coined a word for a feeling most of us have had but never named: *sonder*. The realisation that every person you pass is living a life as vivid and complicated as your own.

In my practice I use a simple framework built on this idea: Stop. Wonder. Sonder. (See figure 11.2.)

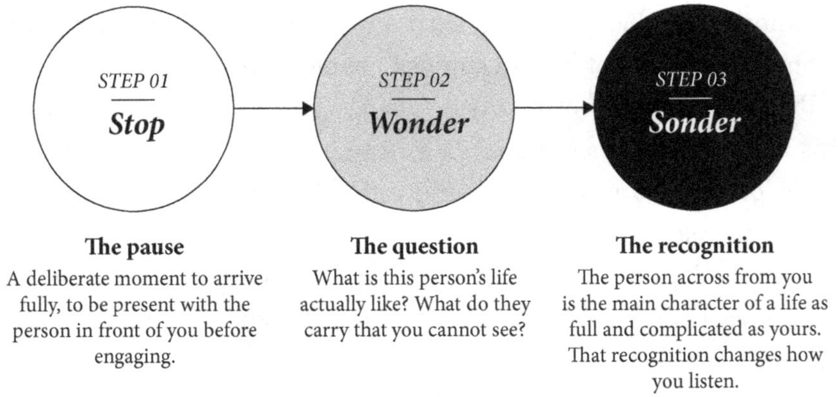

Figure 11.2 Stop. Wonder. Sonder. A three-step practice for presence

Stop is the pause. Wonder is the question. Sonder is what the question opens up.

The person across the table from you is the main character of a life as full and complicated as yours. Holding that recognition, even briefly, changes how you listen and what you see.

The conditions for this kind of attention are harder to find than they should be.

The pull towards distraction is environmental and it requires your attention. Fortunately, the practice of contemplation can be cultivated. Some leaders build it into their morning routine, spending a few minutes thinking about specific people they will interact with that day. Others take contemplative walks, using the time to reflect on their team members' circumstances. My advice is to keep notes about your people, of their whole lives behind their work identity.

When you don't make space for this, urgency rules. The fuller picture of your people stays invisible: what they carry, what their lives actually look like. Then you make decisions about people you only partially know. Which, as discussed, makes things easier. Just not right.

Stage 6: The care that changes everything

The journey from capacity to contemplation leads finally to care. Care is where understanding becomes action and employee wellbeing becomes a concrete commitment to do something about it.

Care is a practice, though feelings often accompany it. It is the consistent choice to act in ways that serve the wellbeing of others, even when other options are easier or more immediately expedient.

Professional care, its design, its expression as investment and accountability, and what distinguishes it from personal care, is examined in depth in Chapter 9. Here it appears as something different: the destination of a personal journey rather than a framework to implement.

In practice, it might mean pushing back on unreasonable deadlines because of what those deadlines will cost people, or questioning initiatives that could harm teams, even when those initiatives come from above. It might mean creating boundaries and buffers that protect people from organisational chaos.

Care also shows up in smaller moments. Someone mentions their mother is unwell on Monday. You ask about her on Wednesday. Daniel Coyle's research in *The Culture Code* shows why these small moments carry disproportionate weight. He calls them belonging cues: signals that tell people they are safe, valued, and that the relationship will continue. Their power peaks in moments of vulnerability. The check-in when someone seems quieter than usual. The adjusted deadline when life gets heavy. These signals determine whether people trust the people they work for.

Care is demanding because it requires energy and attention that could be directed elsewhere and sometimes creates tension with organisational pressures.

The clearest marker of professional care, as distinct from its performance, is altruism: the willingness to do something that costs you something for the benefit of the person you lead. Done consistently, as the default orientation towards how authority is used. Leaders who care professionally are recognisable in 360 reports and reference checks through the specific memories they leave: moments when they chose the harder path because it was better for someone else.

Care is difficult to perform inauthentically over time. People tend to sense whether their leaders care about them or are going through the motions. This is why the earlier stages of the journey matter. Care that flows from capacity, willingness, curiosity, consideration and contemplation feels different from care deployed as a management technique.

Care is the culmination of the journey, but the journey continues. The pressures of organisational life naturally pull towards transactions over relationships and task completion over attention to the people completing them. Choosing care amid these pressures becomes easier with practice but rarely becomes automatic.

Where are you on the journey?

The journey from capacity to care isn't linear. You may find yourself at different stages with different people or in different circumstances. Under pressure, you may regress to earlier stages. With practice, you can develop greater consistency.

Consider these questions:

1. **On capacity:** Do you believe you have the ability to understand what others experience? Have you ever developed this ability through deliberate practice, or do you assume it operates automatically?
2. **On willingness:** How much of your attention goes to understanding your people versus managing your tasks. When did you last ask someone on your team how things really are and stay for the full answer?
3. **On curiosity:** When someone's behaviour puzzles you, do you investigate or make assumptions?
4. **On consideration:** In your last major decision, did you explicitly consider human impact?
5. **On contemplation:** Do you know the life circumstances of the people you lead?
6. **On care:** Would your people say you care about them?

The journey from capacity to care is the foundation upon which everything else in this book rests. Without this developmental work, the strategies and frameworks that follow become empty procedures. With it, they mean something.

When I got it very wrong

I carried the wrong model into my consulting career. The turning point came with a fintech startup where I was advising the founder. Let's call him Tom. He was brilliant, one of the most innovative thinkers

I've encountered. He had convinced himself, and initially convinced me, that culture was built exclusively through presence. If you weren't in the office, you weren't contributing. If you wanted flexibility, you weren't serious. The work was what mattered, and the work happened in one place, together, intensively.

I supported this view. I helped Tom articulate why co-location was essential. I helped him design an office environment that would maximise interaction. I helped him build a culture where being physically present was the baseline expectation and everything else was suspect.

The company grew quickly. Tom's vision was compelling and the product was strong. But something was breaking underneath. The people who thrived were the people whose lives permitted total dedication. Young, unattached, willing to make work their entire identity. Everyone else struggled and eventually left.

A senior engineer, someone with 15 years of experience and genuine expertise, resigned after seven months. She told Tom she couldn't sustain the pace with a child at home. She needed flexibility that the culture wouldn't provide. Tom's response, which I observed directly, was to wish her well and note that maybe the company wasn't the right fit. He wasn't cruel about it. He was matter of fact.

I nodded along. I still believed the philosophy.

What changed my mind was tracking the outcomes over time. Tom's company continued growing, but it developed a reputation. The talent pool narrowed. The people willing to accept the terms were increasingly a particular type: young, male, unencumbered, wired for intensity, homogeneous in ways that limited perspective. The diversity of thought that drives innovation was disappearing, replaced by a monoculture of workaholics.

Meanwhile, I began working with companies that took different approaches. These companies achieved high performance through flexibility, and built diverse teams by designing for different working styles and circumstances.

The results were better. Much better.

The perspective in this book didn't come naturally to me. I had to unlearn a worldview that felt like truth and that had, for a time, served me well. I had to admit that leaders I had admired and advised had been wrong, and that I had been wrong alongside them.

If you're reading this and recognising your own assumptions, you're not alone. Many of us were trained by cultures that equated suffering with seriousness and intensity with effectiveness. Questioning those equations feels like questioning our own histories and the people who shaped them.

I still believe in excellence and high standards and rigorous accountability. The path to all three, the kind that lasts, runs through care. The fintech company continued to grow after I stopped advising it. Tom's vision was strong enough to carry the business forward for years. But the talent pool narrowed. The people who stayed were the ones the conditions had selected. The conditions were measuring endurance. From the outside, endurance and excellence can look identical. The senior engineer who left to accommodate a child at home would have been, by any serious measure, more valuable over ten years than the three people hired to replace her. Tom never saw it that way. I think he still doesn't. That is the cost of a model that mistakes survival for excellence. You stop being able to see the people you are losing because the people who remain confirm everything you already believe.

The six-stage model describes something the human brain is designed for.

CHAPTER 12

Honest assessment

Above all, don't lie to yourself.
—Fyodor Dostoevsky, *The Brothers Karamazov* (1880)

Before you can solve a problem, you must see it clearly. And one of the greatest obstacles to tackling burnout is the difficulty of seeing it clearly: in ourselves, in our teams, and in our organisations.

Burnout hides. It masquerades as normal stress, as temporary busy periods, as the inevitable price of ambitious work. It whispers that everyone feels this way, that asking for help is weakness, and pushing through is what successful people do. By the time burnout announces itself unmistakeably, through resignations or health crises, it has usually been building for months, if not years.

The frameworks that follow provide honest assessment at every level: individual, team and organisational. Use them as ongoing practices rather than one-time diagnostics; burnout is a condition you must continuously monitor and address.

Beyond the engagement survey

Most organisations attempt, mistakenly, to measure employee wellbeing through engagement surveys. The problem with engagement surveys is that they are not built for what we're trying to detect. Typically they're run annually, which misses the burnout dynamics that develop over weeks and months. For reporting purposes, many surveys aggregate data in ways that hide what's happening at team level. They rely on self-reporting from employees who have learned, often from experience, that honesty in a survey doesn't always go the way you would hope. And they measure engagement, which is a positive state, rather than burnout, which is a distinct and negative condition that can coexist with residual engagement long enough to fool the instrument completely.

Only 42 per cent of burned-out workers tell their manager about their burnout (Eagle Hill Consulting, 2025). Of those who do, 42 per cent say their manager takes no action. The channels that should surface the problem are not functioning, and a once-a-year survey won't fix that.

What works is messier and more human. It requires multiple data sources and leaders who are genuinely trying to understand what is happening in their teams.

It also requires psychological safety. Amy Edmondson, professor at Harvard Business School, describes it as the shared belief that speaking up or admitting uncertainty will not result in punishment or humiliation (Edmondson, 1999). Where it exists, people tell you what is actually happening. Where it is absent, they tell you what they think you want to hear.

In many organisations, engagement survey scores feed directly into bonus calculations. When that happens, leaders have a financial incentive to keep scores looking healthy. In some instances, the survey stops measuring engagement and starts measuring the leader's ability to manage their own rating. Just another hiding spot for burnout.

The three dimensions of burnout

The Maslach Burnout Inventory, the most widely validated assessment instrument for burnout, identifies three dimensions that together constitute the syndrome: exhaustion, cynicism and inefficacy (Maslach et al., 1996).

Exhaustion is the most visible dimension: the sense of being depleted, of having little left to give. This is what most people think of when they think of burnout: tiredness that doesn't resolve with normal rest. For many it carries something else alongside the tiredness: a low grade dread. The alarm going off and the body resisting before the mind has caught up. Some people report a kind of restlessness that sits underneath the exhaustion and makes real rest feel just out of reach. Exhaustion affects energy and the capacity for sustained effort.

Cynicism, sometimes called depersonalisation, involves increasing psychological distance from work. The cynical worker may have stopped investing emotionally or believing that their work matters. They may continue to perform tasks even while having withdrawn their engagement. Cynicism can manifest as negativity and sarcasm, or scepticism towards organisational initiatives.

Gallup's 2025 State of the Global Workplace report covers nearly a quarter of a million workers across 160 nations. It found that 62 per cent of the global workforce, a clear majority, is not engaged at work. A further 15 per cent are actively working against their organisation's interests. Global engagement fell to 21 per cent in 2024, the sharpest decline since the pandemic. These are the Maslach cynicism numbers, at scale.

Inefficacy is the sense of reduced personal accomplishment. The feeling that one is no longer doing good work or making meaningful contributions. Even when objective performance remains adequate, the burned-out worker may experience their value as diminishing. What this feels like in practice is a quiet loss. Work that once felt purposeful starts to feel meaningless.

Harvard researchers Teresa Amabile and Steven Kramer analysed nearly 12 000 diary entries from workers across seven companies. The single most powerful driver of motivation at work, above recognition or rewards, is the sense of making progress in meaningful work. Inefficacy is what happens when that sense is lost. The feeling of moving forward disappears.

All three dimensions are typically present in clinical burnout, though any one of them warrants attention. A worker who is exhausted but not yet cynical may be on a trajectory towards burnout. A worker who is cynical but still energetic has likely sustained some damage that could eventually manifest as exhaustion. The dimensions often represent progressive stages of a single process.

Individual warning signs

Assessment at the individual level involves attention to signs that people sometimes minimise or explain away. The symptoms can be physical, cognitive, emotional or behavioural. See table 12.1.

Table 12.1 Burnout indicators in the individual

1. Physical symptoms	• persistent fatigue that doesn't resolve with sleep • frequent illness due to compromised immune function • headaches • gastrointestinal problems or muscle tension without clear medical cause • disrupted sleep patterns including both insomnia and excessive sleeping
2. Cognitive symptoms	• difficulty concentrating or making decisions • forgetfulness and mental fog • reduced creativity and problem-solving capacity • difficulty seeing the big picture or planning strategically
3. Emotional symptoms	• increased irritability and emotional volatility • feelings of dread about work • detachment from colleagues and clients • loss of satisfaction in accomplishments that previously brought joy
4. Behavioural symptoms	• withdrawal from social interaction • procrastination and avoidance • increased use of alcohol or other substances • neglect of self-care including exercise, nutrition and rest

None of these symptoms is definitive on its own. All of them can arise from causes other than burnout. However, patterns of multiple symptoms, persisting over time and specifically connected to work, warrant serious assessment and potential intervention.

Measuring culture: The only way to know

It still surprises me how little most organisations invest in knowing the state of their own culture. Leaders who would never make a financial decision without data make cultural decisions on gut feeling and anecdote.

McKinsey's Organisational Health Index, tracking more than 1500 companies across 100 countries, identified organisational health as the strongest predictor of long-term value creation. Companies in the top quartile deliver three times the shareholder returns of those in the bottom quartile. Culture is the most important driver of organisational health and consequent performance.

Leaders routinely measure financial performance, operational efficiency, customer satisfaction and market share. They would never claim to understand these dimensions of their business based on gut feeling or casual observation. Yet when it comes to culture, the very thing that determines whether all other metrics can be achieved in ways that last, many leaders rely on intuition and wishful thinking.

This has to change. Culture can be measured as rigorously as any other organisational variable. And it must be measured, because the alternative is flying blind into terrain that destroys both people and performance.

In 2019, Australia's Royal Commission into Misconduct in the Banking, Superannuation and Financial Services Industry delivered its final report. Commissioner Kenneth Hayne had examined how some of the country's most trusted financial institutions had systematically failed the people they existed to serve. The Commission found a culture failure at the root of it. Boards could not see it because they had no instrument to measure it.

At The Culture Institute of Australia, we developed CultureHealth™ to address this gap. It is an independent diagnostic that takes employees three to five minutes to complete and delivers a single verified score to the executive and board: the CultureHealth Score, from 0 to 100.

CultureHealth™ measures four dimensions:

1. **Sentiment** captures how people genuinely experience the overall culture.
2. **Safety** measures whether people can speak and challenge without fear, across four sub-dimensions drawn from the psychological safety research of Timothy Clark, author of *The 4 Stages of Psychological Safety : Inclusion Safety, Learner Safety, Contributor Safety, and Challenger Safety.*
3. **Conduct** identifies whether harmful patterns are present across the organisation.
4. **Customer Centricity** measures whether the culture enables or obstructs the outcomes it exists to deliver.

Each dimension was designed with direct reference to Australia's regulatory and governance requirements, including APRA's CPG 220, ASIC's conduct and culture framework, and Safe Work Australia's psychosocial hazards obligations.

The assessment also captures Culture Orientation: the dominant styles shaping how an organisation collaborates and responds to challenge. The score reflects health. Orientation reflects character.

A team can be hitting its targets while the culture beneath them is moving towards failure. By the time the performance metrics register the problem, the damage is usually well advanced. CultureHealth™ surfaces cultural risk early, when the cost of addressing it is lowest.

The safety prerequisite

Honest assessment becomes difficult without psychological safety. If people worry that reporting burnout will be held against them, in performance reviews, promotion decisions or informal judgements, they may not report it. The data may suggest everything is fine while the underlying reality is quite different.

Creating safety is less about policy declaration and more about demonstrated behaviour over time. Leaders build safety by responding constructively to difficult news, expressing appreciation when people raise concerns, acting on the information, and avoiding any perception of punishing messengers. Safety erodes when bad news is unwelcome and when those who only bring good news seem to be favoured.

You may be trying to build psychological safety for your team while operating in an environment where you yourself don't feel safe. Your own manager may punish bad news, and the broader culture may reward those who suppress problems. You may be absorbing exactly the kind of pressure you're trying to shield your team from.

This is one of the hardest positions in leadership, and many readers will recognise it.

You can't guarantee that what you create for your team will be extended to you. What you can do is create a pocket of safety within your sphere of influence, even if that pocket exists within a larger culture that operates differently.

Your team can experience psychological safety with you, regardless of what exists above you. This is exhausting, important work. The people who report to you will remember what it felt like to work for someone who created space for honesty, even when that space was hard fought.

A useful reflection: When was the last time someone on your team shared something you didn't want to hear? If this is difficult to recall, there may be an opportunity to strengthen the conditions for honest communication. The assessment challenge is often less about getting honest answers and more about creating conditions where honest answers feel safe.

Team level indicators

Assessment at the team level requires attention to collective patterns that may not be visible in individual data. Both excessive conflict and complete absence of conflict can indicate problems. The informal channels that healthy teams maintain, the quick messages, the casual check-ins, the spontaneous collaboration, these often dry up when burnout takes hold. Some team members consistently take on more than others, while others disengage. This unevenness often reflects both individual burnout and team dysfunction. See table 12.2.

Table 12.2 Burnout indicators at team level

1. Meeting quality deteriorates	• meetings have become perfunctory • people seem disengaged • conflict has increased or disappeared entirely
2. Communication patterns shift	• email response times lengthen • messages become more terse or defensive • people stop sharing information proactively via quick messages, casual check-ins, spontaneous collaboration
3. Workload distribution becomes uneven	• some team members take on more responsibility while others disengage
4. Recovery capacity diminishes	• After intense periods, healthy teams bounce back. Burned-out teams remain depleted. If your team used to recover quickly from crunch periods and no longer does, take notice
5. Psychological safety erodes	• people stop raising concerns, admitting mistakes or asking for help • ideas that would once have been shared are kept private • the collective intelligence of the team decreases because information stops flowing

Digital signal detection: The data you already have

Most organisations have access to early warning signals they may not recognise as such. The digital tools that enable modern work also generate data about how people are working, and patterns in that data can reveal burnout risk before self-reports or visible symptoms would.

This can be seen as surveillance by the more cynical employees, but it's not. It is simply using aggregate, anonymised patterns to understand organisational health, much like a physician uses vital signs rather than waiting for acute symptoms before taking action.

Email and messaging metadata

Patterns in email and messaging data carry significant information about team health. The relevant data is usage: timing and network patterns. Message content plays no part in this. This data includes:

- **Activity outside normal working hours.** This shows what percentage of communication occurs after hours and whether that percentage is growing.
- **Response time patterns.** These reveal whether people seem constantly available in ways that indicate difficulty disconnecting.
- **Communication volume relative to output.** This may indicate coordination challenges or inefficient processes that are wearing people down.
- **Network isolation.** Individuals becoming disconnected from team communication networks can precede burnout. This may be detectable before the person explicitly signals distress.

Burnout is kryptonite for high performance. Getting on the front foot before it takes hold is both possible and practical.

Calendars

Calendars reveal how time is actually being spent, often in ways that surprise those spending it. Meeting load beyond 40 per cent of working hours makes time for focused work critically insufficient since each meeting generates an estimated 69 minutes of preparation and administration (ViewSonic, cited by Flowtrace, 2025). An employee whose calendar shows five hours of meetings on a given day may actually be losing nine or ten hours to meeting-related activity.

Recommendation

Consider what those meetings produce: 40 per cent of workers receive no follow-up notes or action items after meetings end (Calendly, 2024), and 54 per cent of attendees leave unclear about next steps or responsibilities (Atlassian, 2024). When the total meeting burden exceeds available working hours and most of that time produces nothing, there is only one place the actual work can happen: nights, weekends and the hours that were supposed to belong to recovery. I strongly recommend tracking the real number, not just what appears on the calendar.

The quiet cracking diagnostic

We discussed quiet cracking earlier: less dramatic but equally damaging disengagement and burnout. The following questions help identify it by focusing on change over time rather than current state:

1. Compared to six months ago, do you look forward to work more, the same, or less?
2. Do you feel more, the same, or less connected to your team?
3. Do you feel more, the same, or less confident in your ability to do your job well?

4. Do you find it easier, the same, or harder to concentrate on complex tasks?
5. Do you feel more, the same, or less proud of your work?

Consistently negative trajectories across these questions may indicate quiet cracking even if absolute levels seem acceptable. Someone who is less engaged than they were, but still adequately engaged, may be on a concerning path.

Discretionary effort assessment

Discretionary effort, work beyond minimum requirements, is often the first casualty of quiet cracking. These questions help assess it:

1. When was the last time you voluntarily suggested an improvement to how your team works?
2. When was the last time you helped a colleague with something outside your formal responsibilities?
3. When was the last time you learned something new related to your work because you were curious, not because it was required?
4. When was the last time you stayed with a problem beyond what was strictly necessary because you wanted to solve it well?

Answers of 'weeks' or 'months' rather than days may suggest declining discretionary effort. This decline might not appear in productivity metrics until it becomes significant, but it indicates that the reserves enabling high performance are depleting.

Organisational red flags

At the organisational level, certain patterns indicate systemic burnout risk. See table 12.3 (overleaf).

Table 12.3 Burnout indicators at organisational level

1. Turnover patterns	Rising voluntary departures, particularly among high performers. Exit interview data, if collected and analysed honestly, often reveals burnout as a contributing factor.
2. Absence data	Increased sick leave, particularly short-term absences. Patterns of Monday or Friday absences may indicate people are extending weekends to recover from work.
3. Engagement survey trends	Survey trends matter more than absolute scores. A steady decline over multiple survey periods indicates systemic problems even if current scores seem acceptable.
4. Performance inconsistency	Results become unpredictable. Deadlines slip. Quality varies. Teams that used to deliver become unreliable.
5. Internal mobility decreases	A decline in internal mobility may indicate that people lack the energy to pursue growth opportunities, or are preparing to leave

The assessment conversation

Data and frameworks are necessary but insufficient. At some point, you must have listening-led conversations with people about their actual experience. These conversations require skill that many leaders have never developed:

1. **Before the conversation, create conditions for honesty.** Choose a private setting. Allow enough time that the conversation doesn't feel rushed. Be clear about the purpose: you want to understand their experience so you can support them better.
2. **Prepare yourself emotionally.** You may hear things that are difficult. You may hear that decisions you made contributed to someone's suffering. Commit in advance to listening without defensiveness.

3. **During the conversation, start with explicit reassurance.** Whatever you share with me won't affect my view of your capability or your future here. I'm asking because I care about your wellbeing and because I want to help if I can.
4. **Ask open questions and then be quiet.** How are you really doing? What's your real, everyday experience of working here? What am I not seeing?
5. **Listen more than you speak.** Resist the urge to explain, defend, or immediately problem solve.
6. **Watch for minimisation.** People often downplay their struggles, especially with their managers. If someone says they're fine but their body language or tone suggests otherwise, gently probe further.

What not to say

'Everyone is under pressure right now' minimises their experience. 'Have you tried meditation?' redirects from their experience to your advice. 'I'm sure it will get better after this deadline' asks them to endure current suffering for a future that may not materialise. 'You're one of our best people, I need you firing on all cylinders' communicates that their value is conditional on performance.

What to say instead

'That makes complete sense given what you've been dealing with' validates without minimising. 'What would be most helpful right now?' invites them to identify what they need. 'What can I take off your plate, even temporarily?' signals concrete willingness to act. 'I'm glad you told me. This is important for me to know' rewards the disclosure.

Act on what you learn, even partially. Nothing destroys trust faster than asking for feedback and then doing nothing with it. Even if you can't solve everything, do something visible that demonstrates you took the conversation seriously. Follow up. Check in again within a reasonable time frame.

Making assessment ongoing

Assessment is a continuous practice that must be built into how you lead:

- **Weekly.** Notice energy levels in your team. Who seems depleted? Who seems disengaged? What has changed since last week?
- **Monthly.** Have explicit wellbeing conversations with each direct report. These don't need to be long, but they need to happen consistently.
- **Quarterly.** Review aggregate data: turnover, absence patterns, engagement indicators. Look for trends rather than snapshots.
- **Annually.** Conduct comprehensive culture assessment (e.g. culture sentiment, health, conduct, psych safety). Compare results to previous years. Identify areas of progress and areas of concern.

The trick is catching problems early, when intervention is still possible, rather than waiting for crisis to force attention.

Assessment requires courage: looking at realities you might prefer to avoid, hearing truths that implicate your own decisions, and accepting responsibility for conditions you may have contributed to creating.

Assessment is also the beginning of change. What you see clearly, you can address. What remains hidden continues to cause damage.

You can't lead what you're not prepared to see.

CHAPTER 13

Below threshold

> When a prince's personal conduct is correct, his government is effective without the issuing of orders. If his personal conduct is not correct, he may issue orders, but they will not be followed.
>
> —Confucius, *Analects* 13:6

Most of the conversations I have with leaders about their team's burnout start in the wrong place, with the team. The more useful questions are closer to home. They're about you.

A depleted leader cannot guide others through recovery. A leader working at a pace that cannot be sustained builds a culture that reflects it. What you carry into the work shapes what the work becomes.

Leadership begins with self-leadership: your own relationship to work, your own patterns of stress and recovery. The transformation of organisations almost always starts with the transformation of the person leading them. The better CEOs and leaders I've worked with have known this and done something about it. Others have made themselves conveniently unavailable.

The awareness gap

Research by organisational psychologist Tasha Eurich found that while 95 per cent of people believe they're self-aware, only 10 to 15 per cent actually meet the criteria (Eurich, 2018). The gap is even wider for leaders.

The more power a person holds, the more likely they are to overestimate their own competence, a pattern documented consistently across decades of leadership research and most recently confirmed in Eurich's own work with thousands of leaders across multiple industries.

Leaders who rate themselves substantially higher than their bosses do are more than six times more likely to derail in their careers. Working with colleagues who lack self-awareness can cut a team's chances of success in half and the paradox is that the less self-aware someone is, the more confident they tend to be in their own judgement.

Then there is the question of how work fits into your life:

- How much of your sense of self is tied to your professional identity?
- When you imagine losing your job, do you also imagine losing yourself or self-confidence?
- Can you describe who you are without reference to what you do?

Psychologists use the term 'enmeshment' to describe what happens when the boundaries between a person and their work become so blurred that individual identity loses importance. Deloitte's 2025 global survey found that 46 per cent of millennials and 41 per cent of Gen Z workers say their primary job is central to their identity, second only to friends and family. A 2014 Gallup poll found 55 per cent of all US workers get a sense of identity from their job, rising to 70 per cent for college graduates (Riffkin, 2014).

Overidentification with role is one of the most dangerous patterns for leaders. When work becomes everything, any threat to work becomes existential. Performance anxiety escalates because every project feels like a referendum on your worth. Boundaries dissolve because you can't set limits on something that defines who you are.

The consequences are severe. Decades of research on involuntary job loss consistently link it to increased rates of depression, anxiety and substance abuse, with the effects worsening the longer unemployment continues. Research published in the journal *Psychological Medicine* found that men made involuntarily redundant were significantly more depressed than their employed peers at six month follow up, with a quarter of those still unemployed crossing the threshold into clinical depression (Eales, 1988; Bolton & Oatley, 1987). A separate 2014 Gallup poll found that unemployed Americans were more than twice as likely to say they had been treated for depression as those holding full-time jobs (Crabtree, 2014). A Pew Research Center survey conducted in January 2021 found that 56 per cent of unemployed Americans reported experiencing more emotional or mental health issues, such as anxiety or depression, since losing their job (Parker et al., 2021).

Understand the contagion effect

Self-awareness is important because leadership stress cascades. When leaders are anxious, their teams often become anxious. When leaders operate from scarcity and fear, they can inadvertently create cultures of scarcity and fear.

This contagion operates through multiple channels: the explicit communications that convey stress, the implicit signals of tone and body language, the decisions made under pressure that create pressure for others. Teams absorb their leaders' emotional states whether leaders intend to transmit them or not.

Research by Amit Goldenberg at Harvard Business School shows that negative sentiments spread faster than positive ones, particularly when expressed by those in prominent positions. Anger and frustration intensify as they move through groups. The evolutionary logic holds: fear and anger activate the fight or flight response in the amygdala. Positive emotions move more slowly and with less force.

A 2001 review of over 300 studies by Roy Baumeister and colleagues found that negative events carry greater psychological weight than positive ones of equal magnitude, and humans attend to threats first. Brock Bastian at the University of Melbourne found that shared pain bonds groups with unusual speed and durability. A leader broadcasting anxiety triggers something ancient in the people around them, and the group organises around the threat signal.

The contagion moves in the other direction too, and with deliberate effort. The asymmetry matters: positive climates require intentional building. Negative ones arrive without invitation. The best leaders understand the asymmetry and work with it. They maintain equanimity, that steady composure under pressure, and help their teams find it. They model work at a pace that can be sustained and make those patterns available to others.

What you model matters more than what you say

What leaders do matters more than what they say. The midnight emails override the talk about work–life balance and visible exhaustion overrides wellness initiatives. You can't credibly tell your team to look after themselves while visibly not looking after yourself. Or rather, you can, but nobody will believe you.

Research confirms this gap between intention and behaviour. In her book *Over Work: Transforming the Daily Grind in the Quest for a Better Life*, journalist Brigid Schulte describes a project with the behavioural design firm ideas42 that investigated workplace norms around overwork. Leaders at many organisations expressed a desire for better work–life balance, yet they themselves were often among the worst offenders: texting at 9 pm, emailing over the weekend and rarely taking holidays.

Research by Liuba Belkin at Lehigh University confirms that employees take their cues from observed managerial behaviours. Sending an after-hours email, even without explicitly requiring an immediate response, creates a perception that such availability is expected. These perceptions lead to higher levels of emotional exhaustion, regardless of the actual time spent on work emails after hours.

Modelling work that can be sustained means working in ways that can be sustained, and doing so visibly: leaving at reasonable hours and being open about it, taking holidays and disconnecting, acknowledging limits and asking for help when needed. Belkin's research suggests that if employees observe their manager setting firm boundaries between work and non-work domains, such as not responding to emails after 8 pm, they are more likely to follow suit.

This modelling can be particularly challenging for leaders who reached their positions through patterns that couldn't be sustained. They may believe that their success required their sacrifice, and unconsciously expect similar sacrifice from others. Shifting this pattern involves examining beliefs about what success demands and whether those beliefs are serving anyone well.

I've found that leaders who model healthy patterns often discover something that is predictable but is still, for many, surprising: their performance improves rather than declines. The focused hours produce more value than the exhausted hours. The rested mind makes better decisions than the depleted one.

Research by Alhola and Polo-Kantola, published in *Neuropsychiatric Disease and Treatment*, identifies attentiveness, working memory, alertness, judgement and decision making as the first casualties of inadequate sleep. A landmark 1997 study by Drew Dawson and Kathryn Reid, published in *Nature*, quantifies the scale of that loss: a person who has been awake for 17 hours performs at a cognitive level equivalent to someone with a blood alcohol concentration of 0.05 per cent. The leader who invests in recovery brings materially greater capability to every decision, conversation and judgement call they face.

There is one finding in workplace research that should change how every leader thinks about their role. Gallup's analysis of 27 million employees across 2.7 million work units in 2015, reaffirmed in 2025, found that managers account for at least 70 per cent of the variance in team engagement. The difference between an engaged team and a disengaged one is not the company, the perks or the mission statement. It is who is leading the team.

A 2023 global study by the Workforce Institute at UKG, surveying 3400 employees across ten countries, found that 69 per cent of employees said their manager had the biggest impact on their mental health. That is the same impact as a spouse or partner, and a far greater impact than their doctor (51 per cent) or therapist (41 per cent). When the same survey asked what most shapes a person's overall mental health, work topped the list for 60 per cent of respondents.

The person who assigns work, sets expectations, runs the meeting and writes the review has more influence on the wellbeing of the person across the desk from them than almost anyone else in that person's life. The leader is the environment, and that environment travels home with every team member at the end of every day.

This is what makes self-assessment of impact non-negotiable.

Leaders often underestimate how visible their state is to others. Teams are dialled in to their leader's emotional state because that state directly affects their own. They pick up the edge in your voice and the impatience in your responses before you have finished walking through the door.

Buddhist practice cultivates what is called *metta*, loving kindness, which is sometimes misread as a warm feeling towards people you already like. In practice it is something more demanding: the deliberate cultivation of goodwill towards everyone in your orbit, including the difficult ones. Including on the bad days. What neuroscience calls emotional contagion, contemplative tradition calls transmission. The quality of attention a leader brings into a room is the first thing a nervous system detects. A leader who has cultivated equanimity creates a different field than one who has learned to mask anxiety with authority.

The best way to understand your impact is to ask, and asking requires creating the conditions where honest answers are possible. Anonymous surveys can help. So can third-party conversations with someone trained in gathering and presenting feedback. The gap between how you perceive yourself and how others experience you may be larger than you expect.

Take the mirror test

So, before exploring your team's burnout, you need to explore your own. This kind of honest self-reflection can be challenging but seeing yourself clearly is the work that makes everything else possible.

Begin by asking yourself:

1. How long have you been running at this pace?
2. What does your working week look like?
3. When you are not working, are you still thinking about work?
4. Are you exhausted in ways that sleep doesn't resolve?
5. Have you become cynical about your work, your organisation, colleagues or the people you lead?
6. Do you feel effective, or do you feel like you're going through motions, no longer producing meaningful results?

Even if you feel certain you're not burned out, complete these assessments that follow. The data may surprise you.

Physical symptoms

Begin with physical reality. The body doesn't lie, even when the mind does:

1. How do you feel when you wake up, rested or already tired?
2. Has your baseline energy declined over the past months?
3. Are you getting sick more often?
4. Do you experience regular headaches, muscle tension or stomach problems?
5. Examine your sleep: falling asleep easily, staying asleep, waking refreshed.
6. Have your eating patterns changed?
7. Are you using caffeine, alcohol or other substances more than you used to?

Emotional indicators

Consider your baseline emotional state, not during specific events, but on any ordinary day:

1. Is there an undertone of anxiety that wasn't there before?
2. Do you feel flattened, as though emotions that used to be vivid have become muted?
3. How quickly do you recover from setbacks?

Pay particular attention to Sunday evenings. Mild anticipation is normal but if Sunday evenings bring dread, anxiety or depression, your relationship with work has become problematic.

Cognitive changes

1. Are you having trouble concentrating on complex tasks?
2. Is your memory less reliable than it used to be?
3. Do you find yourself unable to think creatively, stuck in routine responses?
4. Do decisions that used to come easily now feel paralysing?

Behavioural changes

1. Have you withdrawn from colleagues, from friends, from activities you used to enjoy?
2. Are you procrastinating on tasks that used to engage you?
3. Have you neglected relationships or responsibilities outside work?
4. Are you working longer hours but producing less?

Follow your personal recovery plan

If the preceding sections revealed concerns, a plan is needed. Begin with the ten steps listed here:

1. **Take a look at your week.** Pull up your calendar from the last 14 days. Count the hours that were meetings, the hours that were

focused work, and the hours that were recovery. Most leaders are shocked by what they find.

2. **Prune your meetings ruthlessly.** A meeting deserves its slot only if it meets three tests. Is a decision being made or advanced? Are the right people in the room? Could the outcome be achieved with a written update or an asynchronous thread? Anything that fails those tests is recoverable time. Cancel it, shorten it or convert it. Some leaders recover eight hours a week doing nothing but this. Others recover more.
3. **Block one half day a week with no meetings.** Protect it like the most important meeting in your diary. Tell the team what you are doing and why. At The Culture Institute of Australia we all have 'Meeting free Fridays' which means the deep work gets done without interruption and the team can work at their own pace and lead into every weekend with less reactive energy.
4. **Protect a daily focus block.** Ninety minutes, once a day, no meetings, no email, phone face down. Without it, your days can belong to other people's priorities.
5. **Conduct a 'no inventory'.** Look at every commitment you said yes to in the last month. For each one, ask whether you would say yes today. The ones you would not are candidates to delegate, or exit. Most leaders find a third of their workload is built on yeses that no longer make sense, and the freedom in cutting that third loose is its own form of recovery, often more powerful than rest.
6. **Ask your team what you should stop doing.** Never in a town hall. One-to-one, in private, with the people closest to your work. The question is specific. *What am I doing that I should hand off, drop, or do less of?* The answers will sting. They will also be more useful than anything you can work out on your own.
7. **Schedule recovery first.** Block holiday time, evenings, weekends, weekly recovery, before anything else lands on the calendar.
8. **Fix your sleep before anything else.** If you are physically depleted, nothing else on this list will hold. Sleep first. Calendar second.

9. **Take a real break.** A long weekend with email open is recovery theatre. The body and mind need a true disconnection, seven days at minimum, ideally 14, with someone else carrying decisions in your absence. Many leaders cannot remember the last time they did this.
10. **If the job is the problem, name it.** Some roles have been engineered into shapes no human can sustain. No amount of pruning or blocking or saying no will fix a role that is structurally impossible. If after your assessment the role itself is what is breaking you, then the conversation to have is with the chair, the board, your leader or yourself. There are only three options. Change the job. Change how you do it. Change your relationship to it. Pretending there is a fourth option is what keeps leaders trapped, sometimes for years.

Accountability mechanisms help you follow through. Tell someone you trust about the levers you are pulling and schedule a check-in within four weeks to review what changed. Plans made in private and protected by no one have a habit of disappearing.

The leadership practices that sustain

Leadership that can be maintained benefits from practices that maintain the leader's capacity over time. These are the essential disciplines that make everything else possible. Physical health forms the foundation; sleep, nutrition and movement are the conditions under which everything else performs. Leaders who invest consistently in their physical health bring clearer thinking, steadier emotions and sustained effectiveness to their work over time.

Sleep isn't negotiable

Chronic sleep deprivation impairs every cognitive faculty leadership demands: judgement, decision making, memory and attention. Many leaders sacrifice sleep first when time is short, redirecting those hours to work. Cognitive capacity has a finite reserve, and drawing on it consistently without replenishment carries compounding costs.

Movement restores energy

Remember to prioritise movement. Exercise triggers physiological responses that reduce stress hormones, improve sleep quality and enhance cognitive function. A leader who makes time for movement gains that time back through sharper thinking, stronger recovery and greater output throughout the day.

Nutrition affects mental function

Proper nutrition, and respecting meal times, is important. Blood sugar fluctuations affect mood, concentration and decision making. Caffeine creates the sensation of alertness as underlying fatigue continues to accumulate. Alcohol disrupts sleep architecture even when it appears to aid relaxation. These choices affect leadership performance whether or not a leader pays conscious attention to them.

Emotional energy fuels engagement and connection

Sustained conflict, negativity and the effort of suppressing emotional responses all draw on emotional reserves. Positive emotions, authentic expression and meaningful connection restore it. Leaders who suppress emotional responses in the service of professional composure pay a continuous cost: contained emotions draw on energy regardless of whether they are acknowledged. Finding appropriate outlets, through trusted relationships, journaling or other practices, preserves the emotional capacity that leadership demands.

Barbara Fredrickson, professor of psychology at the University of North Carolina, developed the Broaden and Build Theory to explain how positive emotions contribute to wellbeing and performance. Her research demonstrates that positive emotions broaden people's momentary thought action repertoires, which in turn serves to build their enduring personal resources. Deliberately cultivating positive emotional experiences is practical maintenance of the emotional reserves that leadership requires.

Contemplative practices

Contemplative practices, whatever form they take, create space for the mind to settle and restore. Some leaders meditate. Others journal. Others walk. The specific form matters less than the function: creating regular space for mental renewal. Mental energy enables focus, clarity and creative thinking. It's depleted by distraction, multitasking and excessive decision making. It's restored by focused attention, mental rest and reduced decision load.

Daniel Kahneman's research on cognitive systems shows that deliberate, analytical thinking, the kind leadership decisions require, draws on a limited resource. As that resource depletes across a day, the brain defaults to faster, more automatic responses: intuitive shortcuts, familiar patterns, the first answer rather than the best one. This is why leaders who make sound decisions in the morning may make poorer ones by afternoon. Protecting cognitive capacity requires prioritising decisions that genuinely require your attention and delegating the rest. Routines that reduce trivial choices preserve capacity for choices that matter.

Recovery rituals

Recovery must be deliberately designed and consistently practised. Rituals, which are practices repeated regularly enough to become automatic, are the mechanism for embedding recovery into demanding schedules.

How you begin the day shapes its entire trajectory. The first hour establishes the conditions for every hour that follows. A morning ritual creates the conditions for sustained performance. Begin before demands begin. Wake early enough that the first part of your day belongs entirely to you. Use this time for practices that restore: meditation, exercise, reflection or silence. Email can wait. The moment you engage with others' demands, your agenda becomes theirs.

At the end of the workday, create a ritual that signals to your nervous system that work is ending. A walk, a shower, a change of clothes, a call to a family member or a friend from outside work: choose a practice and perform it consistently. The ritual's power comes from its regularity. Done reliably, it becomes a cue that tells your brain to downshift. Transition rituals create the boundaries that make full presence possible. The best leaders separate their days, deliberately bringing full attention to work when working and genuine recovery to rest when the day is done.

At least one day per week must be entirely free from work. Not reduced work or checking in briefly. Completely free. Current demands may make this feel impossible. You can still make it happen. The sabbath principle appears across religious traditions because they understood something about human nature that modern work culture has forgotten. We require rest. We function better when rest is built into our rhythms rather than squeezed in as afterthought.

Courage in action

Leading by example calls for courage: the willingness to push back on demands that would require responses that can't be sustained, to challenge decisions that would harm the team, to speak truthfully about what is and isn't possible.

This courage is tested when those above you in the hierarchy are themselves operating in ways that can't be sustained and expecting you to do the same: when the CEO works around the clock and tacitly expects executives to match that commitment, or the client's impossible timeline is accepted without negotiation.

Courage doesn't mean recklessness, refusing every difficult request or fighting every battle. It means being willing to have hard conversations about what can be sustained and to name the human cost of decisions that might seem costless to those making them.

Leaders who exercise this courage often find more support than they expected, because others were also struggling but were hesitant to speak. Sometimes the situation simply needs one voice to name what others are also seeing... and more importantly, feeling.

When your own boundaries are compromised

You may be reading this while operating in an environment that doesn't respect boundaries. Perhaps you are receiving late-night messages from your own manager, or are expected to be perpetually available, which means you are unable to model the patterns you want to create for your team.

This is one of the hardest positions in leadership: carrying responsibility for others while navigating conditions that test your own capacity.

Consider becoming a boundary buffer. Even if chaos flows down to you, you can choose not to pass it through unchanged. The 10 pm email from your manager doesn't have to become a 10 pm email to your team. The weekend request can be absorbed and translated into a Monday morning task. Your team may never know what you shielded them from, and that's the point.

This approach is demanding and sustainable only as a temporary measure. Use it while you assess whether your own situation can change, through influencing the culture above you or through a broader decision about where you choose to lead. Leadership is ultimately about the people in your care. Absorbing pressure from above to protect those below is costly work. It is also an act of leadership.

Meanwhile, work on your own situation. Can you have honest conversations with your manager about what's realistic? Can you build coalitions with peers facing similar pressures? Can you demonstrate through results that different approaches work? And if none of these paths are available, can you honestly assess whether this environment is one you should remain in?

Identity beyond title

One of the more typical burnout traps is overidentification with one's professional role. When work becomes who you are rather than what you do, any threat to work can feel like a threat to self. When identity is entirely wrapped in a title, losing that title can feel like losing yourself.

Research confirms this vulnerability. A Pew Research Centre survey found that over half of postgraduate workers consider their jobs central to their overall identity. Psychologists warn that when the line between personal identity and professional role blurs, the consequences can be severe: burnout, anxiety, and a troubling sense of psychological disconnection. When careers become unstable due to layoffs, industry shifts or burnout, the identity built on top of them can collapse. Tania, from Chapter 4, had made this trade completely. Her sense of self belonged to the firm, to the title, to the floor she sat on. She had long since stopped noticing the distance between who she had been and who she had become.

Building identity beyond a title means investing in relationships, interests and sources of meaning that aren't contingent on professional position. It means knowing who you are when you're not at work, and spending enough time away from work to discover this.

This may sound like advice to work less, but it's actually advice to *be more*. More than your title. More than your role. More than the function you perform. The leader with identity beyond title may bring more to work precisely because they're not desperately dependent on work for their sense of worth.

A note to leaders under pressure

To the leader who recognises burnout in themselves, or who senses they're on the path towards it: you are not alone. The research shows that leaders burn out at significant rates, and the pressures you face are real. Acknowledging that you're struggling isn't weakness. It's the first step towards recovery.

Recovery is possible. Chapter 3 mapped both the damage burnout does to the brain and the evidence for reversal. The brain can heal. Capacity can be restored. Healing demands specific conditions: sustained reduction in stress, adequate sleep, physical activity, and the one that today's typical leadership culture makes hardest to find: time.

If you're burned out, you need help. This might mean working with a coach who can provide perspective and accountability. It might mean having honest conversations with your peers and executive leaders about what's realistic. It might mean taking medical leave if the situation is severe. It might even mean making changes to your role or your organisation.

What you can't do is power through. The strategies that got you into leadership may not be the strategies that sustain you in leadership. The ability to push through exhaustion, which may have served you earlier in your career, becomes a liability when it prevents you from recognising that you need to stop.

The most compelling reason to protect your own capacity is the people in your care. Their access to your steadiest thinking, clearest judgement and fullest presence depends on what you bring. Recovery is a leadership responsibility.

Lessons from elite sport

What elite endurance sport has discovered about sustained performance over the past two decades offers one of the more precise frames available for understanding how leaders sustain their own. The parallel runs deeper than it first appears. Distance running at the highest level and senior leadership share a defining characteristic: results are built from accumulated performance across time, and the conditions that make that accumulation possible are more specific than most participants assume.

At the centre of that discovery is the work of Marius Bakken, a two-time Olympian turned physician, who developed the method through more than 5500 personal lactate tests conducted across his competitive career and medical practice, and whose findings shaped what became known as the Norwegian double threshold method. Bakken demonstrated something counterintuitive: elite endurance athletes achieve their greatest results by spending 75 to 80 per cent of their training volume at low intensity, deliberately and consistently below their threshold. Operating within reserves builds capacity. Consistent training at or above threshold produces breakdown.

A sustained leadership role is an endurance event. The leaders who perform best across it are those who spend most of their time within reserves, protecting capacity and accumulating what they need for the moments that demand the most from them.

Leadership is an endurance event. Manage yourself accordingly.

Mental health support

Australia

- Beyond Blue: beyondblue.org.au (mental health support, 1300 22 4636)
- Heads Up: headsup.org.au (specifically for workplace mental health)
- Black Dog Institute: blackdoginstitute.org.au

United Kingdom

- Mind: mind.org.uk (0300 123 3393)
- Mental Health at Work: mentalhealthatwork.org.uk

United States

- NAMI: nami.org (988 Suicide and Crisis Lifeline, also covers mental health broadly)
- SAMHSA National Helpline: 1-800-662-4357

CHAPTER 14

The multiplier effect

> It is not your duty to finish the work, but neither are you at liberty to neglect it.
>
> —Rabbi Tarfon, *Pirkei Avot* 2:16 (c. 200 AD)

It is essential to build cultural health that outlasts any single leader's tenure, spreads beyond any single team, and becomes the way the organisation works rather than the exception someone fought to create. But how do you maintain the culture when a strong and successful leader leaves the company?

I've spent my career watching the same mistake being made: a leader invests in their people, strong performance follows, and the lesson is promptly misattributed. The leader's methods are credited to their personality and the results are credited to the people themselves. When the leader moves on, the culture moves with them. In the department down the hall, the manager stoking a furnace stays put. The attrition and poor engagement are absorbed as the cost of doing business.

The Mainfreight story is the example I reach for when someone tells me culture cannot scale. The company has grown from a single truck into operations across more than 26 countries, and the culture has travelled with it. That is the result of deliberate design.

Meaning multiplies: The Mainfreight story

In 1978, a New Zealand accountant named Bruce Plested fell out with management at his freight company and walked out. He then did the only sensible thing a man in his position could do: bought a truck and started a competitor.

Mainfreight is now one of the largest logistics companies in the southern hemisphere, operating across 26 countries. It has never quite become famous outside the industry, which suits Plested. The culture he built is built for people not for press releases.

The word 'management' was banned from the beginning. Budgets were called 'bullshit'. Why spend time preparing figures that are out of date before the ink is dry? Just make more than last year. The full profit and loss posted on the cafeteria noticeboard so everyone could see it. Decisions made by whoever was closest to the customer, not by whoever had the most impressive title. And one more thing: Mainfreight pays the university tuition fees of every employee's children. Not just senior employees or long-tenure staff. Everyone. That single policy says something about the relationship between employer and employee that no values statement has ever quite managed to say as clearly.

21 000 buckets

The most revealing artifact of Mainfreight's culture has no business case, no committee behind it, and no strategic rationale. It started as a thought at an orchard in Hawke's Bay. The apple bucket tradition started when Plested visited his cousin's orchard and found himself thinking about a friend who used to give freshly caught fish to a local doctor who treated his large family for free, because it was the only gift his friend had to give. Plested decided to give buckets of fresh apples to his team and customers. That was one orchard, one team, one season. Mainfreight now distributes more than 21 000 apple buckets, as gifts, globally every year. The tradition has no business case. It has survived for decades because it started as something meaningful.

What's probably most interesting is what Mainfreight does when it acquires a struggling company in a new market. It does not send in a restructuring team or deploy a change program. Instead, it brings the managers of the acquired company to New Zealand and puts them right inside Mainfreight's culture of flat structure and daily habits. Those managers stay there until those things have become natural rather than foreign. Mainfreight calls this 'The Blue Injection'. The managers then go home, carrying with them that Mainfreight company culture. Plested said that knowing they could successfully transplant the culture gave the company more confidence than any financial result.

(Source: Davies, 2013.)

Identifying the culture carriers

Culture spreads best through people it has already changed. Every organisation has people who disproportionately shape its culture. Often they're not the most senior people. They set the tone through their behaviour, transmit norms through their reactions, and model what's possible and expected.

Organisational culture significantly influences employee behaviour, workplace dynamics and performance outcomes. A 2024 systematic review in *Cogent Business and Management* examining studies from 2014 to 2023 found that cultural dimensions, including teamwork, innovation and involvement, repeatedly emerged as key factors shaping organisational effectiveness. What that research describes is downstream of leadership. Leaders set the initial conditions by modelling what gets noticed and what gets rewarded, and culture flows from there through everyone whose behaviour others watch and copy.

Identifying these culture carriers is critical for scaling change. Research by Rob Cross, Professor of Global Leadership at Babson College, on informal organisational networks has consistently found that the people who most shape how work gets done and how norms travel are rarely those with the most formal authority. They are the informal network nodes: the people others turn to for honest advice, for guidance that the organisational chart does not show. In short, the most trusted and positive people.

Our own network analysis work across large Australian organisations has found the same pattern consistently. The culture carriers, the people whose behaviour and emotional state most influence those around them, are rarely on the formal talent register. They are often mid-level, long tenured and overlooked by succession planning. The answer to who they are rarely matches the list of people the organisation has earmarked as high potential. Identifying them requires looking at who people turn to when something matters.

Developing culture carriers means building their capacity to recognise cultural dynamics and to model relational health in their own practice. It means giving them the language to talk about culture and the support to prioritise it. And it means attending to their own wellbeing. Burnout among those in influential informal positions spreads through the organisation as surely as it does from the top. Protecting the health of culture carriers protects the health of the culture itself.

Manager-as-coach

The frontline manager role is often where culture is most directly transmitted and where burnout is most immediately created or prevented. Shifting this role from primarily task supervision towards developmental coaching can be among the most effective interventions.

A 2024 study published in *Frontiers in Psychology* found that leaders who adopt a coaching approach produce measurably higher engagement and stronger performance outcomes. The effect is most pronounced when work is complex and changing quickly

Being a manager-as-coach means reconsidering the primary function of management: moving towards *developing* and *enabling* rather than primarily monitoring and directing, building capacity rather than just ensuring compliance, and buffering teams from chaotic demands when possible.

This shift typically requires both capability development and role redefinition. Managers may need skills they were never formally taught, such as having difficult conversations, providing effective feedback, recognising and tackling burnout, and creating psychological safety. Internal data from The Culture Institute of Australia's coaching practice shows that 87 per cent of recipients reported improved confidence and 71 per cent reported a stronger desire to stay with their organisation.

The International Coaching Federation, in collaboration with the Human Capital Institute, has found that organisations with strong coaching cultures tend to see benefits in employee wellbeing and retention. Their research suggests that solutions targeting only individuals, such as offering employee wellness programs like yoga or mandated social activities, are far less likely to have a sustainable impact on employee wellbeing than more systemic initiatives.

Systems over individuals

The most durable culture change works through systems rather than depending on specific individuals. Ideally, when the leader who built healthy culture moves on, the culture remains. Sadly, this isn't always the case. But it's more likely when healthy patterns have been embedded in structures that operate regardless of who occupies any particular role.

Most organisational processes are designed for efficiency. The meeting is scheduled because it is efficient. The project timeline is set because it is efficient. The health of the people executing the work needs to also be part of the conversation.

The organisations that perform best over time treat efficiency and human health as complementary design goals. Building cultural health into systems means making that balance structural: workload assessment built into project planning from the start, culture measurement as a quarterly discipline rather than an annual afterthought, team health as a standing agenda item.

A note for those without organisation-wide authority: systems thinking applies at every level. If you lead a team, you can build systems for that team. You can establish team norms that become self-reinforcing and create rituals that persist even when you're not present. You can document practices so they survive your departure. The scope may be smaller than organisation-wide transformation, but the principles are identical. A meaningful, well-designed team system is worth more than a grand organisational initiative that exists only on paper.

Systems-level change also involves aligning incentives with relational health. If managers are evaluated purely on team output without regard to team health, they may rationally prioritise output over health. If career advancement appears to require visible sacrifice, ambitious people may sacrifice accordingly.

Research supports the value of systemic approaches. Allianz, one of Australia's largest workers' compensation insurers, reports that mental health claims have risen almost 50 per cent over the past five years, with the average cost of those claims up almost 30 per cent over the same period (Allianz, 2024). Safe Work Australia reports that serious mental health compensation claims reached 17 600 in 2023–24, a 161 per cent increase over ten years (Safe Work Australia, 2025). The median time off work for each mental health claim is 35.7 weeks, nearly five times the median for all other workplace injuries. The Productivity Commission's Inquiry into Mental Health estimated the total cost of mental ill-health and suicide to the Australian economy at $200 to $220 billion annually.

I have sat in many process design workshops, and most share the same uncomfortable truth. The process is usually fine. The culture it operates inside is doing the damage. The data describes what happens when that continues.

Systems built purely for efficiency, with no account taken of what the people inside them can actually sustain, eventually deliver the opposite of what they promised.

Measurement that matters

Australia has some of the most advanced psychosocial and culture health regulation in the world, more comprehensive than the frameworks operating in the United Kingdom or the United States. ASIC, APRA, Safe Work Australia and the ASX Corporate Governance Council have each arrived at the same conclusion through different legislative pathways: culture oversight is a board responsibility and the standard of proof has risen considerably.

Despite this, most boards still rely on an engagement score to meet it. APRA has found that almost 80 per cent of entities under heightened supervision exhibit underlying governance issues. The 2024 Qantas governance review found that the board had extrapolated from a strong safety culture to assume the broader organisational culture was sound. That is not measurement.

Critically, HR teams rarely initiate culture health measurement. It tends not to sit within their authority or their budget. Worth remembering: in any royal commission or regulatory investigation, it's the board and executive team who face the consequences. Not HR.

Accountability frameworks

A manager who delivers results by depleting their team hasn't succeeded. Short-term output at the cost of long-term capacity is, in my view, 'borrowed performance'. Accountability for cultural health means holding leaders responsible for both: what they produced and what producing it cost.

Culture Amp's 2024 analysis of 97 million employee responses across 5000 organisations found that leadership quality is the strongest single predictor of whether people stay. Employees with a great leader and a great manager report commitment to stay at 94 per cent. That figure drops to 35 per cent when the leader is poor, even with a good manager, and falls to 19 per cent when both are poor. The effect persists after leaders move on. Within six months of a leader's departure, affected teams experience 40 per cent higher attrition than teams with no change at the top. A change of manager produces a 16 per cent increase over the same period.

This has structural implications. Boards can build cultural health metrics into executive performance reviews and compensation alongside financial returns. When the people at the top are assessed on how they led as well as what they produced, that signal travels through every team below them.

Building coalitions

Individual leaders pushing for change are easy to dismiss. Groups of leaders presenting shared concerns are harder to ignore.

Damon Centola's research at the University of Pennsylvania on how behaviour spreads through organisations explains why. Behavioural change is a complex contagion. Unlike a rumour or a virus, which can spread from a single contact, changing how people behave requires reinforcement from multiple independent sources before it takes hold. One voice saying the same thing five times registers as repetition.

Five different voices saying the same thing once registers as evidence. That is why coalitions change things and persistent individuals often don't.

Start by identifying potential allies. Who else seems to care about these issues? Who has pushed back on demands that couldn't be sustained? Who has built pockets of health within their own teams? These are your potential coalition partners. Then build relationships deliberately. Have conversations about what you're seeing. Share what you're trying. Ask about their experiences. Over time, these individual relationships can become an important network that amplifies everyone's impact.

The long game

Cultural transformation takes time. Often more time than leaders initially want to invest, more time than quarterly thinking allows. The changes described in this book may require sustained effort over years, not months.

That said, an aligned and action-oriented team, department or organisation can expect meaningful improvement within a 12-month period. In 2025, my firm, The Culture Institute of Australia, halved negative culture sentiment and increased cultural health by 52 per cent in a division of a leading Australian bank. Change is possible, and it can happen faster than sceptics suggest, but it requires sustained attention.

The mechanism that turns 12 months of effort into 12 months of measurable improvement is deceptively simple. We train and certify the leaders themselves in cultural leadership.

Most attempts at culture transformation stall for a single underlying reason. Senior leaders inherit cultural authority by virtue of position. Few have been formally trained in how culture actually forms. Certification closes that gap. Leaders prove, through observable behaviour and applied practice over time, that they understand the mechanics of culture: how values become behaviours, how behaviours become norms, how norms become the felt sense of what it is like to work somewhere. The standard creates accountability. The accountability produces consistency.

No other intervention we have tested produces faster movement.

Certified leaders make different decisions about meeting design, recognition practice, hiring criteria, conflict resolution, and the dozens of small culture-shaping moments that pass through a leader's calendar each week. The bank result above emerged from exactly this approach. The culture shifts through the leadership layer. Each certified leader is a culturally educated champion of change. Sustainability follows because the conditions are now set by the people who shape every team.

Playing the long game means maintaining commitment when early results are disappointing, when other priorities compete for attention, and when the urgency of transformation fades against daily demands. It means building cultural health into strategic planning horizons rather than treating it as an optional initiative.

The long game also means accepting that the full results of what leaders build may not manifest until many months or even years after they have moved on. This requires a different relationship to achievement, by finding satisfaction in planting rather than only in harvesting.

Research supports longer term approaches. A 2024 systematic literature review examining 70 peer-reviewed articles found that a strong, adaptive organisational culture was positively associated with enhanced organisational performance and that culture and communication provide the foundation for collaboration, cohesion and sustainable outcomes. Similarly, Gallup's research has consistently shown that organisations with higher employee engagement and wellbeing see benefits in retention, productivity and profitability over time.

The multiplier effect turns individual leadership into systemic change. It transforms personal practice into organisational culture and helps ensure that the work of building culturally healthy workplaces outlasts any individual's tenure.

The highest aspiration of leadership is to build something that outlasts you. A system that continues serving the people inside it long after you have moved on.

The burnout crisis will be addressed by leaders who build organisations where *cultural health* and *strong performance* are simply the way things work because they are designed and integrated into the system and do not require heroic maintenance.

A leader who leaves and takes the culture with them built a following, not a culture.

CHAPTER 15

When organisations got it right

A path is made by walking on it.

—Zhuangzi, c. 300 BCE

Burnout has many theorists. The proof comes from organisations that got it right. Most fought their way back. One never had to.

These case studies share common features: leadership commitment at the highest levels, the courage to challenge conventional assumptions about productivity and performance, and results that silenced sceptics. They also offer lessons that can be adapted well beyond the specific industries involved.

What stands out across these examples is how consistently the evidence contradicts the assumptions that perpetuate burnout culture. The assumption that 'wellbeing investments are costs' collapses under scrutiny, and the belief that the old ways still work disintegrates the moment you measure exactly what those old ways are quietly destroying.

These organisations chose differently. Their experiences illuminate what becomes possible when leaders have the courage to question conventional wisdom about work. These case studies are the evidence-based wake-up call for leaders who, often through no fault of their own, have drifted into redundant and suboptimal cultural habits. My sincere hope is that these stories of cultural triumph provide the basis for change and the courage for action.

Blackmores: A 90-year wellness culture

In 1932, a Brisbane naturopath named Maurice Blackmore founded a company on the position that human beings are whole systems and the work of health is the work of supporting the whole. His profession was not widely respected at the time and the idea that wellness was something to cultivate over a lifetime was considered eccentric. He persisted. The company he started is now Australia's largest nutritional supplement company, with 1200 employees across 13 markets in the Asia Pacific, more than 90 years of natural therapy behind it, and a culture that still operates from that original conviction he held.

Japanese beverage group Kirin Holdings acquired Blackmores in August 2023 for A$1.88 billion, paying a 23.7 per cent premium for the shares. The founder's son, Marcus Blackmore, voted his stake in favour. Kirin Holdings wanted the brand and the CEO who had been running the company since 2019, Alastair Symington. Symington came to Blackmores after 12 years at Procter and Gamble in Shanghai and Singapore. He brought with him a familiarity with how a different kind of culture operates, and the judgement to recognise that what the founder had built was worth protecting.

The wellbeing approach is anchored by the RISE program. RISE is organised around the four pillars of mental, spiritual, physical and emotional health. The program includes naturopathic training, meditation classes, goal-setting workshops, gym sessions, and access to in-person resources through a digital portal that staff can reach from anywhere in the 13 markets. Underneath RISE sits Sonder, the 24/7 wellbeing platform that gives every employee and their immediate family access to nurses, doctors, psychologists and safety professionals, all within a 10-second response time. Eighty-plus health practitioners work inside the company itself, which means the organisation selling natural health to the world is also the organisation living inside it. People at Blackmores practise what they preach, in part because there are practitioners on the next desk.

The everyday rhythms reflect the same orientation. Monthly town halls keep senior leadership accessible to anyone with a question. The Warriewood campus has a wellness centre with treatment rooms for massage and naturopathy, a yoga and pilates space, a gym, and a 20-metre lap pool. Each permanent employee receives a Wellbeing Day every year to use for family, community, religious or cultural commitments. The giving program lets employees direct 0.5 per cent of their taxable pay to a charity of their choice, with Blackmores matching the contribution. In FY21 the program delivered $181 000 to causes employees nominated themselves.

Then there is the small detail that holds the larger truth. At 5.30 each evening a tenured security employee walks the floor encouraging people to pack up and go home. The practice has continued long enough that everyone in the building knows the invitation is real. Going home is what the organisation wants, and the walk is the daily reminder.

Symington describes Blackmores as 'a little big company', a phrase that captures what the size makes possible. A 1200-person enterprise can know its people in a way a 60 000-person multinational cannot, while being large enough to fund the infrastructure that supports them. The short-termism that wears

(*continued*)

down so many listed companies has been buffered here by Japanese ownership that values heritage, and by a CEO whose definition of success is shaped by what Maurice Blackmore wrote down 90 years ago.

Symington is one of those loved CEOs, human and commercially formidable. On the closing of our interview he said something I've been wanting all CEOs to say, 'Performance is only possible when a healthy culture is the foundation'.

(Source: Interview with CEO Alistair Symington – 14 May 2026)

Microsoft Japan: The four-day revolution

We met Microsoft Japan's Work Life Choice Challenge earlier in this book, in Chapter 6. The headline is worth holding in mind as the first case study here. In August 2019, the company closed its offices every Friday for a month and gave 2300 employees a paid day off. Productivity rose by nearly 40 per cent against the same month a year earlier. Electricity use fell by more than 20 per cent. An impressive 92.1 per cent of employees reported satisfaction with the four-day week. The full account of how that happened sits in Chapter 6. What matters here is the assumption it broke, an assumption every burnout culture quietly relies on: that longer hours produce more output. One radical experiment, in one of the world's most overworked countries, proved that assumption wrong.

The United Kingdom: The world's largest trial

Microsoft Japan demonstrated what was possible in a single company. Between June and December 2022, the UK conducted the largest coordinated four-day-week trial in history, involving 61 companies and approximately 2900 employees. The research, led by academics from the University of Cambridge and Boston College in partnership with 4 Day Week Global and Autonomy, would provide the most compelling evidence yet for working time reduction.

Stellar Asset Management, a UK financial services firm, joined the trial under the 100:80:100 model: 100 per cent of pay for 80 per cent of hours, with employees committing to 100 per cent productivity. To make it work, the firm invested in technology to streamline and automate processes. COO Daryl Hine said the four-day offer also gave Stellar an advantage in recruiting and retaining staff. Other companies adapted the model to fit their own work. Platten's, a fish and chip shop on the Norfolk coast, split its team into two rotating groups working two days on and two days off, which kept the shop open seven days a week. The 61 organisations involved spanned online retailers, animation studios, consultancies, housing groups, IT firms, skincare manufacturers, recruitment agencies, marketing businesses and healthcare providers. The breadth was deliberate, testing whether the model worked across very different kinds of work.

By the end of the trial, 71 per cent of employees reported reduced burnout, and 39 per cent reported being less stressed. Mental and physical health both improved on every measure the researchers tracked. Sixty per cent of workers found it easier to combine paid work with care responsibilities, with similar gains for social and

(continued)

household commitments. Satisfaction with relationships and time management also rose.

Revenue rose 1.4 per cent during the trial, and ran 35 per cent higher than equivalent periods in earlier years. Staff turnover dropped by 57 per cent over the same window, and sick days fell by 65 per cent. The cost savings from those two figures alone offset the reduction in working hours.

Fifteen per cent of employees said no amount of money would persuade them to return to a five-day week. Of the 61 participating companies, 56 continued the four-day week after the trial ended, and 18 of those committed to it permanently. Once people had experienced the alternative, going back was the minority choice.

Follow-up research more than a year after the trial ended found the benefits had held. Health and life satisfaction stayed at improved levels, and job satisfaction sat higher than where it had started.

(Sources: Lewis et al., 2023; Lewsey, 2023; Forsdick, 2022; Young & Milliken, 2023; Bonnell, 2023; Pignon et al., 2024)

Unilever: Building comprehensive wellbeing

Successful intervention does not always require reducing working hours. Unilever, the multinational consumer goods company, demonstrates what becomes possible through sustained wellbeing investment within conventional work structures.

Unilever's UK and Ireland operation spans head offices, factories and research sites employing many thousands of people. The company recognised that mental health had become a leading cause of sickness absence and was one of the top three reasons employees claimed through the private medical insurance scheme. This was a measurable problem that demanded response.

The company's approach was holistic. Their Wellbeing Strategy focused on four interconnected dimensions: mental, emotional and physical wellbeing, and sense of purpose. You cannot look after one of these effectively without attending to the others.

Sitting alongside the strategy was Lamplighter, Unilever's global preventive health program that screens employees for early signs of poor mental and physical health before they escalate to illness. Lamplighter has scaled to cover more than 76 000 Unilever employees across over 75 countries since its launch in 2001. Its results include measurable improvements in indicators such as smoking, obesity and diabetes.

Within the UK and Ireland, Mental Health First Aid training became embedded as a core leadership discipline. The company took a distinctive approach by making this training mandatory for line managers across key sites, using a bespoke half-day course. At the time of reporting, Unilever had trained over 50 per cent of its line managers in mental health first aid skills. Feedback was strongly positive. The training changed how managers approached conversations with their teams. Instead of jumping straight into performance discussions, managers learned to ask how employees were doing and gain a sense of their current wellbeing before addressing tasks.

Leadership modelling was essential. Senior executives shared their own personal stories about mental health, demonstrating that these conversations were legitimate and valued at the highest levels. Paul Polman, then CEO of Unilever, captured the philosophy directly. By listening and responding to employees' emotional needs, the company gave people a much better chance of fulfilling their true potential.

(*continued*)

Beyond management training, Unilever established peer support networks called Time to Talk teams. These comprised volunteer employees who had attended the full two-day Mental Health First Aid training program. The teams provided employees with improved access to wellbeing resources and helped destigmatise mental health discussions in the workplace.

Unilever's approach worked because of its comprehensiveness. The strategy systematically transformed how the organisation thought about and supported employee wellbeing. It was sustained over years, refined based on results, and embedded in organisational culture rather than treated as an HR add on.

(Sources: MHFA England, 2023; Unilever UK & Ireland, 2026; UN Global Compact Business & Human Rights Navigator, 2026; Nair, 2020)

Salesforce: The Ohana philosophy

In the late 1990s, a 31-year-old Oracle executive named Marc Benioff asked his boss for time off. He had been the company's youngest-ever vice president, named at 26, and was earning over a million dollars a year. He felt lost. He took a six-month sabbatical and travelled to India and Hawaii. In Hawaii he immersed himself in local culture and learned about a Hawaiian concept called *Ohana*. The word translates as 'family', and in Hawaiian tradition it carries the idea that family members, whether by blood or by choice, are bound together and responsible for one another.

Benioff founded Salesforce in March 1999, in a San Francisco apartment. He wrote Ohana into the company's foundations from day one. Decades later, Salesforce had grown into the world's largest customer relationship management company, and *Ohana* had become the organising principle of its culture: employees, customers, partners and the wider community were spoken of as one extended family, with the company's success understood to depend on the success of every member of it.

That cultural foundation shaped how Salesforce treated wellbeing. Employees were given monthly wellbeing days on top of standard paid leave, and reimbursements for things like gym memberships and nutrition counselling. At one point the company gave employees access to a 75-acre wellness retreat centre. Across Salesforce offices, dedicated spaces called Mindful Zones were built into the floorplan, designed for employees to unplug or find quiet time during the working day. Mental restoration was central to their culture and seen as part of the work.

When the COVID pandemic struck in 2020, Salesforce moved quickly. The company expanded its mental health resources and introduced flexible work schedules with dedicated mental health days, bringing the new programming together under a virtual wellbeing hub called Camp B Well.

Communication did much of the work behind these outcomes. Regular feedback loops and wellbeing surveys gave the company a continuous view of how employees were faring, and open channels meant that problems were surfaced and addressed before they became crises.

What Salesforce demonstrated was that culture itself can be a wellbeing intervention. When an organisation treats wellbeing as a value, that value works its way into countless small decisions: how meetings are scheduled and what the workforce feels permitted to ask for.

The *Ohana* philosophy has been tested. On 4 January 2023, Salesforce announced a restructuring plan that reduced its

(*continued*)

workforce by approximately 10 per cent, around 8000 employees, after a period of pandemic-era over-hiring. How a company conducts itself in moments like this reveals what its culture is made of. Benioff told staff directly that the company had hired too many people and that he took responsibility for it. Departing employees received a substantial package, including nearly five months of pay, health benefits and career transition support, with comparable provision in other markets.

That response did not undo the pain of the layoffs, and no organisation is exempt from the moments when cultural values collide with business pressures. The *Ohana* values held under the pressure that most often breaks them. Organisations that build wellbeing into their cultural DNA outperform those that don't, and Salesforce has spent more than two decades proving that the difference matters.

Note: I personally came to know Ohana through a different route. Over the years I competed in seven world surf ski championships in Hawaii, racing across the Kaiwi Channel from the small island of Molokai, a former leper colony, to Hawaii Kai just east of Waikiki. It's recognised as the most demanding ocean race on Earth, and surf ski is one of the most individual extreme sports there is. Yet before each channel crossing every competitor formed a circle, held hands, and stood as one before facing the channel alone. It moved me every time.

(Sources: Salesforce Staff, 2024; Salesforce Staff, 2020; Kohner, 2017; Salesforce, 2024; Jacoby, 2023; Salesforce, n.d.; Robbins, 2017; Kohner, 2016; Salesforce, Inc., 2023a; Benioff, 2023b)

My own experience: REA Group

I had the privilege of working closely with four of Australia's leading technology companies over many years. REA Group taught me more about culture than any of them. What made them remarkable was that no turnaround was ever needed. From the beginning, the leadership cherished its people. That orientation was embedded in how decisions were made and how leaders were evaluated. Creating a thriving culture was treated as foundational to business performance.

One individual embodied this more than anyone I have encountered in my career: the company's long-serving Chief Strategy Officer, Henry Ruiz. When I met Henry, he had been with the organisation for 10 years. He had a background in psychology and an analytical mind that few in the business could match. He held strategic rigour and human wellbeing in balance as a matter of practice.

What set him apart was authenticity. He cared about people because he was the kind of person who cared. When he asked how someone was going, he wanted to know. When difficult decisions had to be made, and they always do, he weighed the wellbeing of the people involved alongside the needs of the business. He made hard calls, and he made them with a deep consideration for the humans affected.

Henry was not the only one. Natalie Feehan led marketing strategy at REA before going on to rebrand MYOB and then to join SEEK, where she works today. At REA, she built cultural health inside her teams while the always-on pressure of an Australian tech unicorn punched above its weight. Val Brown ran consumer product for 13 years and did the same on her side of the business. The three of them, each in their own register, shaped the culture by

(*continued*)

the way they showed up. They were strategic and analytical when the business called for it, and human in every conversation that followed. They understood that the culture was what produced the performance, and they led from that conviction.

Their impact compounded across more than a decade. People knew what good leadership looked like because they had experienced it. New leaders were measured against that standard. The culture perpetuated itself because its exemplars were visible every day.

The real test came when the company faced the kinds of disruption that destabilise other organisations. They changed strategy. They brought in new leaders. They expanded into unfamiliar markets. Any of these shifts could have caused the cultural fractures I have witnessed elsewhere: identity loss, eroded trust, the turnover spike that follows uncertainty.

None of that happened. Performance remained market leading. The people who had built the company's success continued to thrive as the context around them shifted. The reason was cultural health, and the leaders who had built it. The organisation invested consistently in its people because that was the operating principle, and that consistency built a resilience that could absorb change.

Henry, Nat and Val have all moved on. The cultural leadership chairs at REA are now held by fine cultural leaders in their own right. This is the multiplier effect from Chapter 14, visible in one company across more than a decade: culture that outlasts any one leader because it was never the work of any one leader.

The Culture Institute of Australia: A bank transformation

In late 2024, one of Australia's Big Four banks engaged The Culture Institute of Australia to lead a culture transformation across a 900-person division.

The methodology was REFORM™, The Culture Institute's six phase model that moves an organisation from research through to long term maintenance. The measurement was CultureHealth™, the diagnostic that gives a division the granular evidence base needed to design and track its own transformation. The intervention deployed a Leadership Certification program, a structured five wave change program, behavioural micro nudges embedded into daily work, and continuous progress tracking.

Twelve months later, the October 2025 CultureHealth™ diagnostic showed healthy culture sentiment up 59 per cent, unhealthy sentiment halved, and culture toxicity down 40 per cent. Psychological safety lifted across all four established quadrants of inclusion, learner, contributor and challenger. The Customer Centricity Index rose 21 per cent. Every target set at the start of the engagement was exceeded.

What changed in this division in 12 months is what most organisations are still hoping to achieve in five years. The difference is the disciplines developed at the leadership level and the commitment from every level of the division.

What these cases teach us

Across these diverse examples, several patterns emerge that can guide other organisations seeking to address burnout:

- **Leadership commitment is essential.** In every case, change was driven from the top. Senior leaders didn't merely approve initiatives. They championed them, modelled them, and protected them from organisational pressures that would have diluted their impact.
- **Comprehensive approaches outperform isolated interventions.** Unilever's success came from addressing mental, emotional and physical wellbeing together. Salesforce embedded wellbeing in culture rather than treating it as a program. The UK trial combined hour reduction with process improvement and flexibility.
- **Speed is possible when the disciplines are present.** Cultural transformation has long been described as a three-to-five-year endeavour. The Australian bank case shows that 12 months can produce the kind of shift most organisations are still hoping to see at the five-year mark.
- **Measurement matters.** Every successful case involved rigorous tracking of outcomes. Microsoft Japan measured productivity per employee. The UK trial measured burnout, stress, revenue and retention. What gets measured gets managed, and these organisations measured what mattered.
- **The business case is proven.** Across these examples, wellbeing investments produced returns. Productivity increased. Turnover decreased. Healthcare costs dropped. Revenue was maintained or grew. The argument that organisations can't afford to prioritise wellbeing has been refuted by the evidence.
- **Adaptation is necessary.** Microsoft Japan's four-day experiment looked different from Unilever's program, which looked different

from Salesforce's cultural approach. There is no single template. Each organisation must find the approach that fits its context, its challenges, and its people.

- **Culture can outlast its architects.** REA Group demonstrates this most clearly. The cultural exemplars who shaped the company more than a decade ago have moved on, while the culture has continued under new leaders. This is the multiplier effect from Chapter 14, visible across a real timeline.
- **The changes were sustained.** These weren't temporary initiatives that faded when attention moved elsewhere. They became embedded in how these organisations operate.
- **Courage was required.** Each of these cases involved challenging conventional assumptions. Microsoft Japan challenged the assumption that Japanese workers needed to be in the office five days a week. The UK trial companies challenged the assumption that full-time work required five days. Unilever challenged the assumption that mental health was a private matter outside the employer's concern.

You don't need permission

You may have read these case studies with a mixture of inspiration and frustration. Inspiration because they demonstrate what's possible, and frustration because they mostly describe company-wide transformations driven by CEOs, senior executives or company-wide mandates. If you don't occupy those roles, you might wonder what relevance these examples hold for you.

Look past the scale of these interventions to the principles beneath them. Every principle in these case studies can operate at the team level. You can:

- question productivity assumptions within your own team
- experiment with meeting-free time within your sphere of control

- model wellbeing conversations with the people you directly manage
- track outcomes for your team even if nobody is tracking them at the organisational level.

The leaders who eventually drove the company-wide transformations didn't start with company-wide authority. They started with conviction, evidence, and a willingness to demonstrate results on whatever scale they could control. Many began exactly where you may be now: leading a team or managing a department; influencing without commanding.

The case studies show what becomes possible when authority and conviction align. Your situation may require building the factual case that eventually earns that alignment. The work you do at your level, the team you protect from burnout, the results you produce in ways that can be sustained and the example you set, becomes the proof that makes larger change possible.

The burnout conversation

All the frameworks in the world won't help if you can't have the conversation.

You can assess burnout accurately, and design structural interventions and build cultural frameworks that look beautiful on slides. But eventually, you will need to sit down with a human being who is struggling and talk to them about what's happening. That conversation is where burnout intervention succeeds or fails.

I have watched hundreds of these conversations and actively participated in many of them. Some of them have gone spectacularly wrong. Eventually, I have learned to get most of them right.

Remember that before you say a word, the conversation has already begun. Everything that came before, including your history with this person, your reputation as a leader and the culture you have created, shapes whether truth is possible. If you punished people for honesty in the past, they won't be honest now. If you dismissed their concerns as weakness or excuses, they will manage their presentation to avoid that judgement.

Creating conditions for truth requires preparation: clear your calendar so you are present, choose a private space where you won't be interrupted, and turn off your phone completely. These actions signal that this conversation matters.

What these organisations built is available to anyone willing to do the work.

CHAPTER 16

The leader's toolkit

> Dare to declare who you are. The path is not long, but the way is deep.
>
> —Hildegard of Bingen

Across 15 chapters this book I've argued that burnout is structural, the predictable output of organisations that were built with inadequate regard for what humans can sustain, run by leaders who inherited a model of work that was already broken when they arrived. The leaders who effectively address burnout only do so by treating it as an organisational design problem.

Specific challenges require specific tools. More suggestions than tools, the following 11 frameworks have made a substantial difference to burnout and performance across many organisations, regardless of sector or size. They have given teams a way to surface what had been going wrong quietly for years, and given leaders a way to see and act on what they had previously missed. Importantly, none of the frameworks drive change without the right leader showing up to use them with real intent. The frameworks are how that intent gets converted into structural change.

The frameworks fall into three stages. **Assessment** is where you see clearly what is happening in your organisation before you change anything. **Redesign** is where you change the conditions producing the burnout. **Sustainability** is where you make sure the change holds across the years that follow. Table 16.1 (overleaf) lays the toolkit out at a glance.

Table 16.1 The leader's toolkit — at a glance

#	Framework	Purpose
1	**The Burnout Risk Radar**	See burnout clearly at the individual, team and organisational levels.
2	**The Energy Map**	Track energy across your team to spot patterns the engagement survey will miss.
3	**The Stay Interview Guide**	Find out why your best people stay, while there is still time to act on it.
4	**The Visibility Trap Audit**	Name the habits in your organisation that reward being seen over doing the work.
5	**The Workload Justice Test**	Force the honest conversation about whether the work fits the capacity to do it.
6	**Meeting Pruning**	Manage your calendar as ongoing discipline rather than a one-off cull.
7	**The Boundary Umpire**	Draw the line between working and non-working time, and enforce it.
8	**The Psychological Safety Sprint**	Build the conditions under which honest signals reach the leader.
9	**The Culture Health Check**	Measure culture with the rigour you apply to financial performance.
10	**The Drift Stocktake**	Catch the small reversions weekly before they become structural.
11	**The CEO Culture Mandate**	The apex work that no one else in the organisation can do.

These frameworks are tools rather than mandates, and your ability to implement them will vary based on your role, your organisation, and the constraints you operate within. Some can be applied immediately within your sphere of control. Others will require negotiation and coalition building with peers and superiors. A few may simply be unavailable to you given your current position, in which case documenting what you would do differently can build the case for future change.

Read what follows with two questions in mind:

1. What can I implement directly?
2. What requires me to influence others?

The goal is progress, within your constraints. Adapt these frameworks to your context, combine them as needed, and bring yourself fully to the work. The frameworks return more than you expect when used that way, and very little when used any other way.

Framework 1: The Burnout Risk Radar

I met many burned-out leaders who, when I have walked them through this radar, have said some version of 'I tick almost all of these'. They have then looked at me with an expression of guilt, self-contempt and helplessness, because maybe for the first time someone had named what they had been pretending was not happening. That recognition is the first thing this framework is designed for. The second is helping you turn it outward, to scan your team and your organisation with the same honesty you have just brought to yourself.

The radar scans three levels.

1. Individual signals

You are looking for patterns in the people you lead, sustained over weeks or months rather than the occasional bad day. The signals cluster into four bands.

1. *Physical.* Persistent fatigue that does not lift with sleep. Increased illness and slower recovery. Headaches or muscle tension that have become a feature of the working week. Disrupted sleep, changes in appetite, increased reliance on caffeine or alcohol to get through the day.

2. *Cognitive.* Difficulty concentrating on complex work. Memory becoming less reliable. Creative thinking giving way to routine responses. Decisions that used to come easily now stalling, sometimes for days.
3. *Emotional.* Irritability disproportionate to the trigger. Emotional flatness, as if the colour has drained out. Anxiety that sharpens on Sunday evening. Loss of enthusiasm for work that used to engage them. A quiet hopelessness about whether anything will change.
4. *Behavioural.* Withdrawing from colleagues. Procrastinating on tasks they used to handle without thinking. Neglecting things they used to care about, inside or outside work. Working longer hours, producing less.

For each person you are responsible for, note where the signals are present (i) occasionally, (ii) frequently, or (iii) constantly. Three or more signals at frequent or constant level mean that person is in significant burnout risk and needs your attention now.

2. Team signals

Burnout shows up in team behaviour and climate before it shows up in survey results. Notice whether meetings have become perfunctory. Whether communication has shifted towards terse or defensive messages. Whether workload distribution has become uneven, with the same people carrying the load while others have quietly checked out. Whether the team's capacity to recover from a hard week has diminished. Whether people stop raising concerns or asking for help, because psychological safety has eroded and the cost of speaking up has become too high.

3. Organisational signals

Every organisation tracks the numbers that reveal burnout. The problem is that those numbers usually get read as performance problems, or HR problems, or market problems.

The first thing to notice is who is leaving. When your best people start walking, that is the loudest signal your organisation will ever give you. High performers do not leave meaningful jobs in good cultures. They leave when they have run out of reasons to stay, and by the time they hand in notice the decision was made months ago.

The second is who is calling in sick. Even small increases in sick leave matter. People take sick days for reasons that have nothing to do with being sick, and the trend in those days tells you something the daily attendance numbers will not.

Engagement scores trending down matter more than the aggregate, often benchmarked number. An organisation can have a score of 70 and be in real trouble if last quarter it was 76. Most boards focus on the level, when the slope or angle tells you the real story.

And then there is performance itself. When quality starts varying in ways that used to be predictable, when the same team that hit every number last year is suddenly inconsistent, the temptation is to read that as a commitment problem and respond by adding pressure. It is almost never a commitment problem. Depleted people do depleted work, and turning the screws on depletion just increases the likelihood of collapse.

Key organisational signals checklist:

- voluntary departures rising, particularly among high performers
- sick leave trending up, even by small amounts
- engagement scores trending down, regardless of where they sit
- performance becoming inconsistent in ways that used to be reliable.

When two or more of those are present in your organisation right now, you have a burnout challenge.

Framework 2: The Energy Map

HR people (and regulators) love to talk about leading and lagging indicators. When it comes to burnout, energy is one of the more reliable leading indicators. By the time someone is exhausted, the pattern that produced the exhaustion has typically been running for months. Energy levels tend to shift before anything else. They shift before survey results land or resignations start. If you are looking for them, you can see what's happening to your team while there is still time to do something about it.

The Energy Map turns that watching into something practical. It's the simplest framework in this toolkit, and one of the most revealing.

For three weeks, ask every member of your team to log their energy level at the end of each working day. A simple scale from one to ten, one is empty and ten is fully charged. Alongside the number, a single line on what drove the day's energy up or down. That is all. No formal survey. A shared spreadsheet or a group chat will do.

Two things will happen:

1. People will start paying attention to their own energy in a way they have not before. The act of logging it daily makes the patterns visible to the person living them, which is itself an intervention.
2. You, as the leader, will see the shape of your team's working life in a way no engagement survey will ever give you.

After three weeks of collecting data, sit down with the spreadsheet, pop the (anonymised) results into any AI platform and get ready to learn a lot about your team. You will see which days of the week consistently produce the deepest energy dips. You will see which meetings drain the team and which give them something back. You will see the people running on fumes long before they would have told you. And after enough weeks you will know whether the recovery built into your team's week is enough to restore them, or whether they are losing ground week after week.

What you do with the picture is the work of frameworks 5 The Workload Justice Test, 6 Meeting Pruning, 7 The Boundary Umpire, and 8 The Psychological Safety Sprint.

Framework 3: The Stay Interview Guide

The exit interview is one of the great corporate rituals of futility. By the time someone is sitting in one, the decision was made months ago, the damage is done, and the answers they give are diplomatic at best. The organisation collects polite reasons for departure, files them, and moves on.

On the other hand, the stay interview reverses the timing. You sit down with someone who is still in the building, who still has reasons to be there, and you find out what those reasons are and what might be eroding them while there is still time to do something about it.

Done well, a stay interview reads as an honest conversation between two people who both want things to work. The leader is curious, the person feels safe enough to be honest, and the leader leaves with a clearer picture than any survey will give them.

How you set up the conversation matters more than the questions.

Make it private and unhurried. Open by being explicit about why you are having the conversation. Something like I want to understand how things are going for you, properly, so I can support you better and so we can keep what is working and change what's not.

From there, the questions are simple, and designed to surface what most stay interviews miss:

1. What do you look forward to when you come to work?
2. What do you dread?
3. When in the past year have you felt most energised?
4. Most depleted?
5. What would make this a better place to work for you?
6. If you were thinking about leaving, what would be driving that thinking?

Six questions. You may not get to all of them in one conversation. The questions you do get to will tell you more about the person and the organisation than any engagement survey ever has. Most leaders' instinct in these conversations is to fill the quiet with reassurance, which collapses the conversation before it has started. Let it breathe.

What you do afterwards is what determines whether the framework was worth running. Take notes during the conversation, with their permission. Within a week, write back to them with what you heard and what you intend to do about it, even if the answer to some of it is I cannot fix that, but I have heard it. Then do what you said you would do.

The fastest way to destroy the trust this conversation builds is to ask the questions, hear the answers, and let them sit in a file you never return to.

Framework 4: The Visibility Trap Audit

A visibility trap is an organisational habit that rewards the appearance of work, and most organisations are full of them. The unwritten rules demand busyness as the proof of value. The midnight email that signals dedication. The meeting that exists so the right people are visible to each other. They consume time and energy that could have produced real work.

Visibility traps are particularly dangerous because they feel natural. Each one made sense when it started. The meeting was scheduled because something needed discussing. The fast email response was rewarded because once it did matter for something. The five-day office week was the only way work happened in 1972. Then the original reason faded, and the habit stayed, and now an entire generation of leaders is operating inside a set of conventions that no one designed and no one has questioned.

The audit names the most common traps and gives you an action for each. Work through table 16.2 with your leadership team. Be honest about which traps your organisation has fallen into. Then commit to acting on at least three of them inside the next quarter.

Table 16.2 The visibility traps

The trap	The action
1. **The meeting default.** When a decision needs to be made or information shared, is the answer always to call a meeting?	Eliminate one recurring meeting this week. Do not replace it. Watch what happens. If nothing breaks, eliminate another.
2. **The responsiveness illusion.** Does your organisation implicitly reward fast email response?	Establish communication norms that distinguish between urgent and non-urgent channels. Define what genuinely requires immediate response and give explicit permission for everything else to wait.
3. **The always on expectation.** When was the last time you sent a work message after 7pm?	For one month, schedule all your after-hours emails to send at 9 am the next morning. Ask your team to do the same. At the end of the month, ask whether a single business outcome was affected.
4. **The open plan assumption.** Count the places in your office where someone can do two hours of uninterrupted deep work.	Designate quiet hours when conversation and interruption are discouraged. Give people explicit permission to work from home when they need sustained concentration.
5. **The annual review ritual.** Does your performance review process inspire your people to improve, or to manage perceptions?	Supplement or replace the annual review with weekly or fortnightly feedback conversations. Five minutes of specific, timely feedback is worth more than five hours of annual documentation.
6. **The office mandate reflex.** If your organisation has mandated a return to office, what specific evidence informed that decision?	Measure the impact on productivity, retention and engagement. Compare the data to what was promised. If the outcomes do not match the expectations, revisit the policy.

(continued)

Table 16.2 (*continued*)

The trap	The action
7. **The brainstorming default.** When your team needs creative ideas, do you default to putting everyone in a room together?	Give the problem to each team member individually. Ask them to spend 20 minutes generating ideas alone, in writing. Collect and combine the results before any group discussion. Use the group session to evaluate and build on the ideas, not to generate them.
8. **The five-day assumption.** Has your organisation ever questioned whether five days is the right structure for the work you do?	Designate one Friday per month (or fortnight) as a no-meeting, deep workday. Track productivity and wellbeing over three months. If the results are positive, expand the experiment.

When you have completed the audit, count the traps your organisation has fallen into. Four or more, and you have a culture that has probably optimised for visibility over value.

The good news is that every trap on the list has a known alternative, tested across industries and organisation sizes. The question is whether your organisation has the appetite to question habits that feel like the way things have always been done.

Return to this audit every quarter.

Framework 5: The Workload Justice Test

This is where the redesign work begins, with the most common cause of burnout in any organisation. Too much work for the people doing it. Almost every other structural problem you will identify in this chapter is either a symptom of this one or a symptom of trying to compensate for it.

Workload is also the hardest problem to fix honestly, because fixing it means someone in the organisation has to do less of something they have already committed to, or accept that something will not get done at all. Most leadership teams reach for harder work as the answer before they will reach for less work, which is why the same workload conversations recur quarter after quarter without changing anything.

The Workload Justice Test asks you to do these four things, in this order:

1. **Ask your people to track their working hours for two weeks.** Not just the hours on the timesheet, but the hours spent checking email at night, thinking about a problem in the shower, taking a call on the weekend because the timing across markets did not allow anything else. Most leaders significantly underestimate the total. Two weeks of honest data will show you the size of the gap between the official week and the lived one.
2. **Determine what work is invisible to the system.** Emotional labour rarely makes it onto a timesheet. Neither does recovery time, the minutes and hours the brain takes to decompress after a hard conversation, or to rebuild focus after the fifth interruption of the morning. None of it shows up in the operating system, and all of it consumes capacity the work assignment assumed was available.
3. **Assess whether the workload sits within sustainable limits.** John Pencavel's research at Stanford, replicated and extended many times since, found that productivity per hour falls sharply above 50 hours per week, and that someone working 70 hours produces no more than someone working 55. If your team is routinely working past those thresholds, you do not have a productivity problem you can solve by adding pressure. You have a structural workload problem that is destroying capacity faster than you are creating output.
4. **Assess whether the workload exceeds capacity.** If yes, there are three possible solutions. Add resources. Reduce scope. Extend timelines. The conversation about which of the three to choose determines whether the framework works or fails.

An interesting and common reaction to these is for leaders to start explaining why none of them is available right now. Sometimes that's true. More often it is the first time the organisation's management has had a conversation about what it is asking of its people, and the discomfort of that conversation is what is being avoided rather than the choice. The conversation, even when it does not resolve in the moment, is worth having.

Framework 6: Meeting Pruning

The meeting problem is the most quantifiable structural problem in any organisation, and the most quietly catastrophic.

We know the toll of what meetings cost knowledge workers across an average week, what proportion of those meetings are unnecessary by the attendees' own assessment, and how much focused work time has been consumed by meeting preparation, meetings, chat and email combined. None of it is news, and yet in most companies, calendars get heavier rather than lighter with each passing quarter.

The framework and practice that addresses this is called pruning rather than culling because the work is ongoing. I have sat with leadership teams who eliminated two hours of meetings per person per week in a single sitting, discovered that nothing broke, and then quietly reinstated the same meetings six months later because the urgency that drove the original exercise had faded. Pruning is what you do to keep something healthy. Cuts are what you do once. The difference is the difference between a habit and an exercise and as we know, culture is nurtured by habits, patterns and norms.

Apply these three tests to every recurring meeting in your function's calendar. Ask:

1. **What does the meeting produce?** If a decision is not being made, an outcome is not being advanced, or a question is not being resolved, the meeting is performing rather than producing. Performing meetings exist for reasons of habit, hierarchy and

visibility, and they consume hours without producing anything in return.

2. **Who needs to be in the room?** Most meetings have at least two people present who could read the notes afterwards without any loss of information or decision quality. Halving the attendance list of every meeting in your function would recover thousands of hours a year without affecting a single outcome.
3. **Could the same result be reached without a meeting at all?** This is my personal favourite. A shared document or an asynchronous thread does the same job for most updates. The leaders who run organisations well have learned that meetings are the most expensive form of communication available to them, and they reserve that expense for the moments when nothing else will do.

What you do with the results matters more than the audit itself. Cancel the meetings that fail the tests, shorten those that pass, and move the ones that could be asynchronous out of the calendar entirely. Then come back to this exercise every quarter (ideally with your independent coach) because meetings regenerate like weeds. Without ongoing attention, your calendar will be back to where it was inside two quarters.

One last thing. The meetings you yourself created are the hardest to cut, because cutting them admits they were less useful than they felt at the time. Lead with those. When it comes to meeting pruning, the signals to prune matters as much as the pruning itself.

Framework 7: The Boundary Umpire

In Australian Rules Football (AFL), the boundary umpire has one job. They run the perimeter of the oval, watching where the ball goes, and the moment any part of the ball crosses the white line, they signal it. The game stops. The ball is thrown back in. Play resumes. The boundary umpire does not invent the rule about the white line. The rule was set before the match started. Their job is to enforce it, consistently, for the full 2.5–3 hours, while the play happens at speed all around them.

Every organisation needs a Boundary Umpire. Without one, the line that separates working time from personal time moves quietly outward, week by week, until the boundary that existed at the start of the year is no longer where anyone thinks it is. Most organisations have policies that describe these boundaries on paper and behaviours that often ignore them every night. The best leaders are also boundary umpires.

Before there is a line to umpire, the line has to be drawn. Four areas need attention:

1. **What counts as working hours?** Most organisations have never explicitly answered this question, which means every employee answers it for themselves, and the answer creeps wider every year. Define the hours during which work communication is expected, in writing, and make those hours match the hours people are paid for
2. **How does the organisation handle communication outside of working hours?** Most messages that arrive at 10 pm did not need to arrive at 10 pm. Most messages that arrive on Sunday afternoon did not need to arrive on Sunday afternoon. Decide what counts as an emergency that justifies after-hours contact, write that down, and treat every message that does not meet the bar as a violation of the boundary you have just set. The list of true emergencies in most knowledge organisations is short.

   In Australia the boundary umpiring has moved from being a wellbeing nicety to a legal requirement. *The Fair Work Legislation Amendment (Closing Loopholes No. 2) Act 2024* introduced a Right to Disconnect that came into effect on 26 August 2024 for organisations with 15 or more employees, and on 26 August 2025 for those with fewer. Employees now have a protected workplace right to refuse to monitor, read or respond to contact from their employer or third parties outside working hours, unless that refusal is unreasonable. Australia is not alone in this. France brought in similar protection in 2017, Portugal made out-of-hours contact a finable offence shortly afterwards, and several other jurisdictions have followed.

3. **Is the technology configured to support what the policy says?** Email scheduling is the cheapest, highest impact intervention available. If your team's emails sent after 7 pm are automatically queued to deliver at 8 am the next morning, the perceived pressure to respond outside hours disappears almost overnight. Status indicators that show when people are unavailable do similar work for chat platforms. And the leave policy needs to mean what it says. If someone on annual leave is still receiving and answering messages, they are not on leave. They are working from a different location at a discount.
4. **You.** Your behaviour as a leader is the policy that governs your organisation in practice, whatever the handbook says. What an umpire ignores becomes the new boundary. The midnight email, the weekend message, the reply that came in 12 minutes after a message was sent on a Saturday night, all of it is read by your team as the line you have just redrawn. People learn what the organisation will tolerate from what its most senior people do rather than from what its most senior people write. As any umpire will tell you, the rules are straightforward, upholding them can be very difficult. Drawing the line is a one-off exercise. Riding the boundary, calling the breaches when they happen, throwing the ball back in time after time, doing it consistently in front of your team, week after week, year after year, is what determines whether the line is real or decorative.

Framework 8: The Psychological Safety Sprint

Of the four redesign frameworks in this chapter, this is the one that determines whether the others stick.

Workload Justice, Meeting Pruning, the Boundary Umpiring, none of them last unless the team feels safe enough to tell you the truth. Psychological safety is the condition under which honest signal reaches the leader. Without it, every other framework runs blind and probably adds to any existing performative influence.

Importantly, psychological safety has nothing to do with comfort. The teams with the highest psychological safety also tend to have the highest accountability and the most direct disagreements. Amy Edmondson's research found that high safety teams have more open disagreement, because the people on those teams know the disagreement will not cost them. What changes is the cost of speaking up. When that cost is high, people stay silent and errors stack up until they cannot be hidden. When the cost is low, problems surface while they are still problems, rather than once they have become disasters.

Edmondson's foundational hospital research, the work that established the field, found something the researchers had not expected. The best performing nursing teams reported more medication errors than the worst performing ones. They had built the conditions where mistakes were safe to name, surface and learn from.

Google's Project Aristotle reached the same conclusion through different data. The team studied 180 of Google's own teams across two years from 2012 to 2015, examined every team attribute its researchers could measure, and found that the strongest predictor of team performance was psychological safety.

The research is now 30 years old and the finding has been replicated across industries, countries, and team types. Yet most organisations still treat psychological safety as a soft topic that belongs to HR rather than as a structural condition that determines whether anything else they invest in will work.

The Sprint is a four-week intervention. It doesn't build psychological safety from nothing. It accelerates the conditions under which safety can establish itself, by changing the leader's behaviour in deliberate sequence.

- **Week One: Your own vulnerability.** Pick something specific from the past quarter that did not work, and where you had a hand in it. Share this with your team plainly, with no lesson tacked on.
- **Week Two: How you respond.** When someone raises a concern, admits a mistake or pushes back on a decision in week two, your first words are, thank you for bringing this up. Then you ask a question that shows you have taken the contribution seriously. You do this every time, even when the contribution is poorly timed, awkwardly phrased, or about something you would rather not deal with. Ask for feedback on a current decision you are still working through, the way you would have wanted feedback on a decision when you were earlier in your career. Your team is watching to see whether the new behaviour is a new cultural leadership norm.
- **Week Three: The structure.** Before your next significant project starts, sit the team down and ask what could go wrong, where the project is most likely to fail, and what is being underestimated. Schedule a retrospective at the end of each major cycle so that the team has a regular forum for what worked and what did not. Add an anonymous feedback channel as a way to surface what they need to surface. Structure is the safety net in case behaviour slips.
- **Week Four: Measurement.** Run a short pulse survey using Edmondson's seven-question Likert scale, which asks about willingness to take risks, admit mistakes and surface difficult issues. Compare the result to where you thought the team was. Most leaders find the gap larger than they expected. Share what you find back with the team and ask what they need from you in the next quarter to close it.

The Sprint is four weeks of deliberate work followed by years of consistency, because what you put in place in four weeks has to be supported by consistent reinforcement and cues of authenticity.

Framework 9: The Culture Health Check

Cultures revert. Workload creeps back up, meetings reappear in calendars, boundaries dissolve as new people arrive who do not know the rules, and psychological safety degrades the moment a senior person punishes someone for raising a concern. Any leader who runs 'culture change' and then turns their attention elsewhere will, inside 18 months, normally find themselves running the same type of initiative again, wondering why the first one didn't stick.

Consistent, prioritised focus is what long-term culture change and culture optimisation relies on. I recommend a three-step process: 1. Measurement (Framework 9); 2. Drift Stocktake (Framework 10); and 3. Apex Accountability (Framework 11).

The Culture Health Check is the first.

Chapter 12 introduced CultureHealth™, the diagnostic developed by The Culture Institute of Australia that produces a single verified score from 0 to 100, measured across the four dimensions of Sentiment, Safety, Conduct and Customer Centricity. The Health Check is the practice of running that diagnostic on a discipline that matches the seriousness of what it is measuring.

Most organisations want to understand their culture and many of them try, usually through an annual engagement survey. These instruments tell you something useful at the moment they are run. The trouble is that culture does not sit still for 12 months waiting for the next survey, which means the picture you act on is always some months behind the reality your people are living.

The Health Check sets a different rhythm. Run the full CultureHealth™ diagnostic every six months. Read the results in the same week they arrive. Share them with the people who participated, in their actual numbers, including the parts you would rather not share. Then have the conversation about what the data is telling you, and decide what changes you are going to make before the next assessment.

When it comes to culture assessment, I've observed three typical traps:

1. **Measuring and not acting.** The data arrives, the conversation gets scheduled, the conversation happens, and then not much happens. The next round of measurement asks people to make the effort again, and people remember what happened to their honesty and efforts last time. When this happens response rates drops, and the instrument that was supposed to surface truth becomes just another workplace duty with little benefit.
2. **One day in 365.** Annual measurement is too infrequent to catch drift, monthly too frequent to let change register between rounds. Six monthly for the full diagnostic and quarterly for pulses sits in the right place for most organisations.
3. **Treating the score as the goal.** A score is just a signal. The moment leaders start managing the score itself rather than the culture, the score loses its value as a diagnostic and starts measuring something else entirely. As I noted in Chapter 12, the score reflects health and orientation reflects character. The work is knowing what the numbers tell you about the organisation, and how you respond to what they reveal.

The Health Check depends on the seriousness of the executive who commissions it. Treated with the rigour applied to financial reporting, it produces insight the organisation can act on. Anything less, and it becomes another HR exercise the executive tolerates rather than owns.

Framework 10: The Drift Stocktake

Cultures rarely break. They drift.

Cultural drift has been written about widely. Most authors describe the same pattern: cultures rarely break in any visible way, they decay slowly through a series of small accommodations that no one quite intends to make. What follows is my own contribution to that conversation, focused on what the leader does between the formal culture measurements to catch the drift while it can still be reversed.

The redesign work in Stage 2 produces visible change inside 90 days when applied with intent. The trouble is that visible change is a high-water mark. Once the urgency that drove the work fades and attention shifts to the next quarter's priorities, or new people join who never witnessed the original problem, the conditions that produced the effort begin to reassert themselves. And quietly. A meeting that was cancelled gets reinstated for a reason that sounds sensible. An after-hours email that would have been unthinkable in week one of the new policy becomes thinkable. The boundary umpire stops making calls because the breaches feel small and there is always something else more pressing to attend to. None of these moves looks like backsliding. They all look like pragmatism, and together they are how cultures lose what they have just built. I watch it every single year.

Framework 9's Health Check will catch this, but on a six-monthly cadence. By the time the diagnostic catches up, the work to recover the lost ground is harder than the work that built the original position.

What I call the Drift Stocktake helps close that gap. It's the leader's weekly scanning practice between the formal measurements, short and informal, designed for vigilance rather than precision.

Set aside 20 minutes at the end of each week to walk through these three questions:

1. **What has reappeared this week that you had previously removed?** A meeting back on the calendar. An after-hours message thread you tolerated because the timing seemed urgent. A piece of feedback you brushed past in a one-to-one because the day was busy. Write down what you notice. Most weeks the list will have one or two items, and most leaders will be tempted to dismiss them as one-offs. The early signal of drift looks exactly like that, a list of small forgivable exceptions, each of which would not matter on its own.

2. **What has crept in for the first time?** A new recurring meeting that someone added with good intentions. A new expectation about response times that no one explicitly set but everyone now seems to follow. A new piece of work that has been quietly distributed to the same person who is already at capacity. These additions matter because they are how cultures rebuild the conditions they were just redesigned to remove, without anyone making a deliberate decision to do so.
3. **What have you done this week that contradicts the redesign you just put in place?** The answer is rarely zero. It is the email you sent at 10 pm because the day got away from you. The concern someone raised in a meeting that you closed down before you understood why they raised it. Your behaviour is the loudest signal your function reads, and the small contradictions are the ones that erode the new culture fastest because very few are likely to tell you about them directly.

The Stocktake produces a working list of small concerns. Most resolve quickly when named. A reinstated meeting can be cancelled again. Your own contradictions can be acknowledged, and the act of acknowledging them is itself the reinforcement the culture redesign needs to survive.

The items that don't resolve in a week or two are the ones that require harder conversations. Take those into your monthly leadership team meeting, and into your quarterly review. They are the seeds of culture drift and, ultimately, of dysfunction if allowed to grow.

Framework 11: The CEO Culture Mandate

This framework is for those at the apex of the organisation: the CEO, the board or the senior executive team. If you are not in those roles, you can read it anyway, because the leaders above you are the variable that will determine whether everything else you have implemented in this chapter survives.

Culture work that doesn't start at the top, doesn't start. My team, clients and probably my friends are no doubt tired of hearing me say that culture is the responsibility of the CEO, and if the shaping and governance of culture has been delegated to HR, it is essentially in foster care, separated from its natural owner. I say this as I open every annual CultureCon™ and I wrote it very clearly in The Australian Workplace Culture Guidelines. Despite this, as mentioned previously, many CEOs continue to pay culture lip service and pass the ball to HR for assessment, development and governance (boundary umpiring).

The first ten frameworks in this toolkit can be implemented at function or team level by leaders at any tier. Framework 11 is different. It is the work only the people at the top of the organisation can do, and the work that determines whether the rest of the toolkit holds across the enterprise or stays trapped inside a few enlightened pockets.

There are five things that fall to the CEO and the board alone.

1. **Own culture.** Culture sits on your reporting line, alongside finance and risk, with the same cadence and the same seriousness. You do not delegate it. You commission the measurement, you read the data, you report culture health to the board every quarter.
2. **Apply financial grade rigour to culture data.** You would not run your business without financial statements. Running it without culture data is the equivalent, except the losses do not show up on a balance sheet until it is too late to act on them. Track CultureHealth™ scores quarterly. Know which parts of your organisation are healthy and which are quietly burning. Discuss culture health in the same meetings, with the same intensity, as financial performance.
3. **Make culture health a condition of leadership advancement.** The single most powerful signal you can send to the organisation is who you promote. If the leaders who consistently build healthy, high performing teams are the ones who rise, every other leader

will calibrate their own behaviour accordingly. If the leaders who burn their teams out for short-term results are the ones who rise, no amount of wellness programs or training will compensate. Promote on culture as deliberately as you promote on performance.

4. **Model what you ask of everyone else.** Your behaviour is the loudest signal in the building, and it reaches further than you think. The midnight email, the holiday that isn't really a holiday, the meeting that runs over because your time is the only time that doesn't get protected, all of it is watched and replicated. The leaders below you read your behaviour as the policy that governs the organisation, regardless of values promised in the lift.
5. **Resource culture properly.** Organisations spend money on what they value. Fund the measurement, fund the cultural leadership development, and fund the work that addresses root causes.

The capacity for cultural leadership can be developed by most executives willing to take it seriously. The business case for doing so has been made more times, in more industries, in more countries, than any reasonable sceptic could dismiss. Every leader at the apex of an organisation has access to the information they would need to act.

What separates those who do from those who do not is character, and this is the very thing most of us judge one another on.

Conclusion

From firestorm to flourishing

I know you're tired but come, this is the way.

—Rumi

If you've made it this far, you now know more about burnout than most of the people running the organisations that produce it. You've seen the data. You've seen the neuroscience. You've seen the economics. You've seen the systems that make burnout predictable and the choices that make it reversible. You have, in short, lost the luxury of not knowing.

Now, what will you do with what you know?

The moral imperative

Beyond economics and strategy lies a moral reality that should move every leader. The burnout epidemic is a humanitarian crisis unfolding in cubicles and conference rooms. Real people, your people, are suffering. Their health, their relationships, the years of their lives: work is consuming all of it, and work was supposed to sustain them.

You have the power to reduce this suffering. Every choice you make as a leader either contributes to burnout or counters it. Every decision about workload, boundaries and culture, about what you reward and what you tolerate: these decisions have human consequences.

Leadership is stewardship, not extraction. The people who work for you are not resources to be optimised but human beings entrusted to your care. What you do with that trust matters, to them, and to the kind of leader you are.

The performance imperative

Beyond the moral case lies a performance reality that should compel every leader who cares about results. The approaches most leaders believe create high performance, including pressure, control, intensity and internal competition, destroy the very outcomes they seek. The relentless pursuit of excellence generates unsustainable spikes followed by decline.

And beyond the performance case lies a legal reality that most leaders haven't fully absorbed. In Australia, the UK and across the European Union, employers are now legally required to prevent psychological harm at work, not simply to respond to it once it occurs. The organisations that have done the cultural work described in this book are the organisations closest to meeting their legal obligations.

Professional care and curiosity are the foundation that high performance requires. People with cognitive capacity rather than chronic stress think clearly. Those offering discretionary effort rather than mere compliance contribute fully. Psychological safety enables creative risk taking. Trust enables real coordination. And when people have genuine capacity, they extend real care to customers.

You face a choice. Leaders who squeeze everything from this quarter leave their successors with less, whereas leaders who support are creating something that grows stronger over time.

Sustainable achievement, innovation, deep collaboration, real customer centricity: these become possible when leaders choose investment over extraction.

The evidence that change works

Hope is warranted by the evidence.

Companies implementing sustained interventions report 71 per cent burnout reduction while maintaining revenue (Autonomy/4-Day Week, 2023). Mental health programs generate returns of approximately £5 for every £1 invested (Deloitte, 2020). The WHO estimates a return of US$4 for every US$1 invested in treatment for depression and anxiety (Chisholm, 2016; WHO, 2016). Employees in organisations that have actively invested in workplace mental health report better outcomes across burnout, presenteeism and turnover (Deloitte and Workplace Intelligence, 2024).

Change works. These organisations made the journey by investing in their people, and the success they built will outlast the leaders who began it

You can join them.

The mandate for leaders

Culture health is the core responsibility of leadership. Creating conditions where people can do their best work, contribute fully without being destroyed, thrive rather than merely survive: this is what leaders are for. Leaders who lack either the will or the capacity to build healthy cultures cause active harm. For every day they prioritise extraction, they diminish their people and the organisation that depends on them.

Perfection isn't the standard. Every leader makes mistakes, faces constraints, and operates within systems they didn't design. The question is whether you are determined to build something healthy, to learn from failures, and to treat the people you lead as people rather than resources.

The CEO's responsibility

To chief executives specifically: this book is a call to action that only you can answer.

No one else in your organisation has the authority to transform culture at scale. No one else can set the tone from the top, align incentives with relational health, hold leaders accountable for how they treat their people, and make the sustained investment that genuine culture change requires. Your CHRO, HRD, CPO or HR team can all support and advise you, and they can implement what you decide. But the decision, the commitment and the leadership: these must come from you.

The human cost of burnout is devastating. The economic cost is staggering. The trajectory, if nothing changes, leads to outcomes that should be unacceptable to any leader with a conscience. You know this now. What you do with this knowledge defines who you are as a leader and what legacy you will leave.

Will you be the CEO who transformed your organisation's relationship with its people?

Or will you be the CEO who read the evidence, understood the stakes, and chose to do nothing?

The choice is yours. But please understand: choosing to do nothing is still a choice. And it's a choice with consequences for every person in your organisation.

A vision of work that enhances life

Throughout this book, Buddhist philosophy has informed my perspective on work and suffering. The Buddhist concept of *Right Livelihood* describes work that serves life rather than consuming it.

Imagine workplaces where people grow rather than diminish. Where relationships with colleagues enrich rather than exhaust, and the purpose of the work connects to purposes worth serving.

Imagine coming to work with energy and leaving with satisfaction. Having time for the people you love, the activities that restore you, the dimensions of life that make living worthwhile. Bringing your full self to your work because your work doesn't require the sacrifice of everything else.

None of this is utopia. It's just what work looks like when we design it for human beings rather than against them. It's available now, to any leader with the courage and conviction to build it.

The invitation

You may be burned out yourself. You may have read this book while exhausted, squeezed into margins of days that have no margin. You may be feeling the impossibility of adding one more initiative, one more change effort, one more thing to manage.

I'm not asking you to do more. I'm asking you to *do differently.*

Start small. Choose one practice from these pages and implement it this week. Have one honest conversation about wellbeing. Protect one boundary you've been violating. Model one pattern that can be sustained where before you modelled one that couldn't.

Small changes accumulate. Consistent attention compounds. The path from firestorm to flourishing isn't a single dramatic transformation but countless small choices, made daily, that gradually reshape what's normal and possible.

And if your scope is limited, if you lead a team rather than a company, a department rather than an enterprise, know that your work matters. The people on your team don't experience 'the organisation'. They experience you. It is your decisions, your behaviour, and your care or indifference that shapes their daily reality. A healthy team can exist inside an unhealthy organisation. It shelters the people in it, and often plants the seed of broader change.

You may have read this book over several weeks in the stolen moments of exactly the kind of workday this book describes. You may have underlined sentences at midnight that you agreed with completely and felt unable to act on by morning.

That is where most of us are. That is not a reason to put the book down. It is the reason this book exists.

The platform is burning

Life isn't a rehearsal. The hours you spend burned out, the years you give to work that can't be sustained, the health and relationships you sacrifice: these don't come back. Time moves in one direction, and every day spent in the fire is a day of your finite life that you won't get back.

The same is true for the people you lead. Their lives are finite and precious, and they deserve conditions that allow them to live well.

The modern workplace platform is burning. You can stand on it and burn with it. You can watch others burn while telling yourself it's someone else's problem. Or you can grab a bucket and encourage others to do the same.

I wrote at the beginning of this book that work should be one of the best parts of life. I still believe that. I've seen it, in teams that trust each other, in organisations that treat people as people, in leaders who figured out that care and excellence are the same thing wearing different clothes.

It's possible. It's proven. The people you lead deserve it. And you deserve it too.

My dad told me to do what moves you. He spent 40 years sitting with people in their worst moments and helping them find a way through, which means he understood something most leadership books never quite get to: what moves us is simpler and harder to argue with. It is the person in front of us, and whether we are willing to see what they are carrying and act on it.

Do what moves you.

If you've read this far, something moved you.

Start there.

Afterword

Workplace burnout is a structural problem with a behavioural cure. The simplest word for the behaviour is consideration. Consideration is what happens when a leader looks past the title on the badge and notices the person who carefully chose their outfit for the day. It's what happens when an executive thinks about the downstream effects of a decision on the people who will live with it.

Consideration is treated in most organisations as a soft skill. It is the hardest discipline I know. It requires the leader to slow down, to listen properly, and to take responsibility for what they hear. The frameworks in chapter 16 are how that discipline gets converted into structural decisions. The frameworks return what you put into them, and they return little when the leader using them brings something less than consideration to work.

I've been working on this concept for 30 years. I started inside aged care facilities, where I watched what happens when consideration is withdrawn from a population that no longer has any economic value to the system around it. The day rooms were the most efficient possible arrangement for the staff and the most inconsiderate possible arrangement for the residents. People sat facing walls. Nobody spoke to them. The room had been designed without due consideration about what the humans inside it might need.

Once a week I would put a record on in one of those rooms and dance with Olive, who was 88. The dancing mattered less than the act of consideration. Someone had looked at her, recognised that she was still in there, and made the small behavioural decision to bring three minutes of the thing she loved most back into her life.

Workplaces are doing the same thing to people many decades younger than Olive, at scale, every day. The architecture may be different but the outcome is the same. People who used to bring energy to the work are sitting in their own version of the day room, waiting to be seen.

Two pieces of research have shaped my thinking on this more than any others.

The first is Self-Determination Theory, developed by Edward Deci and Richard Ryan over 40 years of research and now one of the most empirically supported frameworks in psychology. It identifies three basic psychological needs that human beings require in order to function well: autonomy, the sense that they have meaningful agency over their work; competence, the sense that they are getting better at something that matters; and relatedness, the need to feel connected to the people around them, to feel safe enough to engage, to know that the people they spend their working lives with have positive intentions towards them. Workplaces that thwart any of these needs produce predictable consequences: disengagement, declining wellbeing, and eventually burnout. Workplaces that meet all three produce something rare and very valuable.

The second is the Harvard Study of Adult Development, the longest study of human happiness ever conducted, now running for over 80 years. Its central finding, replicated across eight decades of data, is that the strongest predictor of human happiness is the quality of a person's relationships. Stronger than wealth. Stronger than IQ. Stronger than social class.

Autonomy, competence and connection. Those are what people want from a working life.

The leaders I work with now are the ones who understand this. They commission measurement, and ask the harder questions. The cultures they are quietly building are the ones their best people refuse to leave.

The most reliable obstacle to culture health has nothing to do with budgets or strategy. It is power intoxication, the slow distortion of perspective that comes when a leader has been deferred to for long enough that they stop hearing what their organisation is trying to tell them. Almost every cultural failure I have walked into has it sitting near the centre. The leaders who address it are the ones who stay curious and who keep listening.

I should say plainly that I have spent time on the fringe of burnout myself. My job is demanding, the cases are heavy, and the standard I hold the work to is high. The radar and the toolkit in Chapter 16 are how I stay back from the edge. I use them on myself, regularly, and I would not be able to write a book like this honestly without that experience sitting underneath it.

The introduction to this book describes the day in 1998 when I was 22 and an avalanche came down on the car I was driving in New Zealand. I was buried under snow for several hours, with no idea whether anyone knew where we were. What arrived in the silence, once the fear settled, was a single question. What have you done with your time alive on this planet?

The promises I made under the snow that day are the same promises that drive the work I do now and the writing of this book. My hope is that the rest of us don't need a mountain to find a better way to be with one another. Consideration, kindness, and the resolve to make structural decisions for the people we lead are available in any moment, and the return dwarfs the cost.

The headwind is intensifying. The two pressures named at the start of this book, AI-era job insecurity and the financial wellbeing crisis, are turning what was already a structural challenge into a generational one. The workforce I am writing for is anxious, financially stretched, and watching their roles get reshaped around them.

What I want you to take from this is simple. The people you lead need safety, and they need to be seen. Both of those are inside your gift as a leader. Kindness is the most underrated starting point I know of, and consideration is the discipline that turns kindness into structural decisions.

The next generation is watching to see whether the workplaces they are about to inherit are worth inheriting. So is mine, the generation old enough to remember when work was meant to make life better. So is Olive, whose three minutes of dancing taught me what consideration looks like when it costs almost nothing and means almost everything.

References

AARP Public Policy Institute & National Alliance for Caregiving (2025). 'Caregiving in the US 2025.' www.aarp.org/pri/topics/ltss/family-caregiving/caregiving-in-the-us-2025/

ADP Research (2026). 'Today at Work 2026,' Issue 1. *Global Workforce Survey*, 39,000 respondents across 36 markets, data collected July–August 2025. Released 25 March 2026. https://mediacenter.adp.com/2026-03-25-ADP-Research-Only-22-of-Workers-Confident-Their-Job-is-Safe-from-Elimination

ADP Research Institute (2025). 'People at work 2025: A global workforce view.' https://au.adp.com/resources/insights/people-at-work-2025-a-global-workforce-view.aspx

Afsharian, A, LaMontagne, AD, Milner, A & Butterworth, P (2025). 'The effect of psychosocial safety climate on depression: A prospective cohort study.' *Journal of Occupational and Environmental Medicine.*

Alhola, P & Polo-Kantola, P (2007). 'Sleep deprivation: Impact on cognitive performance.' *Neuropsychiatric Disease and Treatment* 3(5): 553–67.

Allianz Australia (2024a). 'Mental health claims analysis.'

Allianz Australia (2024b). 'Unpacking the new workforce.' https://www.allianz.com.au/business-insurance/workers-compensation/workplace-mental-health/unpacking-the-new-workforce.html

Amabile, TM & Kramer, SJ (2011). *The progress principle: Using small wins to ignite joy, engagement and creativity at work*. Harvard Business Review Press.

American Institute of Stress (AIS) (2023). 'Workplace stress statistics.' https://www.stress.org/workplace-stress

Atlassian (2024). 'Workplace woes: Meetings – Inside Atlassian.' https://www.atlassian.com/blog/workplace-woes-meetings

Australian Bureau of Statistics (ABS) (2026). 'Recorded crime — Offenders 2024–25.' www.abs.gov.au

Australian Prudential Regulation Authority (APRA) (2025). *APRA Corporate Plan 2025–26*. www.apra.gov.au/apra-corporate-plan-2025-26

Autonomy/4 Day Week Global (2023). Lewis, K et al. 'The results are in: The UK's four-day week pilot.' https://autonomy.work/portfolio/uk4dwpilot/

Backhaus, I et al. (2025). 'Mental health effects of unemployment and re-employment: A systematic review and meta-analysis of longitudinal studies.' *BMJ Public Health*. https://pmc.ncbi.nlm.nih.gov/articles/PMC12505101/

Bakir, S, Dogru, T, Bilgihan, A & Ayoun, B (2025). 'AI awareness and employee-related outcomes: A systematic review of the hospitality literature and a framework for future research.' *International Journal of Hospitality Management* 124:103973. https://doi.org/10.1016/j.ijhm.2024.103973

BambooHR Research (2024). 'The new surveillance era: Visibility beats productivity for RTO & remote.' www.bamboohr.com/resources/data-at-work/data-stories/2024-return-to-office

Baron Cohen, S (2011). *The science of evil: On empathy and the origins of cruelty*. New York: Basic Books.

Bartlett, S (2026). *Thriving minds in the age of AI*. Brisbane: Phineline Publishing.

Bastian, B, Jetten, J & Ferris, LJ (2014). 'Pain as social glue: Shared pain increases cooperation.' *Psychological Science* 25(11): 2079–85.

Baumeister, RF & Tierney, J (2011). *Willpower: Rediscovering the greatest human strength*. New York: Penguin Press.

Baumeister, RF, Bratslavsky, E, Finkenauer, C & Vohs, KD (2001). 'Bad is stronger than good.' *Review of General Psychology* 5(4): 323–70.

Belkin, LY, Becker, W & Conroy, SA (2016). 'Exhausted, but unable to disconnect: After-hours email, work-family balance and identification.' *Academy of Management Proceedings* 2016(1): 10353. DOI: 10.5465/AMBPP.2016.10353abstract

Benioff, M (2023). 'Letter to Employees.' Exhibit 99.1 to Form 8-K. Salesforce, Inc. Filed 4 January 2023. US Securities and Exchange Commission. https://www.sec.gov/Archives/edgar/data/0001108524/000110852423000003/ex991-lettertoemployees.htm

Bernstein, ES & Turban, S (2018). 'The impact of the open workspace on human collaboration.' *Philosophical Transactions of the Royal Society B* 373(1753): 20170239.

Beyond Blue (2025). '1 in 2 Australians facing workplace burnout – young adults and caregivers leading the trend.' Media release, 17 July 2025. www.beyondblue.org.au/about/media/media-releases/1-in-2-Australians-Facing-Workplace-Burnout

Bloom, N, Han, R & Liang, J (2024). 'Hybrid working from home improves retention without damaging performance.' *Nature* 630:920–25.

Bolton, W & Oatley, K (1987). 'A longitudinal study of social support and depression in unemployed men.' *Psychological Medicine* 17:453–460.

Bond, FW & Bunce, D (2003). 'The role of acceptance and job control in mental health, job satisfaction, and work performance.' *Journal of Applied Psychology* 88(6): 1057–67.

Bonnell, C (2023). '4-day work week trial yields overwhelming success in U.K., researchers say.' *PBS NewsHour*, 21 February 2023. https://www.pbs.org/newshour/world/4-day-work-week-trial-yields-overwhelming-success-in-u-k-researchers-say

Brown, B (2018). *Dare to lead: Brave work. Tough conversations. Whole hearts.* New York: Random House.

Brunell, AB, Gentry, W, Campbell, WK, Hoffman, B, Kuhnert, K & DeMarree, K (2008). 'Leader emergence: The case of the narcissistic leader.' *Personality and Social Psychology Bulletin* 34(12): 1663–1676.

Calderone, A, Latella, D, Impellizzeri, F, de Pasquale, P, Famà, F, Quartarone, A & Calabrò, RS (2024). 'Neurobiological changes induced by mindfulness and meditation: A systematic review.' *Biomedicines*, 12(11), 2613. https://doi.org/10.3390/biomedicines12112613

Calendly (2024). *The state of meetings 2024*. Conducted by Brand Over Matter, June–July 2024. https://calendly.com/newsroom/press-release/report-state-of-meetings-2024

Carpenter, R (2024). 'A viewpoint on the impact of fundamental attribution error in organizational learning.' *Development and Learning in Organizations: An International Journal*. DOI: 10.1108/DLO-12-2023-0281

Cascio, WF (2006). 'The high cost of low wages.' *Harvard Business Review*, December 2006. https://hbr.org/2006/12/the-high-cost-of-low-wages

Centola, D (2018). *How behavior spreads: The science of complex contagions*. Princeton University Press.

CFO.com (2018). 'PE firms' role in Toys R Us collapse questioned.' Informa TechTarget.www.cfo.com/news/pe-firms-role-in-toys-r-us-collapse-questioned/658864/

Chartered Management Institute (CMI) & YouGov (2023). 'Taking responsibility: Why UK PLC needs better managers.' www.managers.org.uk/wp-content/uploads/2023/10/CMI_BMB_GoodManagment_Report.pdf

Chisholm, D, Sweeny, K, Sheehan, P et al. (2016). 'Scaling-up treatment of depression and anxiety: A global return on investment analysis.' *The Lancet Psychiatry* 3(5): 415–24. https://doi.org/10.1016/S2215-0366(16)30024-4

Chung, H & Yuan, S (2025). 'Return to office mandates: What is at stake for gender equality?' King's College London, Global Institute for Women's Leadership. www.kcl.ac.uk/giwl/assets/return-to-office-mandates-what-is-at-stake.pdf

Clark, TR (2020). *The 4 stages of psychological safety: Defining the path to inclusion and innovation.* Oakland: Berrett-Koehler Publishers.

Covey, SR (1989). *The 7 habits of highly effective people: Powerful lessons in personal change.* New York: Free Press.

Coyle, D (2018). *The culture code: The secrets of highly successful groups.* New York: Bantam Books.

Crabtree, S (2014). 'In U.S., depression rates higher for long-term unemployed.' Gallup, 9 June 2014. https://news.gallup.com/poll/171044/depression-rates-higher-among-long-term-unemployed.aspx

Cross, R & Parker, A (2004). *The hidden power of social networks.* Harvard Business School Press.

Cross, R, Nohria, N & Parker, A (2002). 'Six myths about informal networks.' *MIT Sloan Management Review* 43(3): 67–75.

Culture Amp (2024). *2024 State of the manager report.* www.cultureamp.com/resources/reports

Culture Institute of Australia (2023). *Coaching impact survey 2023.* https://cultureinstitute.com.au

Darley, JM & Batson, CD (1973). '"From Jerusalem to Jericho": A study of situational and dispositional variables in helping behavior.' *Journal of Personality and Social Psychology* 27:100–108.

Davies, K (2013). *Ready, fire, aim: The Mainfreight story.* Auckland: Random House.

Dawson, D & Reid, K (1997). 'Fatigue, alcohol and performance impairment.' *Nature* 388:235. https://doi.org/10.1038/40775

Dayen, D (2018). 'Private equity: Looting 'R' Us.' *The American Prospect,* March 20, 2018.

Deloitte (2022). 'Mental health and employers: The case for investment, pandemic and beyond.' www.deloitte.com/uk/en/services/consulting/analysis/mental-health-and-employers-the-case-for-investment.html

Deloitte (2025). '2025 Gen Z and Millennial survey: Living and working with purpose in a transforming world.' www.deloitte.com/gr/en/issues/work/genz-millennial-survey-2025.html

Deloitte & Workplace Intelligence (2024a). 'The important role of leaders in advancing human sustainability.' 18 June 2024. https://www.deloitte.com/us/en/insights/topics/talent/workplace-well-being-research-2024.html

Deloitte UK (2020). 'Mental health and employers: Refreshing the case for investment.' Deloitte LLP. https://www2.deloitte.com/uk/en/pages/consulting/articles/mental-health-and-employers-refreshing-the-case-for-investment.html

Deloitte UK (2024b). *Mental health and employers: The case for investment* (4th ed.). London: Deloitte LLP. https://www.deloitte.com/uk/en/about/press-room/poor-mental-health-costs-uk-employers-51-billion-a-year-for-employees.html

Dery, K & Sebastian, I (2017). 'Building business value with employee experience.' *MIT Centre for Information Systems Research Briefing* Vol XVII, No 6. https://cisr.mit.edu/publication/2017_0601_EmployeeExperience_DerySebastian

DHR Global (2024). *2024 Global leadership report: The burnout epidemic.* https://www.dhrglobal.com/insights/balancing-engagement-burnout-what-dhr-globals-2024-report-reveals/

DHR Global (2025). *2025 Workforce trends: Leadership and wellbeing.* https://www.dhrglobal.com/insights/workforce-trends-report-2025/

Ding, Y et al. (2025). 'Return to office mandates and brain drain.' Baylor University / Hankamer School of Business. https://hankamer.baylor.edu/news/story/2025/return-office-mandates-and-hidden-cost-brain-drain

Dunbar, RIM (1992). 'Neocortex size as a constraint on group size in primates.' *Journal of Human Evolution* 22(6): 469–93.

Dutton, JE, Workman, KM & Hardin, AE (2014). 'Compassion at work.' *Annual Review of Organizational Psychology and Organizational Behavior* 1:277–304. https://doi.org/10.1146/annurev-orgpsych-031413-091221

Dyrbye, LN, Thomas, MR, Massie, FS et al. (2008). 'Burnout and suicidal ideation among US medical students.' *Annals of Internal Medicine* 149(5): 334–341.

Eagle Hill Consulting (2025). *Workforce burnout survey 2025.* www.eaglehillconsulting.com/news/workforce-burnout-survey-2025/

Eales, MJ (1988). 'Depression and anxiety in unemployed men.' *Psychological Medicine* 18:935–45.

Edmondson, AC (1999). 'Psychological safety and learning behavior in work teams.' *Administrative Science Quarterly* 44(2): 350–383.

Edmondson, AC (2019). *The fearless organization: Creating psychological safety in the workplace for learning, innovation, and growth.* Hoboken: John Wiley & Sons.

Edmondson, AC & Lei, Z (2014). 'Psychological safety: The history, renaissance, and future of an interpersonal construct.' *Annual Review of Organizational Psychology and Organizational Behavior* 1:23–43.

Edwards, D (2026). *How to be happy.* Melbourne: John Wiley & Sons.

Erikson, T (2022). *Surrounded by narcissists.* New York: St. Martin's Essentials.

Eurich, T (2017). *Insight: The surprising truth about how others see us, how we see ourselves, and why the answers matter more than we think.* New York: Crown Currency.

Eurich, T (2018). 'What self-awareness really is (and how to cultivate it).' *Harvard Business Review*, 4 January 2018. https://hbr.org/2018/01/what-self-awareness-really-is-and-how-to-cultivate-it

Flowtrace (2025). 'Meeting statistics for 2026: 100 data points on time, cost and collaboration.' Flowtrace Collaboration Blog. https://www.flowtrace.co/collaboration-blog/50-meeting-statistics

Fonagy, P, Luyten, P, Moulton-Perkins, A, Lee, Y-W, Warren, F, Howard, S et al. (2016). 'Development and validation of a self-report measure of mentalizing: The Reflective Functioning Questionnaire.' *PLOS ONE* 11(7): e0158678. https://doi.org/10.1371/journal.pone.0158678

Forrester Research (2023). 'The cost of not being customer obsessed.' https://www.forrester.com/report/the-cost-of-not-being-customer-obsessed/RES179393

Forsdick, S (2022). 'It would be impossible to go back: Inside the UK's four-day work week trial.' *Raconteur*, 1 September 2022. https://www.raconteur.net/future-of-work/inside-the-uk-four-day-week-trial

Fredrickson, BL (2001). 'The role of positive emotions in positive psychology: The broaden and build theory of positive emotions.' *American Psychologist* 56(3): 218–226.

Frollova, N et al. (2024). 'The leadership fallacy: How misattribution of leadership leads to a blaming game.' *Journal of Economic Psychology* 104:102753. https://doi.org/10.1016/j.joep.2024.102753

Frost, PJ & Robinson, S (1999). 'The toxic handler: Organizational hero and casualty.' *Harvard Business Review* 77(4): 96–106.

Gallup (2013). *State of the American workplace: Employee engagement insights for US business leaders.* Washington DC: Gallup Press.

Gallup (2015). *State of the American Manager: Analytics and advice for leaders.* Washington DC: Gallup Press.

Gallup (2018). *State of the global workplace 2018.* Washington DC: Gallup Press.

Gallup (2019). 'More harm than good: The truth about performance reviews.' *Gallup Workplace.* https://www.gallup.com/workplace/249332/harm-good-truth-performance-reviews.aspx

Gallup (2020). *Employee burnout: Causes and cures.* Washington DC: Gallup Press.

Gallup (2022). *State of the global workplace 2022 report.* Washington DC: Gallup Press.

Gallup (2024). *State of the global workplace 2024 report.* Washington DC: Gallup Press.

Gallup (2025). *State of the global workplace 2025 report.* Washington DC: Gallup Press.

Gartner (2025). 'HR's behaviors and actions are a key differentiator in sustaining employee productivity during RTO.' Media release. www.gartner.com/en/newsroom/press-releases/2025-05-12-hrs-behaviors-and-actions-are-a-key-differentiator-in-sustaining-employee-productivity-during-rto

Gartner HR Practice (2024). 'The data is in: Return-to-office mandates aren't worth the talent risks.' www.gartner.com/en/articles/the-data-is-in-return-to-office-mandates-aren-t-worth-the-talent-risks

George, B (2024). 'Why Boeing's problems with the 737 MAX began more than 25 years ago.' Harvard Business School Working Knowledge. https://www.library.hbs.edu/working-knowledge/why-boeings-problems-with-737-max-began-more-than-25-years-ago

Gerlich, M (2025). 'AI tools in society: Impacts on cognitive offloading and the future of critical thinking.' *Societies* 15(1): 6. https://doi.org/10.3390/soc15010006

Gino, F (2018). 'The business case for curiosity.' *Harvard Business Review* 96(5): 48–57.

Global Corporate Challenge (GCC) Insights (2015). 'Presenteeism: The problem we ignore.' Validated against the WHO Workplace Health and Productivity Questionnaire (WHO-HPQ).

Goh, J, Pfeffer, J & Zenios, SA (2016). 'The relationship between workplace stressors and mortality and health costs in the United States.' *Management Science* 62(2): 608–28.

Goldenberg, A (2023). 'The social spread of emotion.' Harvard Business School Working Paper.

Golkar, A, Johansson, E, Kasahara, M et al. (2014). 'The influence of work-related chronic stress on the regulation of emotion and on functional connectivity in the brain.' *PLOS ONE* 9:e104550. https://journals.plos.org/plosone/article?id=10.1371/journal.pone.0104550

Goodhart, CAE (1975). 'Problems of monetary management: The UK experience.' *Papers in Monetary Economics* Vol I. Reserve Bank of Australia.

Grant Thornton Australia (2024). *Retail industry workforce report 2024.*

Grow Therapy (2025). *State of mental health in America: Workplace edition 2025 to 2026.*

Hagtvedt, LP, Dossinger, K, Harrison, SH & Huang, L (2019). 'Curiosity made the cat more creative: Specific curiosity as a driver of creativity.' *Organizational Behavior and Human Decision Processes* 150:1–13.

Han, S, Shanafelt, TD, Sinsky, CA, Awad, KM, Dyrbye, LN, Fiscus, LN, Trockel, M & Goh, J (2019). 'Estimating the attributable cost of physician burnout in the United States.' *Annals of Internal Medicine* 170(11): 784–790.

Haraldsson, GD & Stronge, W (2021). 'Going public: Iceland's journey to a shorter working week.' Autonomy and Association for Sustainability and Democracy (Alda). https://autonomy.work/portfolio/icelandsww/

Harrison, SH, Pinkus, E & Cohen, J (2022). 'Research: 83% of executives say they encourage curiosity. Just 52% of employees agree.' *Harvard Business Review.* https://hbr.org/2022/08/research-83-of-executives-say-they-encourage-curiosity-just-52-of-employees-agree

Health and Safety Executive (HSE), UK Government (2025). *Work-related stress, depression or anxiety statistics in Great Britain, 2025.*

Howe, GW (2015). Research program on unemployment and depression. Summarised in: 'Unemployment and depression: Inside an unsettling partnership.' George Washington University, Columbian College of Arts & Sciences. https://columbian.gwu.edu/unemployment-and-depression-inside-unsettling-partnership

Huberman, AD (2025). Various episodes on stress, neuroscience, and performance. *Huberman Lab Podcast*, 2021–25.

IBM Smarter Workforce Institute & Workhuman (2016). *The employee experience index: A new global measure of a human workplace and its impact.* www.workhuman.com/resources/reports-guides/the-employee-experience-index/

Institute for Corporate Productivity (i4cp) (2023). *Culture fitness: Healthy habits of high-performance organizations.* https://go.i4cp.com/culturefitness

Insurance Council of Australia (2024). 'The economic cost of mental illness in Australia.'

International Coaching Federation and Human Capital Institute (ICF) (2019). 'Building a coaching culture for increased employee engagement.'

Ipsos (2023). *Global views on AI 2023: A 31-country Global Advisor survey.* www.ipsos.com/sites/default/files/ct/news/documents/2023-07/Ipsos%20Global%20AI%202023%20Report-WEB_0.pdf

Jacoby, D (2023). 'A winning sales culture: Lessons from Salesforce & Netflix.' SBI Growth Advisory, 15 March 2023. https://sbigrowth.com/insights/blog/building-a-winning-sales-culture-lessons-from-salesforce-and-netflix

Kahn, WA (1993). 'Caring for the caregivers: Patterns of organizational caregiving.' *Administrative Science Quarterly* 38(4): 539–63.

Kim, BJ & Lee, J (2024). 'The mental health implications of artificial intelligence adoption: The crucial role of self-efficacy.' *Humanities and Social Sciences Communications* 11, Article 1561. DOI: 10.1057/s41599-024-04018-w

Kim, J & de Dear, R (2013). 'Workspace satisfaction: The privacy-communication trade-off in open-plan offices.' *Journal of Environmental Psychology* 36:18–26.

Kivimaki, M & Steptoe, A (2018). 'Effects of stress on the development and progression of cardiovascular disease.' *Nature Reviews Cardiology* 15(4): 215–29.

Koenig, J (2021). *The dictionary of obscure sorrows*. New York: Simon & Schuster.

Kohner, J (2016). 'How and why Salesforce took the day off to be mindful.' *Medium*, 7 November 2016. https://medium.com/@salesforce/how-and-why-salesforce-took-the-day-off-to-be-mindful-3aa7462e206d

Kohner, J (2017). 'The real meaning behind Salesforce community.' *Salesforce Blog*, 6 February 2017. https://www.salesforce.com/blog/what-is-salesforce-ohana/

Kong, DT et al. (2023). 'Electronic performance monitoring and employee outcomes: A meta-analytic investigation.' *Personnel Psychology* 76(4): 1149–80.

Kotter, JP & Heskett, JL (1992). *Corporate culture and performance*. New York: Free Press.

KPMG International (2024). *CEO outlook survey*. https://assets.kpmg.com/content/dam/kpmg/sg/pdf/2024/09/kpmg-ceo-outlook-2024-executive-summary.pdf

LaMontagne, AD (2024). 'Work-related suicide: Evolving understandings of etiology and intervention.' *American Journal of Industrial Medicine*. doi: 10.1002/ajim.23624

Lancaster University Work Foundation (2025). *Shifting challenges? How cost of living pressures are impacting workers in 2025*. www.lancaster.ac.uk/work-foundation/news/blog/shifting-challenges-how-cost-of-living-pressures-are-impacting-workers-in-2025

Lazonick, W & Sakinç, ME (2019). *Boeing's shareholder value orientation has resulted in an unprecedented catastrophe*. The Academic-Industry Research Network / The American Prospect.

Lee, D-W, Lee, J, Kim, H-R & Kang, M-Y (2020). 'Association of long working hours and health-related productivity loss, and its differential impact by income level: A cross-sectional study of Korean workers.' *Journal of Occupational Health* 62(1): e12190.

Lembke, A (2021). *Dopamine nation: Finding balance in the age of indulgence*. London: Dutton/Penguin Random House.

Levine, M (2025). 'The story of Boeing's failed corporate culture.' *The CPA Journal*, August 2025. https://www.cpajournal.com/2025/08/12/the-story-of-boeings-failed-corporate-culture-3/

Lewis, K et al. (2023). *The results are in: The UK's four-day week pilot*. Autonomy and 4 Day Week Global, February 2023. https://autonomy.work/wp-content/uploads/2023/02/The-results-are-in-The-UKs-four-day-week-pilot.pdf

Lewsey, F (2023). 'Would you prefer a four-day working week?' University of Cambridge, 21 February 2023. www.cam.ac.uk/stories/fourdayweek

Li, X et al. (2023). 'How does CEO curiosity affect firm innovation?' *Technovation.* DOI: 10.1016/j.technovation.2023.102816

Lievens, F, Harrison, SH, Mussel, P & Litman, JA (2022). 'Killing the cat? A review of curiosity at work.' *Academy of Management Annals* 16(1): 179–216.

Lilius, JM, Worline, MC, Maitlis, S, Kanov, J, Dutton, JE & Frost, P (2008). 'The contours and consequences of compassion at work.' *Journal of Organizational Behavior* 29(2): 193–218. https://doi.org/10.1002/job.508

Lin, L & Parker, K (2025). *US workers are more worried than hopeful about future AI use in the workplace.* Washington, DC: Pew Research Center. www.pewresearch.org/social-trends/2025/02/25/u-s-workers-are-more-worried-than-hopeful-about-future-ai-use-in-the-workplace

Liston, C, McEwen, BS & Casey, BJ (2009). 'Psychosocial stress reversibly disrupts prefrontal processing and attentional control.' *Proceedings of the National Academy of Sciences* 106(3): 912–17.

Lloyd's Register Foundation & Gallup (2021). *World risk poll 2021.* www.lrfoundation.org.uk/wrp/themes-and-reports/2021-world-risk-poll

Lyra Health (2025). *Workforce mental health trends 2025.* www.lyrahealth.com

Ma, M et al. (2024). 'Return to office mandates.' University of Pittsburgh working paper. https://papers.ssrn.com/sol3/papers.cfm?abstract_id=4675401

Mark, G (2023). *Attention span: Finding focus for a fulfilling life.* New York: Hanover Square Press.

Maslach, C & Leiter, MP (1997). *The truth about burnout: How organizations cause personal stress and what to do about it.* San Francisco: Jossey Bass.

Maslach, C, Jackson, SE & Leiter, MP (1996). *Maslach burnout inventory manual* (3rd ed.). Consulting Psychologists Press.

Matsuo, T et al. (2022). 'Prevalence of burnout among healthcare workers in Japan: A systematic review.' *Environmental and Occupational Health Practice* 4(1).

McChrystal, S, Collins, T, Silverman, D & Fussell, C (2015). *Team of teams: New rules of engagement for a complex world.* New York: Portfolio/Penguin.

McEwen, BS (2002). *The end of stress as we know it.* Washington, DC: Joseph Henry Press.

McKinsey & Company (2022a). *Addressing employee burnout: Are you solving the right problem?*

McKinsey & Company (2022b). *Women in the workplace 2022.*

McKinsey & Company (2023). *Diversity matters even more: The case for holistic impact.* www.mckinsey.com/featured-insights/diversity-and-inclusion/diversity-matters-even-more-the-case-for-holistic-impact

Mental Health UK & YouGov (2024). *The burnout report 2024.* https://mhukcdn.s3.eu-west-2.amazonaws.com/wp-content/uploads/2024/01/19145241/Mental-Health-UK_The-Burnout-Report-2024.pdf

meQuilibrium (2024/2025). *State of the workforce report: Winter 2025.* Boston. meQuilibrium. https://go.mequilibrium.com/meQ-winter-2025-state-of-workforce-report_content_submit.html

Mercer (2024). *Global talent trends 2024.*

Merrill, RM et al. (2025). 'Presenteeism and absenteeism as a function of health risk and employee productivity.' *American Journal of Preventive Medicine* 68(1): 117–26.

MHFA England (2023). 'Unilever.' Case study, 7 March 2023. https://mhfaengland.org/mhfa-centre/case-studies/unilever/

Microsoft (2022). *Work trend index 2022: Great expectations: Making hybrid work work.* https://www.microsoft.com/en-us/worklab/work-trend-index

Microsoft (2025). *2025 Work trend index annual report: The frontier firm is born.* https://www.microsoft.com/en-us/worklab/work-trend-index/2025-the-year-the-frontier-firm-is-born

Microsoft Japan (2019). *Work-life choice challenge Summer 2019.* Microsoft Japan Press Release.

Milner, A, Spittal, MJ, Pirkis, J & LaMontagne, AD (2013). 'Suicide by occupation: Systematic review and meta-analysis.' *British Journal of Psychiatry* 203(6): 409–16.

Mind Share Partners (2025). *2025 Mental health at work report.* In partnership with Qualtrics. https://www.mindsharepartners.org/2025-mental-health-at-work-report

Miranda, L (2018). 'How Wall Street bought Toys 'R' Us and left 30,000 people without jobs.' *BuzzFeed News*, 27 April 2018.

Momentum Intelligence (2019). *Legal firm of choice survey.* In partnership with Lawyers Weekly.

Moodle (2025). *State of workplace learning report 2025.*

Mullen, B, Johnson, C & Salas, E (1991). 'Productivity loss in brainstorming groups: A meta-analytic integration.' *Basic and Applied Social Psychology* 12(1): 3–23.

Nair, L (2020). 'How we take care of our people at Unilever.' LinkedIn, 2020.

NALP Foundation (2017). *Update on Associate Attrition.* National Association for Law Placement.

Nartey, J (2025). 'The Boeing 737 MAX crisis: An ethical analysis of corporate governance failures.' *SSRN.* https://papers.ssrn.com/sol3/papers.cfm?abstract_id=5316121

National Alliance on Mental Illness (NAMI) (2025). *2025 NAMI workplace mental health poll.* Conducted by Ipsos, 21–27 January 2025. Washington, DC: NAMI. https://www.nami.org/support-education/publications-reports/survey-reports/the-2025-nami-workplace-mental-health-poll/

O'Reilly, CA & Chatman, JA (2020). 'Transformational leader or narcissist? How grandiose narcissists can create and destroy organizations and institutions.' *California Management Review* 62(3): 5–27.

O'Reilly, CA, Chatman, JA & Doerr, B (2014a). 'When "me" trumps "we": Narcissistic leaders and the cultures they create.' Research Paper, Stanford Graduate School of Business.

O'Reilly, CA, Chatman, JA & Doerr, B (2014b). 'The promise and problems of organizational culture: CEO personality, culture, and firm performance.' *Group & Organization Management* 39(6): 595–625.

Organisation for Economic Cooperation and Development (OECD) (2024). 'Hours worked (Indicator).' OECD Data. https://data.oecd.org/emp/hours-worked.htm

Park, SY et al. (2024). 'Employee monitoring and psychological wellbeing: A systematic review.' *Occupational Medicine.*

Parker, K, Horowitz, JM & Minkin, R (2021). 'Unemployed Americans are feeling the emotional strain of job loss; most have considered changing occupations.' Pew Research Center, 10 February 2021. https://www.pewresearch.org/short-reads/2021/02/10/unemployed-americans-are-feeling-the-emotional-strain-of-job-loss-most-have-considered-changing-occupations/

PDI Ninth House/University of Minnesota (2012). 'You're not all that: Self-promoters six times more likely to derail.' *PR Newswire*, 17 April 2012. https://www.prnewswire.com/news-releases/youre-not-all-that-self-promoters-six-times-more-likely-to-derail-according-to-pdi-ninth-house-and-university-of-minnesota-study-147742375.html

Pega, F, Nafradi, B, Momen, NC et al. (2021). 'Global, regional, and national burdens of ischemic heart disease and stroke attributable to exposure to long working hours.' *Environment International* 154:106595.

Pencavel, J (2014). 'The productivity of working hours.' *Economic Journal* 125(589): 2052–76.

Perry, BD & Winfrey, O (2021). *What happened to you? Conversations on trauma, resilience, and healing.* New York: Flatiron Books.

Pew Research Center (2010). 'The impact of long-term unemployment: Lost income, lost friends — and loss of self-respect.' Pew Social Trends, 9 July 2010. https://www.pewresearch.org/social-trends/2010/07/09/the-impact-of-long-term-unemployment/

Pew Research Center (2024). *Baby Boomers approach age 65.*

Pignon, T, Lewis, K, Mullally, L, Kikuchi, L, Kellam, J & Western, G (2024). *Making it stick: The UK Four-day week pilot one year on.* Hampshire: Autonomy Research Ltd, February 2024. https://autonomy.work/wp-content/uploads/2024/02/making-it-stick_-1.pdf

Pink, DH (2009). *Drive: The surprising truth about what motivates us.* New York: Riverhead Books.

PricewaterhouseCoopers LLP (2026). *2026 employee financial wellness survey.* www.pwc.com/us/en/services/consulting/business-transformation/library/employee-financial-wellness-survey.html

Private Equity Stakeholder Project (2018). 'KKR, Bain Capital, Vornado repeatedly rewarded themselves for adding debt to Toys R Us.' https://pestakeholder.org/news/kkr-bain-capital-vornado-repeatedly-rewarded-themselves-for-adding-debt-to-toys-r-us

Qantas (2024). *Qantas governance review report*, 8 August 2024. www.qantas-board-governance-review-report.pdf

Reclaim.ai (2023). *Productivity trends report: The state of meetings in* 2023.

Riffkin, R (2014). 'In US, 55% of workers get sense of identity from their job.' Gallup, 25 August 2014. https://news.gallup.com/poll/175400/workers-sense-identity-job.aspx

Rizki, DF et al. (2024). 'Organizational culture, leadership style, and organizational communication on organizational performance: A systematic literature review.' *Dinasti International Journal of Economics, Finance & Accounting* 6(5): 4597–4609.

Robbins, C (2017). '5 Culture lessons from 100 best company salesforce.' *Great Place to Work*, 20 March 2017. https://www.greatplacetowork.com/resources/blog/5-culture-lessons-from-100-best-company-salesforce

Robison, P (2024). Cited in: Levine, M (2025). 'The story of Boeing's failed corporate culture.' *The CPA Journal*, August 2025. https://www.cpajournal.com/2025/08/12/the-story-of-boeings-failed-corporate-culture-3/

Rogoff, S, Moulton-Perkins, A, Warren, F, Nolte, T & Fonagy, P (2021). '"Rich" and "poor" in mentalizing: Do expert mentalizers exist?' *PLOS ONE* 16(10): e0259030. https://doi.org/10.1371/journal.pone.0259030

Rohleder, N (2014). 'Stimulation of systemic low grade inflammation by psychosocial stress.' *Psychosomatic Medicine* 76(3): 181–9.

Rovelli, P & Curnis, C (2021). 'The perks of narcissism: When behaving like a star speeds up career advancement to the CEO position.' *The Leadership Quarterly* 32(3): 101489.

Rupprecht, S, Falke, P, Kohls, N, Tamdjidi, C, Wittmann, M & Kersemaekers, W (2019). 'Mindful leader development: How leaders experience the effects of mindfulness training on leader capabilities.' *Frontiers in Psychology* 10:1081. DOI: 10.3389/fpsyg.2019.01081

Safe Work Australia (SWA) (2025). *Key work health and safety statistics Australia 2025*. https://data.safeworkaustralia.gov.au/insights/key-whs-statistics-australia/latest-release

Safe Work Australia and Dollard, M et al. (2019). *Psychosocial safety climate and workplace mental health*.

Salesforce (2024). 'Marc and Lynne Benioff's philanthropy in Hawai'i.' *Salesforce Newsroom*, 16 July 2024. https://www.salesforce.com/news/stories/marc-and-hawaii/

Salesforce (n.d.). 'Salesforce wellbeing headquarters.' *Trailhead*. https://trailhead.salesforce.com/content/learn/modules/wellbeing-at-work/wellbeing-at-salesforce

Salesforce, Inc. (2023). Form 8-K: Current Report. Filed 4 January 2023. US Securities and Exchange Commission. https://www.sec.gov/Archives/edgar/data/0001108524/000110852423000003/crm-20230104.htm

Salesforce Staff (2020). 'The history of Salesforce.' *Salesforce Newsroom*, 19 March 2020. https://www.salesforce.com/news/stories/the-history-of-salesforce/

Salesforce Staff (2024). 'Salesforce Ohana and Hawaiian culture: Embracing community.' *Salesforce Blog*, 2 August 2024. https://www.salesforce.com/blog/salesforce-and-hawaii/

Schein, EH (2017). *Organizational culture and leadership* (5th ed.). Hoboken: John Wiley & Sons.

Schneiderman, N, Ironson, G & Siegel, SD (2005). 'Stress and health: Psychological, behavioral, and biological determinants.' *Annual Review of Clinical Psychology* 1:607–28.

Schulte, B (2024). *Over work: Transforming the daily grind in the quest for a better life*. New York: Henry Holt.

Schultz, W (2024). 'A dopamine mechanism for reward maximization.' *Proceedings of the National Academy of Sciences* 121(20). DOI: 10.1073/pnas.2316658121

Scullen, SE, Mount, MK & Goff, M (2000). 'Understanding the latent structure of job performance ratings.' *Journal of Applied Psychology* 85(6): 956–97.

Securities and Exchange Commission (SEC) (2005). Toys R Us Inc., Form 8-K, 17 March 2005. https://www.sec.gov/Archives/edgar/data/0001005414/000119312505057772/dex991.htm

SelectSoftwareReviews (2023). '85 must-know performance management statistics.' https://www.selectsoftwarereviews.com/blog/performance-management-statistics

Shanafelt, TD, Dyrbye, LN, Sinsky, C et al. (2021). 'Suicidal ideation and attitudes regarding help seeking in US physicians relative to the US working population.' *Mayo Clinic Proceedings* 96(8): 2067–80.

Sharma, V et al. (2025). 'Psychological impacts of AI-induced job displacement among Indian IT professionals: A Delphi-validated thematic analysis.' *International Journal of Qualitative Studies on Health and Well-being*, 2 September 2025. DOI: 10.1080/17482631.2025.2556445

Simkin, D & Hunter, T (2026). *Full stack human.* John Wiley & Sons.

Slack Workforce Lab (2023). 'The surprising connection between after-hours work and decreased productivity.' *Slack Workforce Index, Winter 2023.* https://slack.com/blog/news/the-surprising-connection-between-after-hours-work-and-decreased-productivity

Slack Workforce Lab (2024). 'Case study: What happened when we took a break at Slack.' https://slack.com/blog/productivity/case-study-what-happened-when-we-took-a-break-at-slack

Society for Human Resource Management (SHRM) (2019). 'The high cost of a toxic workplace culture.' Alexandria, VA: SHRM. https://www.shrm.org/topics-tools/research/2021-workplace-culture-report

Society for Human Resource Management (SHRM) (2025). 'Gen Z mental health expectations at work.'

Spill (2024). *Tech industry mental health report 2024.*

Strathern, M (1997). 'Improving ratings: Audit in the British University system.' *European Journal of Education* 32(3): 305–321.

Sull, D, Sull, C & Zweig, B (2022a). 'Toxic culture is driving the great resignation.' *MIT Sloan Management Review*, 11 January 2022.

Sull, D, Sull, C, Cipolli, W & Brighenti, C (2022b). 'How to fix a toxic culture.' *MIT Sloan Management Review*, 28 September 2022.

TalentLMS (2025). *The state of employee engagement 2025.*

Taren, AA et al. (2024). 'Neurobiological changes induced by mindfulness and meditation: A systematic review.' *Biomedicines* 12(11): 2613. doi.org/10.3390/biomedicines12112613

The Happiness Index (2026). *The global workplace happiness report 2026.* www.thehappinessindex.com

The Workforce Institute at UKG, in partnership with Workplace Intelligence (2023). 'Mental health at work: Managers and money.' Survey of 3400 employees across ten countries, January 2023. https://www.ukg.com/about-us/newsroom/managers-impact-our-mental-health-more-doctors-therapists-and-same-spouses

Ton, Z (2024). 'Costco and other retailers prove a "good jobs" strategy works.' Harvard Business School Institute for Business in Global Society. www.hbs.edu/bigs/costco-and-other-retailers-prove-a-good-jobs-strategy-works

Trapnell, PD & Campbell, JD (1999). 'Private self-consciousness and the five-factor model of personality: Distinguishing rumination from reflection.' *Journal of Personality and Social Psychology* 76(2): 284–304. DOI: 10.1037/0022-3514.76.2.284

Treasure, J (2014). *Sound business* (2nd ed.). Management Books 2000 Ltd.

Twenge, JM & Campbell, WK (2010). *The narcissism epidemic.* New York: Atria.

UKG (Ultimate Kronos Group) (2023). *Mental health at work: Managers and money.* UKG Workforce Institute.

UN Global Compact Business & Human Rights Navigator (2026). 'Unilever: Health and wellbeing programme.' https://bhr-navigator.unglobalcompact.org/case_studies/health-and-wellbeing-programme/

Unilever UK & Ireland (2026). 'Health & wellbeing.' https://www.unilever.co.uk/sustainability/health-wellbeing/

US Bureau of Labor Statistics (2024). *Remote work and total factor productivity analysis.* Washington DC: US Department of Labor.

US Bureau of Labor Statistics (2026). Employment cost index — March 2026. Washington, DC: US Department of Labor. www.bls.gov/news.release/eci.htm

ViewSonic (2024). 'Wasting time in meetings? And what to do about it.' *ViewSonic Library.* www.viewsonic.com/library/business/wasting-time-meetings/

Vyas, A, Mitra, R, Shankaranarayana Rao, BS & Bhattacharyya, S (2002). 'Chronic stress induces contrasting patterns of dendritic remodeling in hippocampal and amygdaloid neurons.' *Journal of Neuroscience* 22(15): 6810–18.

World Economic Forum (2023). *The future of jobs report 2023.* Geneva: World Economic Forum.

World Economic Forum (2025). *The future of jobs report 2025.* Geneva: World Economic Forum. www.weforum.org/publications/the-future-of-jobs-report-2025/

World Health Organization (WHO) (2016). 'Investing in treatment for depression and anxiety leads to fourfold return.' WHO news release, 13 April 2016. https://www.who.int/news/item/13-04-2016-investing-in-treatment-for-depression-and-anxiety-leads-to-fourfold-return

Young, S & Milliken, D (2023). 'How four-day-week trials are working out in the UK.' *World Economic Forum*, 19 May 2023. https://www.weforum.org/stories/2023/05/how-four-day-week-is-working-in-uk/

Zhang, Y et al. (2024). 'Organisational culture and performance: A systematic review 2014 to 2023.' *Cogent Business and Management* 11(1).

Zhou, L et al. (2024). 'Coaching leadership and employee engagement in uncertain work environments.' *Frontiers in Psychology* 15.

Zhu, DH & Chen, G (2015). 'CEO narcissism and the impact of prior board experience on corporate strategy.' *Administrative Science Quarterly* 60(1): 31–65.

Made in United States
North Haven, CT
05 November 2026

21757841R00077